The Invention and
Reinvention of
Big Bill Broonzy

The Invention and Reinvention of Big Bill Broonzy

Kevin D. Greene

The University of North Carolina Press CHAPEL HILL

© 2018 The University of North Carolina Press
All rights reserved
Set in Merope Basic by Westchester Publishing Services
Manufactured in the United States of America

The University of North Carolina Press has been a member of the
Green Press Initiative since 2003.

Library of Congress Cataloging-in-Publication Data
Names: Greene, Kevin D., author.
Title: The invention and reinvention of Big Bill Broonzy / Kevin D. Greene.
Description: Chapel Hill : University of North Carolina Press, [2018] |
 Includes bibliographical references and index.
Identifiers: LCCN 2018011168 | ISBN 9781469646480 (cloth : alk. paper) |
 ISBN 9781469646497 (pbk : alk. paper) | ISBN 9781469646503 (ebook)
Subjects: LCSH: Broonzy, Big Bill, 1893-1958. | African American
 musicians—Biography. | Blues musicians—United States—Biography. |
 African Americans—Race identity. | Blues (Music)—History and criticism. |
 Celebrities in popular culture. | Harlem Renaissance.
Classification: LCC ML420.B78 G73 2018 | DDC 782.421643092 [B]—dc23
 LC record available at https://lccn.loc.gov/2018011168

Cover illustration: 1951 head shot of William "Big Bill" Broonzy
(author's collection).

For Casey, Thomas, and Yates

Contents

Acknowledgments xi

Introduction 1

CHAPTER ONE
Southern Blues 17

CHAPTER TWO
Carving Out a Home in the Promised Land 33

CHAPTER THREE
Southern Migrant Blues 49
Lee Bradley and the Black Metropolis

CHAPTER FOUR
The Rise of Big Bill 69

CHAPTER FIVE
I Come for to Sing 96

CHAPTER SIX
We Love the Blues, but Tell Us about Jazz 115

CHAPTER SEVEN
Big Bill Broonzy 131
The Making of a Legend

CHAPTER EIGHT
Escaping the Folk 148
The "Authentic" Career of a Black Pop Star

Epilogue 173
This Is Your Father's Guitar

Notes 181
Bibliography 207
Index 219

Illustrations

Broonzy, ca. late 1920s–early 1930s 70

John Lee "Sonny Boy" Williamson, Walter Davis, and Broonzy, ca. 1939 77

Broonzy, ca. mid-1930s 79

Broonzy and Rosetta Howard, 1947 86

John Lee "Sonny Boy" Williamson and Broonzy, ca. early 1940s 94

Broonzy and Michael van Isveldt, 1957 132

Broonzy, ca. mid-1950s 150

Michael van Isveldt and Broonzy's guitar, 2013 174

Broonzy playing guitar with Michael van Isveldt, 1957 175

Michael van Isveldt, the author, and Bettina Weller, 2016 176

Acknowledgments

Most projects of this scale materialize only through the exhaustive efforts of many, many people. From beginning to end, I have constantly relied on the unmatched wisdom and unending support of a chorus of patient colleagues, friends, and family, whose contributions have made this study far better than I could have alone. I am forever grateful for their encouraging words and pointed criticisms, which have shaped the direction of this book from cover to cover.

Studies of this nature are impossible without tremendous help from scholars, archivists and librarians and their incredible, encyclopedic knowledge of the resources from which this work draws. I want to thank the institutions and their representatives that made this investigation possible, including the American Folklife Center at the Library of Congress; the Alan Lomax Audio Archive at the Association for Cultural Equity; the Blues Archive at the Chicago Public Library; the Blues Archive at the University of Mississippi; Jazz at Lincoln Center; the DuSable Museum of African American History; the Lippmann+Rau-Musikarchiv in Eisenach, Germany; the University of Chicago Library; the Southern Historical Collection at The University of North Carolina; the Chicago History Museum; the Newberry Library; the Parks Library-Special Collections at Iowa State University; the Illinois Office of Cook County Clerk; and the Michael van Isveldt Collection in Amsterdam, the Netherlands. I would like to give special thanks as well to Roger House and Bob Riesman for their pioneering works on Big Bill. The spirits of their projects have guided this study. I hope I may one day repay the favor to all of the individuals who gave so freely their time and efforts to push this piece across the finish line.

All of my mentors, whose sage advice and stern honesty kept this burgeoning academic from running things off the rails, share a collective voice in the pages that follow. First, I am endlessly indebted to Kathleen "Kit" Cooke and N. E. Bou-Nacklie for convincing me that studying history is far more fascinating and rewarding than studying jazz guitar. Don and Jo Ann Parkerson, too, will always hold a special place in my life for pushing me to embrace academia and intellectual pursuits, even in those times when I felt as if I never really belonged. Thank you for being my adopted academic parents.

Benjamin Filene's guidance as my doctoral adviser taught me how to overcome my fear of messiness in historical thinking. Thankfully, he convinced me to actively seek out the tensions in the past and embrace them as the "good stuff" of history. Likewise, I would not be where I am today without the persistent wit and wisdom of Chuck Bolton. More than once, I walked into his office ready to hang up my academic "cleats," only to have him put my shattered pieces back together and send me excitedly back to my work. Unfailingly kind and generous, Chuck still accepts my panicked calls and worried emails as I navigate the travails of becoming a young faculty member and research-center administrator. He is the example scholar, teacher, administrator, and family man from whom I have molded my own life and career. Finally, Davarian Baldwin graciously helped transform my disparate and disconnected ideas into the fluid concepts that would become this monograph. Thank you for taking the time to evaluate my book proposal and sample chapters for the academic publishing market. Your work is an inspiration and has changed my approach to research and scholarship forever.

For many of us, learning never stops once we finish our education. My gratitude toward my colleagues at the University of Southern Mississippi and their steadfast support of my work and career is unbounded. There is insufficient space here to thank them all, but there are a few whose contributions to this project are immense. First, thank you, Andrew Haley, for being an intellectual's intellectual and for helping me set the tone for this project. You remained my most trusted sounding board at every stage of this process, and I am so very grateful for it. Similarly, Heather Stur and Ken Swope read all or parts of this manuscript at various stages, ultimately providing both brilliant feedback and biting criticism where needed. Allison Abra, Matthew Casey, and Rebecca Tuuri have also suffered my ranting drivel as I worked through, in both polite and annoying conversation, the protean path and shifting terrain this manuscript has followed over the past few years. No longer my colleague at Southern Miss but forever a great friend, Paul Linden leant his incredible ear and gift for music to a few porch sessions that helped me rediscover Big Bill's unprecedented talents as performer and composer in a way I never had before. I am equally thankful for Max Grivno's help in illustrating how to converse and negotiate with university presses. Finally, although I never asked them to spend their scant free time evaluating my work, several seasoned colleagues—namely, Andrew Wiest, Kyle Zelner, Susannah Ural, and Marek Steedman—have remained resolutely supportive of all of my endeavors at USM. In many ways, their mentorship has provided the fertile environment in which all academic pursuits can flower.

The staff at the University of North Carolina Press has been nothing short of remarkable in their support of this project. Above all, Mark Simpson-Vos has remained loyally committed to me as an aspiring author, even as I evolved from the doe-eyed graduate student he first met several years ago into a university faculty member. At every step of the way, he has been but an email or phone call away as I trod through the frighteningly unfamiliar waters of academic publishing. Both he and the press obtained first-rate reviewers for the manuscript whose insightful suggestions and candid critiques have shaped the scope and aim of this book as much as anyone. I would also like to thank Brandon Proia for the inspiring conversations we shared covering topics on publishing, music, books, and food as we crossed paths around the country at the occasionally dull academic conference. Finally, I would like to give special thanks to Matthew Somoroff for his patience and prudence in assisting the final revisions for the project. Matthew, I owe you one.

For nine days in the early summer of 2010 and for a weekend in the summer of 2016, I had the remarkable pleasure of visiting the home of Michael van Isveldt and Bettina Weller, Big Bill Broonzy's Dutch children. Graciously, they opened their lives to an American stranger who spent hours analyzing Michael's personal collection of letters, correspondence, ephemera, and memorabilia shared between his parents and the close-knit community of friends that supported Broonzy's tours of Europe in the 1950s. For the budding historian, the collection provided a window into the personal life of a very public figure. More important, the discovery of this nearly untouched archive, the welcoming warmth of its owners, and the miraculous experience of conducting history on another continent drove the writing of this book and serve as a reminder of the past's very real connection to both the present and the future. Michael and Bettina have taught me as much about history as any of my degree-granting institutions have.

Finally, to my own family and my in-laws, please accept the sincerest apologies for those filial moments I missed during holidays and parties as I sacrificed family time to read one more chapter or eke out another paragraph or two. In no small part is your love and support a component of this book. Of course, none of this—the book or my career—would be possible without the unwavering encouragement from my spouse and partner in all things brilliant and insane, Casey Greene. Many years ago, we started down this path together, and you and our two boys are a daily reminder of why history matters in all things, both big and small.

The Invention and
Reinvention of
Big Bill Broonzy

Introduction

> And oh, how I wondered about the artist himself, that irreproachable magician! . . . Was he a worldling smothered in success? Was he coldly calculating, knowing how to tickle people in exactly that delicate, sensitive spot between their tear glands and their purses, which makes tears and dollars fall like rain, if one but understands the magic? Or was he a humble servant of the art, too modest to permit himself a judgment of his own, willingly and helpfully playing his role, making no protest against fate? Or had he perhaps, after profound experience and reasoning, come to doubt the worth of music in modern life and the possibility of its being understood, and was his purpose to begin by leading men beyond all music once more back to the beginnings of the art, to the naked sensuous beauty of the tones, to the naked force of primitive feelings? It was too much for me to decipher. I am still puzzling over it today.
> —HERMANN HESSE, "A Virtuoso's Concert," 1929

On December 23, 1938, in front of a packed house in New York City's Carnegie Hall, the Chicago bluesman Big Bill Broonzy and a host of other twentieth-century black musical legends performed in a live review of the history of black music in the United States. Featuring "spirituals, holy roller hymns, harmonica, blues, boogie-woogie piano playing, early New Orleans jazz, and soft swing," the concert, "From Spirituals to Swing," promised to educate its integrated audience on "The Music That Nobody Knows."[1] Filled with recording-industry giants, music promoters, university intellectuals, and government and academic folklorists, this event represented an important moment for the history of American music and racial integration. Organized for the political and intellectual Left and promoted by members of the recording industry, an integrated audience witnessed a publicly performed history of black music. For decades, black American music had remained at the margins of American life. But after this evening, black music and Big Bill Broonzy quickly moved into the mainstream music industry.

The show's first act featured "African Tribal Music" interpreted by Count Basie and his Orchestra from Hugh Tracey's West African "scientific recordings" expedition. Then Mitchell's Christian Singers and Sister Rosetta Tharpe offered spirituals and holy-roller hymns, followed by the Kansas City Six's take on soft swing. Saunders "Sonny Terry" Terrell harmonica helped steer the evening's performances toward the segment before intermission, simply titled "Blues." At last, situated among Ruby Smith with James P. Johnson on the piano, Joe Turner featuring Pete Johnson on the piano, and James "Jimmy" Rushing and his Kansas City Five, came the show's rural blues component. Introduced as an Arkansas sharecropper, Big Bill Broonzy performed on vocals and acoustic guitar, accompanied by the pianist Albert Ammons (with Broonzy playing in the style of the late and increasingly mythical Robert Johnson, the bluesman whom Broonzy replaced in the lineup at the last minute).[2]

The Columbia Records producer John Hammond, who organized the show with the intentions of a promoter more than those of a historian, offered Broonzy his "first performance before a white audience," where he played one of his latest unrecorded blues, "Just a Dream," to much acclaim.[3] This particular performance of the song featured Broonzy offering a moderately slow, twelve-bar blues in the key of D major. Ammons provided the performance's harmonic framework with a steady rhythmic backing, allowing Broonzy to alternate between strumming and single-note melodies on his guitar in nearly every measure. Broonzy's vocal delivery was smooth and controlled both rhythmically and melodically; he did not include the melisma or falsetto that emerged in later performances. The powerful and amusing lyrics captivated the audience with stories of Broonzy's experiences standing on the precipice of exaltation only to find out that they were dreams.[4] As he would countless times throughout his career, Broonzy shared through his performance of "Just a Dream" the realities of black life and the disappointment felt by African Americans as they loved and upheld a country that refused to grant them full citizenship. That night in Manhattan, Broonzy shared his dream of visiting the White House to shake the president's hand, only to wake up and realize that in the Jim Crow United States, such an occurrence was impossible. Hammond had intended for the crowd to witness the majesty of the country blues that evening, but instead those in the audience heard the bedrock arrangement that made up the Chicago blues sound and a performance reverberating the expression of a modern black artist's evolving consciousness.

According to Harry "Sweets" Edison, trumpeter and member of Count Basie's Orchestra who performed at the concert, Broonzy was scheduled to play another song later in the show. But when the time came for his second performance, Broonzy was nowhere to be found; when the evening's performers gathered after the show, Broonzy still had not surfaced. John Hammond had assumed the entire cast would leave Carnegie Hall to hit the streets of New York and carry on the air of celebration throughout the night. "From Spirituals to Swing" represented a prophetic moment for the future of black music in the United States and set Broonzy down an interesting path. Hammond and the producer Eric Bernay had hoped to share with the audience black music's critical importance in any understanding of American popular music, past or present. Anyone in attendance would rave to the success of such a magical night in New York for its use "of music in pursuit of social change."[5] The circumstances, then, were ripe for more magical musical moments. Christmas was two days away, and it was opening night at the very first integrated music club in the United States, Greenwich Village's Café Society.[6] But as the audience filtered out of New York's premier music hall and the performers gathered en masse for their venture into the cold December night, Big Bill Broonzy had vanished. Hammond searched the performance hall, asking anyone he could about Broonzy, only to hear that the man introduced simply as "Big Bill" had caught the earliest bus back to Arkansas in hopes of making it home for Christmas.[7]

In many ways, Arkansas served as crucible for Broonzy's personality; he grew up near Little Rock, poor, rural, and black at the height of Jim Crow segregation in the United States. Indeed, Broonzy had family near Little Rock, lending credence to his role as the replacement for the Delta blues legend Johnson and to his claims that he was returning home for Christmas after the 1938 concert. But he did not return to Arkansas that day. In reality, he was heading to Chicago, where he was one of the most significant members of the city's blues community and where December 25 marked the biggest party of the year for the blues stalwarts living in Bronzeville, Chicago's black South Side community. Every year, Broonzy's close friend and blues colleague Hudson "Tampa Red" Whitaker held his birthday party on Christmas in Bronzeville, and every year, all of the great Chicago musicians would show up to "eat and drink, talk about different blues songs, and give [Tampa Red] a good beating."[8]

This single anecdote, with the sharp contrast it depicts between the myth of the country rube and the realities of the urban migrant, captures the amazing fluidity of this important black musician. Was he William "Big Bill" Broonzy from Arkansas or just plain "Big Bill" from Chicago? Broonzy made sure the answer to that question remained quite unclear within the legions of his devoted audiences and fans. The Chicago media personality and Broonzy's close friend Studs Terkel once said that Broonzy "always" told the truth but skeptically called it "his truth."[9] In actuality, Broonzy's public persona was a continual work in progress, one that involved constantly inventing and reinventing himself throughout his long career. Broonzy actively shaped his identity, performances, networks, and other dimensions of self-presentation in response to public tastes and audience influences. Over the course of three decades, he navigated the music industry in the United States and Europe by cannily creating personas that suited the expectations of individuals who could help sustain his career. Across much of the twentieth century, Broonzy carried his music and larger-than-life personality out of Jim Crow Arkansas to Chicago's Black Metropolis and across the Atlantic to Europe. The Great Migration pulled Broonzy to Chicago, where he transformed his country fiddling into sophisticated urban blues. After decades as a black popular artist who had pioneered the Chicago blues sound, he became a hip, "down home" folkster, a vanguard of the emerging folk music revival of the 1950s, embodying its fascination with classic blues. In Europe, he became something else, a touchstone for European absorption of the classic blues and urban jazz culture that had documented the black experience for decades. Ultimately, Broonzy embodies "the pressures of celebrity and the effort to please across racial and [and national] class lines."[10] And because of this, when he is investigated within the context of the twists and turns of his career, Broonzy offers historians a pathway to understand how musicians shaped the black experience under the weight of Jim Crow. Over his long career, Broonzy achieved escalating levels of renown among varying groups. As an in-demand guitarist, Broonzy became a celebrated accompanist at buffet flats and rent parties across Chicago. From there, Broonzy became one of the most prolifically recorded blues artists between 1932 and 1942, selling tens of thousands of records across the United States, ultimately becoming one of Chicago's urban blues pioneers. As his career evolved again in the 1940s, he became a celebrity among the political Left and their growing affection for folk music.

Beneath the surface of "From Spirituals to Swing" lay a crucible for creating what became an important but equally troublesome American folk music revival that appropriated ownership of black music in a manner that masked Broonzy's contributions to black popular culture under the banner of authenticity. Only from 1946 to 1958 did he become an acclaimed artist among American folk audiences and an international success to European audiences, yet his entire life is typically depicted as an exemplar of the folk—a touchstone to black music's past, when solo black bluesmen performed acoustic southern music in the vein of Blind Lemon Jefferson and Robert Johnson. From the 1920s to the 1950s, Big Bill Broonzy continually reinvented himself in ways that cut across the color line, even becoming a blues ambassador of sorts as one of the first black blues artists to tour post-World War II Europe. At each turn, Broonzy was the prism through which various world citizens, from rural black southerners to European hipsters, refracted their own ideas about race, belonging, national identity, and the blues. And Broonzy negotiated a successful and lengthy career by navigating each group's cultural expectations through a process that continually transformed his musical, professional, and personal lives. This book recovers the adventures of Bill Broonzy during the Great Migrations, the black modern experience in the Windy City, and the travails of expatriate life in Europe, and it reconsiders the meanings of race and celebrity through the larger-than-life exploits of a major, but largely forgotten, blues artist who transformed his experiences into words and music.

Tracing Broonzy's rise from isolated obscurity to international celebrity reveals the ways in which "popular culture can simultaneously subvert and reproduce hegemony."[11] The arena of performance became one of the first places where African Americans became engaged in the American cultural marketplace, as that space within the market system required little market capital.[12] Nevertheless, black participation in this cultural marketplace was considerably limited by white control of the recording and production of music, ensuring that black artists such as Broonzy rarely benefited financially from their artistry before World War II. Broonzy's lifelong reinvention as a musician—from old-time fiddler to country blues artist to black pop artist to American folk revivalist and European jazz and blues hero—provides a fascinating window through which to view how African Americans made music and struggled to assert race pride, manhood, and economic independence in the growing music marketplace by creating a unique celebrity as "New Negroes" in the shadow of Jim Crow. Part of Broonzy's legacy, and what *The Invention and Reinvention of Big Bill Broonzy* contributes to our understanding of both the man and musician, is that Broonzy carved out renown from the limited opportunities and racial pressures he faced in this contested cultural marketplace in a manner that not only expanded his own awareness of what it meant to be black during the first half of the twentieth century but also expanded (and challenged) the nation's race consciousness. Broonzy's perpetual reinvention across the twentieth century gives meaning to self-conscious artistry and celebrity in a world that viewed African Americans as "inherently" musical and, by definition, merely skilled tradesmen.[13]

Essentially, Broonzy's story exemplifies black musicians' tortured path from obscurity to celebrity. Sociologists have challenged the academic world's reluctance to acknowledge the importance of studying celebrity's value in unlocking deeper historical meaning and understanding. These sociologists, although in varying terms, define a celebrity as someone recognized "by a critical mass of strangers,"[14] essentially arguing that the entertainment arts industry is important for academic study simply because entertainment has become so unusually rationalized. Since the turn of the twentieth century, many of the country's most popular celebrities have emerged from film, radio, television, and music industries.[15] For some sociologists, moreover, celebrity culture reveals the promise and limits of social and racial mobility.[16] At those times when the audiences identified in this book paid attention and wanted more of Broonzy, his story illuminates a form of celebrity rooted in race, cultural appropriation, romanticism, and authenticity. For the historian, then, celebrity culture may be "rationalized," but it is also nebulous; *The Invention and Reinvention of Big Bill Broonzy* suggests that the meaning of celebrity is "like perfume that takes on a slightly different scent with each wearer."[17] To understand how black Americans were at times able to effectively exploit celebrity to advance both personal ambitions and collective racial consciousness, one needs to recognize that the lives of men such as Big Bill Broonzy both shaped and were shaped by celebrity and that American consumers' shifting tastes have ensured that identifying celebrity's meaning and function in a given culture, as well as its relationship to Broonzy, remains difficult. In multiple ways, this book attempts to peel back the opaque layers masking this process.

First, *The Invention and Reinvention of Big Bill Broonzy* argues that a chorus of white record-company executives, academic folklorists, journalists, record collectors, rock musicians, music critics, and others have invented the blues in a manner that has never reflected the music's real history. In fact, the blues as a twentieth-century art form constantly shifted in style and form, as black and white audiences in the United States and Europe demanded or rejected the creative output of the many black musicians whose works came to represent "blues" in the twentieth century.

Consider Robert Johnson, the famed and often-studied Mississippi delta blues icon whom Broonzy replaced at "From Spirituals to Swing." Until 1961,

Johnson's life and legacy amounted to a footnote in the annals of popular blues history; he was a figure known by only a select few outside of the Mississippi Delta, where he based his career from 1929 to 1938. Dead at twenty-seven, Johnson recorded only twenty-nine songs in his lifetime. In comparison to the popularity of performers such as the classic women blues singers of the 1920s and 1930s and their male contemporaries (such as Big Bill Broonzy)—all of whom were household names, at least in African American homes—Johnson was virtually unknown. Yet the ambiguity surrounding his death, the mythic sale of his soul to the devil for improved musicianship, and his general obscurity have made Johnson one of the most recognized blues artists of all time. When John Hammond and Alan Lomax decided to release and promote a collection of Johnson's small body of recordings, they intended to market the record to the then-thriving folk music revival of the early 1960s, participants of which were eager to soak up such a mysterious figure. The plan failed, but it did begin a long and steadily increasing obsession among the aforementioned chorus that over time catapulted Johnson into legendary status. Thanks in large part to Peter Guralnick's 1988 book *Searching for Robert Johnson*, the 1990 release of Johnson's *Complete Recordings* (a remastered collection of his all-too-brief recording career), and Alan Lomax's 1993 book *The Land Where the Blues Began*, Mississippi Delta musicians such as Johnson emerged in 1990s scholarship as the most mystified and sought-after blues performers in history, ultimately overshadowing the careers of more popular and successful artists such as Broonzy. By unpacking the mechanisms that have created Johnson's legacy and fueled his historical memory, scholars have made significant strides in uncovering the ways in which culture brokers have constructed the canon and history of the blues and its performers in a manner that masks the contributions of many musicians who were prominent during their lifetimes, thus distorting their influence over African American culture.[18] This work seeks to continue this trend.

Second, Broonzy's life and times provide a concrete example of why the blues—along with jazz music, literature, sculpture, architecture, and the visual arts—was a vital part of public and private interactions in urban areas across the country that provided the aesthetics for the New Negro Renaissance and grounded the movement in everyday practices. In this context, Big Bill Broonzy and the blues are not just nostalgic reflections of a disappeared southern tradition. To the contrary, they embody the inherent tensions between modernity and wistful remembrances of the past, while at the same time reminding historians that black musicians from the early twentieth century were far more than entertainers.[19] The men and women who sang and played the blues pioneered the creation of a commercially successful cultural product and were as professional and sophisticated as any of the contemporary black athletes, poets, writers, sociologists, historians, painters, and others who have defined the leadership of the New Negro movement.[20] Placing the music within this context reveals that parameters such as race, class, and geographic location must shape how interpretations of the blues and its history should be understood, thus situating musical production within the urbanizing and politicizing black communities from which it emerged in the modern twentieth century.

Finally, *The Invention and Reinvention of Big Bill Broonzy* provides a new window through which to observe African American music and its enormous impact on the predominance of white culture in the United States and Europe throughout the long twentieth century. The narrative I present here does not end when the New Negro Renaissance came to a close; instead, it charts Broonzy's career from the mid-1940s until his death in 1958, a period in which he achieved newfound fame among white folklorists, jazz enthusiasts, and blues revivalists in Europe and the United States. Throughout the latter stages of his career, as he did during the 1938 New York revival "From Spirituals to Swing," Broonzy explained and described the history of the blues, how it was constructed, and his opinions on black vernacular music in the United States. As he described these topics, often in intricate detail, he (at times unconsciously) offered lessons in the black experience and crafted for himself a new celebrity image as an ambassador of the folk. In the end, Broonzy became an interlocutor in a performed relationship between two continents fascinated by music, race, and the African American past.

Broonzy and hundreds of other contemporary musicians from the 1920s through the 1950s propelled the American music business into a wholly established mass-market capitalist industry.[21] The creation of this market rested on the development of a mass-produced and mass-consumed world of commercialized leisure. Driving much of this evolution in leisure-time activity (beyond its symbiotic relationship with the ever-increasing expanse of urbanization and industrialized labor) were new technologies that brought public life into closer proximity with the private and, likewise, personal lives closer to the public. These mechanisms of modernity—movie theaters, nickelodeons, shopping malls, and sporting arenas, along with records, motion pictures, and radios—helped make the popular culture and leisure-time activity of the age cheaper and much easier to access. At the same time, these growing technologies allowed cultural consumers to share a real or perceived common heritage and experience.[22] Through this increasingly national culture, Americans across the country could listen to recorded music produced outside their region, buy their clothes from beyond local markets, follow the same national radio programs, share in admiration of their favorite movie stars, or jeer their most loathed sports team or celebrity. The age of celebrity culture in which Broonzy made his mark was born of these cultural and economic transformations, and how he negotiated this new era is an intrinsic part of his story.

Of course, black celebrities existed long before Broonzy's life and journey, and a new generation of historical scholarship devoted to American celebrity culture continues to push that time frame further back in the past, while at the same time urging the field to investigate celebrated blackness in a larger, more transnational context.[23] Some scholars have argued that Broonzy embodied the quintessential working-class bluesman, whose prolific recording career never achieved the fame and renown of other contemporaries whose careers were more lucrative and, therefore, more celebrated.[24] But his becoming an African American international celebrity following World War II was not common and reveals a complexity to his celebrity that a strict focus on his musical oeuvre often masks. Of course, Europe had heralded black American entertainment celebrities long before World War II. The Fisk Jubilee Singers, James Reese Europe, Jack Johnson, Paul Robeson, Josephine Baker, and others graced European stages and sporting arenas decades before Broonzy's first European tour. Indeed, his movements between communities and the ways in which these communities—black and white America, rural and urban, popular and academic, national and transnational—experienced his life and music over his long career were quite common for many African Americans. But the effects of the Great Depression and the Nazi jackboot brought European appearances by black American entertainers to a screeching halt. Once Europe began its long journey toward rebuilding the ravaged continent, Big Bill Broonzy became one of the first black entertainers to tour there. For nearly ten years, he shared his life and music with a new generation of Europeans eager to reconstitute some semblance of popular mass consumer culture, and from this, he emerged as one of the first post–World War II black American international entertainment celebrities. Broonzy's story is not contained by the continental boundaries of the United States, even if it had its roots in the American South and flourished in America's cities.

The Invention and Reinvention of Big Bill Broonzy places Broonzy's celebrity within the context of studies of black urban history and seeks to carve out a new understanding of African Americans' role in transnational history. Much of this scholarship has focused on the cultures forged in southern cities and northern centers of industry following the Civil War through the era of the Great Migration.[25] Studies of northern industrial cities, particularly those focusing on northern black centers of migration such as Chicago, argue that despite these cities' racial difficulties, black urban enclaves experienced remarkable growth on many levels, including community advancement, new cultural ideologies, and black identity development. Only occasionally, however, have these studies integrated the lush musical landscape that gave this period of tremendous change its own soundtrack. With urban history in mind, this study seeks to understand the richness of the black urban experience by exploring the vitality of its music scene.

In this vein, *The Invention and Reinvention of Big Bill Broonzy* contributes to recent studies attempting to discover the New Negro Renaissance beyond Harlem and to form a new temporal framework that begins at the start of the twentieth century and lasts until the beginning of World War II.[26] Investigating Big Bill Broonzy's fascinating career offers an important connection between the creation of the Black Metropolis in Chicago, the impact of the New Negro movement beyond New York, and the importance of blues music in those formations. If the New Negro movement is now defined by historians as the presence among blacks of an emerging race consciousness centered on class, gender, geography, and sexual identity, Broonzy's life and career stand as representative evidence in the historical and sociological transformations that gave birth to the New Negro Renaissance's competing conceptualizations of an urbanized, modern race.[27]

As a young, southern migrant fleeing racism in the Jim Crow South, Broonzy's first reinvention entailed wiping clean his Arkansas past and refashioning himself as an urbane, upwardly mobile black artist and citizen of Bronzeville. Only after the Renaissance waned in the early 1940s did Broonzy shed the carefully crafted, cosmopolitan image he constructed as one of the nation's most successfully recorded and accomplished blues celebrities of the period. From the mid-1920s through the 1940s, recorded blues and live performances infused nearly every segment of black life in Chicago from Maxwell Street to South State Street and became an irreplaceable part of Chicago's cultural and social history. In the spaces of leisure production within the Black Metropolis—recording studios, open-air markets, private homes, buffet flats, bordellos, taverns, saloons, and dance halls—and the markets that produced and promoted them, New Negro blues artists such as Big Bill Broonzy contributed to the transformation of a viable consumer marketplace into New Negro experiences.[28] Of course, Broonzy and his contemporaries—the scores of black men and women who helped pioneer one of the most popular art forms in American history—were often discredited by ever-evolving black aesthetics, including New Negro intelligentsia, the African American leaders who had labeled the blues as too provincial and bereft of sophistication.[29] However, the blues as part of the black consumer marketplace and community identity was not necessarily problematic for black Chicago's emerging New Negro leadership; instead, it offered vibrancy and vitality to black Chicago as a site for New Negro prescience and imagination.[30] As a representative of Chicago's New Negroes, Broonzy revealed the powerful contestations over self-identification and determination that defined how the blues as a form of black popular music for black audiences would transmit across class, race, and transnational boundaries in the twentieth century.[31]

Drawing the connections between Broonzy's music and New Negro experiences associated with the Great Migration, urbanization, industrialization, and engagement with cultural and celebrity commerce forces one to reexamine blues music for what it is: an undeniably modern cultural formation. For far too long, the image of the rural, itinerant, and country bluesman has dominated the nation's public memory of one of the United States' most original art forms.[32] Recent investigations directly challenge older blues historians' arguments centered on the importance of the Mississippi Delta region, their predetermined notions of "authenticity," their romanticized and sensationalized emphases on particular individuals, and their tendency to mythologize musical discoveries. Critical to this new generation's investigations is the idea that the blues, although rooted in southern folk culture, was simultaneously a form of recorded popular music deeply enmeshed within the U.S. and European recording and performance industries. Therefore, by combining analytics rooted in American history, African American studies, ethnomusicology, sociology, and cultural anthropology, this book adds to the growing chorus that calls for an "alternative" to traditional narratives about the blues and Jim Crow United States.

When John W. Work III and his team of Fisk University sociologists and musicologists investigated Coahoma County, Mississippi, in 1941 and 1942, the urban blues from Broonzy's days as a solo black pop artist and sideman for the black pop artist Lil Green peppered nearly every jukebox in Clarksdale. The music created by deep Delta musicians—those who have often come to define America's public memory of the blues—was nearly invisible on Clarksdale's machines and, by extension, black-owned jukeboxes across the country.[33] History seems to have forgotten that Broonzy spent two decades performing and recording urban pop blues on archtop and electric guitars with explicit and humorous lyrics written for black urban audiences that evoked imagery and substance only they would understand.

As white audiences showed increasing interest in Broonzy's music, he seized opportunities to share and examine elements of the black experience including southern history, race relations, agriculture, black urbanization, music, economic conditions, labor relations, intracommunity development, migration, politics, sex, violence, alcohol consumption, and much more. Many of his anecdotes, moreover, became song topics within the vast repertoire he shared night after night in cities all over the world. Songs such as "Black Brown and White," "When I've Been Drinking," "WPA Rag," "Plow Hand Blues," and "I'm Gonna Move to the Outskirts of Town" reflected Broonzy's personal life and experiences while providing important insights to newcomers as he helped steer blues music to new territories. In effect, Broonzy became an important teacher for white American and European blues, jazz, and folk audiences.

Another unique contribution of this book to current blues scholarship is the crosscurrent of transnational history it presents. In 1951, Big Bill Broonzy emerged as one of the most important black bluesmen to tour Europe in the post–World War II era. Europeans had been heavily influenced by black music during World War II, and black blues and jazz had developed a small but loyal following in the United Kingdom and across the continent. These collectors, musicians, and researchers saw Broonzy as an antecedent to the blues and jazz of the era. Not only had Broonzy performed and recorded in the down-home style popular in the late 1920s, but he had also helped pioneer Chicago's urban blues in the 1930s, a style that mixed elements of jazz and swing. To Europeans, then, Broonzy was an icon whose intimate and powerful performing style became a crucible for their understanding of the history of blues and jazz.

Broonzy was a celebrity, shaped by endless negotiations between his audience, his history, his times, and the places he performed. Examining these ideas together, however, one is left with a fundamental question: what was Big Bill Broonzy like in private life? Some who remember him offer a picture of Broonzy as a brilliant musician who was a kind, wise, handsome, and humble friend—and much more intelligent, sophisticated, and complicated than he liked to let on. Others recall him as a heavy drinker and womanizer, who, in his own words, "was a happy man when [he] was drunk and playing with women."[34] A few others have suggested that he was a calculating man who shared many, many partial and half truths about his life, ultimately making his past's veracity impossible to uncover. Without a doubt, Broonzy made a lasting impact on all who knew him.

Big Bill Broonzy was until his death a local celebrity in the black Chicago blues community in which he forged an urbane, cosmopolitan life; yet to the world, he has been remembered as the rural, folk bluesman who showed up at New York's Carnegie Hall at Christmas in 1938. There may be many Bill Broonzys, but the tensions and incongruities in his life and career offer a rich opportunity to explore how black history and culture get shaped and reshaped. Broonzy created, defined, and sustained a world of entertainment in Arkansas, Chicago, New York, and cities across Europe that provided new pathways for African Americans' expanding black consciousness as they engaged the cultural forces contained in black celebrity. Thousands of black musicians followed Broonzy's lead throughout the twentieth century.

By moving beyond a heavy reliance on literary criticism of Broonzy's song lyrics, this work recognizes the importance of black musicians' lived experiences, not just their formations of musical expression.[35] Song lyrics are valuable pieces of evidence but are often taken out of context in a manner that creates a singly interpreted narrative. Furthermore, close readings of Broonzy's song lyrics and their revelation of his role as a working-class, underappreciated, and historically obscure musician overshadow his importance as a cultural and historical architect and limit his relevance in larger historical narratives and questions. Yes, Big Bill Broonzy labored most of his adult life within southern and northern labor industries, but simply relying on literary criticism for analysis of blues artists' compositions masks their contributions to larger narratives rooted in American history and black culture. Essentially, the ways in which Broonzy negotiated his transforming worldview reveal fascinating intersections of a number of important historical currents for twentieth-century African Americans, including New Negro community formation, the importance of the consumer marketplace to black urban life, the transmission of American culture around the globe, and the evolving nature of race in an age of mass consumerism and celebrity.

The book comprises eight chapters and follows a chronological framework tracing Broonzy's life and career. The first three chapters chronicle Broonzy's public and private transformations as a black southerner, Chicago migrant, and emerging blues recording sensation. Chapter 1, "Southern Blues," explores Broonzy's life in the South, including his introduction to black music culture, the politics of race and music making in the Jim Crow South, the impact of his service in World War I, and his burgeoning expectations for the wedding of music and celebrity. Chapter 2, "Carving Out a Home in the Promised Land," examines Broonzy's migration to Chicago and his intellectual transformation from a southern sharecropper, day laborer, and part-time musician into a migrant fully engaged with Chicago's New Negro Renaissance and the public and private spaces where it occurred. Broonzy's pursuance of a professional music career in one of the country's centers for black music and culture is investigated in chapter 3, "Southern Migrant Blues."

Chapters 4 to 6 travel through Broonzy's emergence as a black music celebrity and the ways in which both black and white audiences in the United States and Europe embraced his talents as a black pop star or folk blues songster. Chapter 4, "The Rise of Big Bill," considers Broonzy at the height of his black-pop, Chicago blues celebrity, when he was one of the most prolific blues entertainers of the 1930s and early 1940s and his popularity among black audiences reached its pinnacle. Chapters 5 and 6 trace how a series of unforeseen events, including the great musicians' strike from 1942 to 1944, the meshing of jazz with the blues world, and postwar renewal in European interest in African American music, opened new pathways for Broonzy as he transitioned from black pop music star into a folk blues legend. The rise of the American folk music revival and its increasing interest in Broonzy's prolific but mercurial career is the central focus of chapter 5, "I Come for to Sing," while Broonzy's absorption into Europe's flowering blues and jazz culture is covered in chapter 6, "We Love the Blues, but Tell Us about Jazz."

The last two chapters explore Broonzy's legacy and impact, as he became more known in his final decade as blues-as-folk entertainer, and the ways in which American and European listeners have shaped Broonzy's public memory. Chapter 7, "Big Bill Broonzy," highlights the last few years of Broonzy's life as he wrestled with his growing celebrity in Europe and the United States. Chapter 8, "Escaping the Folk," examines the many ways blues enthusiasts, musicians, ethnomusicologists, folklorists, and other scholars have crafted a historical memory of Broonzy's career that often minimizes the importance he held for black audiences.

Of course, Broonzy would laugh at the language used to describe his life throughout this study. He had his own vocabulary to convey the power inherent in his craft. Black men and women (such as Broonzy) employed this early blues culture to momentarily escape from the world of assembly lines, relief lines, and color lines and to leave momentarily the individual and collective battles against racism, sexism, and material deprivation.[36] In several interviews throughout his career, he echoed these ideas with stern conviction and proud serenity. To understand these negotiations at each level of Broonzy's story—rural Arkansas, black Chicago, the music recording and performance industry, the folk music revival, the explosion of blues in Europe, the evolution of black aesthetics, the emergence of black celebrity—is to understand both "the solidarity black people have shown at political mass meetings" and the "conflicts across class and gender lines that shape and constrain these collective struggles."[37] For Broonzy, the blues always looked toward the future. If by the end of his career he had convinced the world that he was the romantic embodiment of a disappearing blues tradition, his life, nonetheless, was rooted in moving his career forward and shaping his celebrity in ways that might make this possible. In the process, he articulated the hopes, dreams, nostalgias, and fantasies of rural southerners, urban industrial workers, intellectuals, and music-industry professionals. To Broonzy, blues singers always sang of a better and brighter tomorrow "because they figure there's going to be a change in something, that it's not always going to be the same."[38] Exploring how Broonzy navigated the shifting scales of this world demonstrates the centrality of music making as African Americans struggled to turn segregation into congregation. The music of people such as Broonzy, and the communities that made them, redefined the circle of "we" in the United States and became a sonic haunting to remind the nation of its persistent racial dilemma as the country sought to export democracy, American style, across the globe.

Historians of the African American experience seem to have largely forgotten Broonzy in favor of other artists whose professional careers were less prolific and, arguably, less influential and revealing. With his ever-evolving career, Broonzy's story is too messy to fit into these existing narratives. And yet the instability in Broonzy's personas, this book argues, makes his career *more* revealing to historians. Tracing and analyzing the ways Bill Broonzy created and re-created his music, style, life, and image uncovers much about the importance of reexamining understudied American musicians in a larger historical context. Above all, this study aims to bring into relief the cultural terrain that both constrained and enabled twentieth-century African Americans as they lived their lives and shaped their sense of themselves both in the United States and in Europe.

CHAPTER ONE
Southern Blues

> When I got up this morning, I heard that Southern whistle blow
> When I got up this morning, I heard that Southern whistle blow
> Says I'm thinking about my baby, but I sure did want to go—
> —BIG BILL BROONZY, "The Southern Blues" (1935)

Broonzy once told an interviewer that he never decided to become a blues singer because he was, in fact, "born that way."[1] Broonzy's undeniable talent helped his rapid development as a musician, but his playful boast notwithstanding, local black southern musicians had an enormous impact on Broonzy's musicianship. Recalling the "stuff of lore," Broonzy remembered that he had learned how to construct his cigar-box fiddle—it was Broonzy's first musical instrument, as it was for many rural southern musicians—from a local community songster named "See-See Rider."[2] Rider, who took his moniker from the famous, if not notorious, blues song of the same name, was apparently one of the best musicians in the Arkansas River bottoms. A former slave, Rider would visit Broonzy's Arkansas family plantation, looking to earn money or a free meal.[3] According to legend, Rider typically played handmade instruments, including guitar, bass, and fiddle. Broonzy befriended the itinerant musician so that he could "figure out how his guitar and fiddle were made" and find the right construction materials at the local commissary.[4] Once Rider discovered the young Broonzy's interest in his instruments, he began teaching Broonzy how to "fix" the strings and even taught the young aspiring musician to play songs such as "Shortnin' Bread," "Old Hen Cackle," and "Uncle Bud."[5] Broonzy watched Rider carefully and learned a bit more from the songster than just old "fiddle reels." Rider also taught Broonzy about black celebrity in the Jim Crow South. Broonzy later recalled,

> Well, he was just a little short fellow who weighed about 140 pounds. And he played a one-string fiddle all the time. And he'd get on the train, and he'd go from town to town, and he didn't have to pay no fare because he sang all up and down through the train for the white people and the Negroes, too, and they never did charge him nothing. He'd go to town

anytime he got ready. And that get me an idea of learning how to play music, too, because he could ride free, and he get his food and everything free. When he got into town, he'd go into places and start playing, and they would give him food. And I never seen him pay for anything. And I said, well, maybe that would happen to me if I start playing.[6]

His tutelage under See-See Rider led to important events that introduced him to the white community in the sharecropping South as a burgeoning musician in the songster tradition and cemented Broonzy's resolve to become famous.

Big Bill Broonzy was born Lee Conley Bradley on June 26, sometime around the turn of the twentieth century, in and around the Arkansas-Mississippi Delta.[7] The fourth and final boy of ten children, he grew up within a poor and relatively stable sharecropping family with roots in slavery and the era of Reconstruction. By 1910, the family had moved to Lake Dick, Arkansas, a small community situated near the area of Jefferson County today known as Plum Bayou. The details of Broonzy's early childhood are scant and difficult to substantiate. One thing remains clear: Broonzy received very little formal education. Broonzy remembered, "A family like my family, there was so many of us had to work, and they'd send two to school. . . . They sent one of my brothers to school and one of the sisters. [*Inaudible*] went to school, and Frank went to school. But we couldn't go because we had to stay there and work."[8] The 1900 U.S. Census lists his father, Frank Bradley, as a farmer, but ten years later, he is listed as a porter in a local retail store. So Broonzy must have worked in and around farms throughout most of his childhood and adolescence.

Broonzy's introduction to southern music culture began at an early age within a relatively small and intimate community. His uncle Jerry Belcher, a blacksmith and local musician, introduced him to many musical concepts such as rhythm and timbre, using everyday items such as plow blades and brooms from his blacksmith shop. Broonzy's first experience of live performance came from his uncle's blacksmith shop, as Belcher and friends created an ensemble using a washtub, plow points, and a shop broom.[9] Another itinerant musician, a banjo player named Stonewall Jackson, performed with Broonzy's uncle and taught him how to play music "they didn't exactly call" the blues.[10]

Music from the early-twentieth-century American South could be described as one of the region's great "natural resources" and most valuable "exports." Typically, southern secular music in the nineteenth century evolved from the continuing cross-pollination of two powerful and influential cultural strains: the English-Scottish-Irish tradition and the African and African American traditions. Of course, pointing to a map or timeline where these particular strands intersect would be impossible. Nevertheless, one might find a plethora of music in various forms across the region. From the 1830s until the abolition of slavery, minstrelsy, through its nefarious and complicated imagery and symbolism, stood as a center example of both black and white southern musical styles and tastes as minstrel troupes crisscrossed the South performing for large cities and small towns alike. Work songs and field hollers, too, sounded across fields from black tenant farmers and sharecroppers from Arkansas to North Carolina. Broonzy recalled a young man near his family's Arkansas plantation who sang "holler songs," named Doc Reese, "who could be heard for two to three miles."[11] Moreover, in every southern community, there survived the tradition of the "songster": a versatile and skilled black musician with knowledge of English balladry, Irish dance music, black spirituals, blues songs, minstrel numbers, and fiddle tunes. With origins rooted in the slaveholding South, these black men dedicated their talents to performing a wide array of styles at picnics, parties, barbecues, harvest celebrations, dances, weddings, and the like, for both black and white audiences. In time, Broonzy became part of this tradition in rural Arkansas.[12]

One afternoon, a white plantation boss learned that Broonzy was a musician and asked him and his friend Louis Carter to perform for the boss's family and friends. Scared to death, Broonzy and Carter obliged and in so doing earned money, respect, and new Sears and Roebuck fiddles. Within three months, Broonzy and Carter became comfortable with their manufactured instruments and quickly became "the best two Negro musicians around."[13] Broonzy recollected, "We would be playing and sitting under screen porches while the other Negroes had to work in the hot sun," earning the admiration of the white audiences as "their Negroes" and receiving food and "old clothes" as compensation.[14] But the recognition they received as gifted black musicians within their rural community also drew the ire of whites who were offended by the sight of two poor, black children with brand-new instruments. Broonzy remembered one of the "meanest white men" mocking them and arguing, "Them Negroes can't play no real fiddles. Give them their old cigar boxes and make them play them all night or till we get tried and ready to go home!"[15]

Broonzy quickly learned that celebrity had its advantages and disadvantages, especially as it led to closer surveillance by white landowners who kept "their" musicians under a watchful and suspicious eye. Constantly aware of the South's caste system, Broonzy quickly learned that even music could become racialized. This realization ensured that his race consciousness developed quickly.[16]

As a successful working musician, Broonzy could circumvent the physical and economic hardships that challenged the daily lives of his sharecropping and service-industry-laboring parents, which ultimately left him with a sense of earning a "pretty good" living.[17] Popular and skilled black musicians within the Jim Crow South might be offered an escape in the form of "subtle protest against the structural racism" of the region and its economy.[18] Music-making was an alternative to the backbreaking agricultural and unskilled, manual labor of the region; it created an opportunity for laborers "to stop working—or at least to work at a task over which they had much more control."[19] In addition, performing music provided Broonzy with an interested audience (in this case, the white overclass of the Jim Crow South) and time to practice. For the next three or four years, Broonzy and Louis Carter continued to hone their skills as "old-time" southern musicians. At the same time, Broonzy and Carter became involved in their local religious communities as a preacher and a deacon, respectively. Broonzy was frustrated and torn between the choice of whether to stay with the church or to devote himself fully to being a fiddler; he openly lamented, "I can't read or write, and I'm trying to lead people and tell them the right way and don't know what is right myself."[20] By age nineteen, Broonzy gained popularity as a talented musician, earning tips playing for various white functions including picnics, country dances, and even church congregations, "through Arkansas, and Mississippi, and some parts of Texas."[21] Making relatively good money—fifty dollars for a three-day picnic, plus tips—Broonzy performed waltzes, reels, two-steps, and ragtime that often included numbers such as "Missouri Waltz," "Sally Gooden," "On the Road to Texas," "Over the Waves," and "Uncle Bud."[22]

Unlike most black musicians from the region and period, Broonzy never played for all-black audiences in the Deep South as a paid musician.[23] Broonzy's recollections on this fact provide insights about the relationship between race and music in the Jim Crow South: "Why didn't I play for Negro dances? Well you see the way [of?] the white man in this South is this. Anything's good, they thinks it's too good for the Negro, see. . . . When I started playing music, white man told me, he says, 'You too good a musician to be playing for Negroes.' See? 'You should be playing for white people.' And therefore they wouldn't allow me to play for my own people."[24] This passage, from an interview in 1946, reveals the fascinating realities of black music-making in the Jim Crow South. First, it reflects the power and dangers of what one scholar has called the "blues model of individualism": while the end of slavery brought about a tremendous upheaval for the worlds of former bondspersons and white southerners, Jim Crow segregation sought to recapture ownership of black labor as the latter morphed into forms of "cultural self-determination."[25] The blues and other forms of southern music were born of these tensions.

Following the Civil War, the relationship between black musical production, race, and ownership changed tremendously. As black music entered the national consumer culture marketplace in the immediate postwar period, it stripped former slave owners of their control of both the bodies through which and the spaces from which black music echoed throughout the slave-holding South.[26] Nevertheless, if black cultural production in the form of music-making replaced elements of economic determination through labor, whites in the Jim Crow South quite naturally sought to control when and where black music creation might happen, in the same manner that whites controlled southern labor in the South. Alan Lomax, working for the Library of Congress, witnessed this practice firsthand when he was arrested, interrogated, threatened, and harassed for attempting to record Son House at his home in Coahoma County, Mississippi, in the summer of 1942. House, of course, had played for black audiences at this point, but the plantation manager whom he worked for controlled his movements and access to his music.[27]

Playing music in Jim Crow Arkansas held multiple and often conflicting meanings for Broonzy. By his late teens, Broonzy, who was raised in the Baptist church by "good Christian people," served as a country preacher for several Arkansas churches and married "the first woman he ever knew": Gertrude Embrey was an acquaintance from church and a few years his junior.[28] He stopped playing the fiddle altogether, renounced his "devilish ways," and continued his different kinds of work as a sharecropper and part-time preacher. That changed when several white plantation owners who had heard of his talents approached him to perform at a series of white dances. This opportunity allowed him to make far more money than he could have sharecropping. As Broonzy put it, "Christian's one thing but money's another."[29] He quickly learned that playing to the expectations of whites in the South's music industry could provide significant financial reward, even if it meant compromising his religious beliefs and personal values.

Long before Broonzy became a leading celebrity of Chicago blues, he learned valuable lessons about southern musical culture, community leadership, and the expectations of those who controlled music-making in the South. By establishing critical relationships with musicians who held knowledge of the music itself and expected Broonzy to carry on the southern musical tradition, Broonzy began developing patterns of behavior that would help sustain his long career in its various phases. Broonzy's relationship to music formed in the South, and that context strengthened his understanding that managing others' expectations could help bolster his career. Finally, and perhaps most important, he quickly discovered that the recognition and celebration of community musicianship might provide an escape from the endless cycle of labor, poverty, and oppression in the Jim Crow South.

Broonzy's first forays into music happened at a critical moment in both the history of black vernacular music and, more broadly, African American history. The black spirituals that Broonzy had heard most of his life became one of the earliest vessels for the expression of anti-Jim Crow sentiment. Of course, the slave spirituals dated back to older, more sacred cultural forms in slavery as a reflection of black religious values juxtaposed against the horrors of American slavery. Relying on a call-and-response pattern, these songs employed deeply seeded African musical traditions, while at the same time perpetuating a collective memory of the black experience in bondage. During the postbellum period, the Negro spiritual took on new form and meaning.[30] By 1871, the spirituals were beginning to leave the fields and black churches in the South for appearances on the concert stage and in music halls for multiethnic crowds across the country and around the world. For some people, including W. E. B. Du Bois, the spirituals continued to stand "not simply as the sole American music, but as the most beautiful expression of human experience born this side the seas."[31] Yet to some African Americans from the early twentieth century, the slave spirituals had become outdated, at best, and bastardized into "concertized and Europeanized art songs," at worst.[32] The first generation of African Americans to inherit the legacy of emancipation—Broonzy's generation—began moving away from the spiritual world of the old sorrow songs to more modern forms of musical culture that expressed their new condition. The cultural historian Lawrence Levine has suggested that following the Civil War, "less and less did the songs of their forbears express their own world view."[33] Instead, new forms of both sacred and secular music developed following the end of the Civil War and Reconstruction, with sacred music becoming, in effect, a more popular cultural vehicle for African Americans engaging with modernity and expressing their changing worldviews. It is no coincidence that the blues as a genre emerged in the late-nineteenth-century South alongside the rise of Jim Crow racism. Disfranchised, defaced by American popular culture, and denied access to equal or adequate education, southern African Americans sought other means for giving expression to their thoughts, emotions, and humanity.[34] Essentially, the blues moved away from the sacred traditions of spirituals by addressing African Americans' increasing secularity. By doing so, the blues transformed the meaning and importance of black popular music for migrants such as Broonzy in the same manner the spirituals had transformed the valences of sacred music for an older generation. The New Orleans jazz pioneer Sidney Bechet has noted that while spirituals looked toward the heavens for hope and relief, the blues commented on the human condition of blacks in a segregated world. "They were both . . . people's way of praying to themselves" and "praying to be let alone so they could be human."[35]

But the blues was far more than a mere extension of the folk. From Broonzy's childhood to early adulthood, blues music quickly became one of the most important musical genres of the early twentieth century. Its history is a complicated one, but it mirrors so many of the complexities and ambiguities of Broonzy's own career that it bears close examination. For the first fifty years of its existence as primarily black popular music, its main proponents were professional musicians.[36] As much as a generation of scholars tried to convince the nation and world that "authentic blues" was a by-product of the laboring masses of the black South, in reality, the genre was much more contrived.[37] What could be identified as blues music in the late nineteenth and early twentieth centuries stemmed from the ideas and aspirations of popular traveling vaudeville and medicine shows, an important sheet-music industry, and nascent recording technology. From 1908 until the late 1910s, blues music coalesced into a genre, as ragtime began to transition into protoforms of blues and jazz. By 1914, W. C. Handy, dubbed the "Father of the Blues," conquered the sheet-music industry with two of his most famous compositions, "Memphis Blues" and "St. Louis Blues," both of which represented an interesting synthesis of the popular rags of Scott Joplin and black rural southern music that he so famously heard at a Tutwiler, Mississippi, train station.[38] Of course, rural, black, southern music contained identifiable elements of the particular blues style popularized by the mysterious, sinewy Tutwiler musician whom Handy heard—as well as the likes of Blind Lemon Jefferson, Lonnie Johnson, Son House, Jimmie Rodgers, and Robert Johnson—but as Broonzy's early tutelage in vernacular music suggests, the repertoires of southern black (and white) musicians were much more diverse and multifarious.[39]

By the 1910s, within the traveling world of vaudeville, minstrel, and tent-show performers, dozens upon dozens of black and white artists traveled the country singing blues-influenced songs and popularizing the blues among southern and northern audiences. By 1910, the vaudeville veteran Sherman H. Dudley began organizing what was to become TOBA, or the Theatre Owners Booking Association (known pejoratively at the time to African Americans as "Tough On Black Asses"), in hopes of creating a black-operated vaudeville circuit for the increasing popularity of traveling solo performers.[40] Most of these early blues songsters—Ethel Waters, Edith Wilson, Lucille Hegamin, Marion Harris, Morton Harvey, Al Bernard, Bessie Smith, Bo Carter, Ma Rainey—began sharing blues songs with their audiences in this emerging black vaudeville circuit at the exact moment when blues compositions on sheet music began their widespread dissemination from coast to coast. Gertrude "Ma" Rainey, one of the blues-as-pop-music's true pioneers, made her first of many appearances in the *Chicago Defender* in May 1915, as a tent performer leaving a Charlotte, North Carolina, audience of "2,000 to 3,000 people . . . roaring with laughter" from her blues songs and banter in Alexander Tolliver's Smart Set Comedy Troupe.[41] As the recording industry moved past its novelty stage in the 1910s, many of these musicians naturally became the first artists to document the growing blues craze on record.

The very first blues song captured on record was a 1915 vocal rendition of W. C. Handy's "Memphis Blues," performed by the white vaudeville veteran Morton Harvey. The sheer mention of a white performer as the first recorded blues singer might raise eyebrows among many people who have failed to understand that "the history of blues as popular music is not the same as its history as black cultural expression."[42] For historians, however, it stands as evidence of the inaccurate nature of how the country's musical past has been remembered, considering that the follow-up to Morton's "Memphis Blues" was the Irish stage actress Marie Cahill's 1917 hit "The Dallas Blues."[43] In 1920, however, Mamie Smith and her Jazz Hounds' "Crazy Blues" became the first recorded blues song by an African American, sold over one million copies within its first year of production, and earned Smith nearly $20,000 in royalties.[44] "Crazy Blues," however, reflected the earlier styles popularized by white vaudeville singers who purveyed the nascent genre blues; it reflected a smoother, more Europeanized approach to twelve-bar blues forms and flatted thirds and fifths than did the women who were to become the most successful of the early blues queens. Those women—Bessie Smith, Ida Cox, Sippie Wallace, Clara Smith, and Ma Rainey—defined a far more familiar style than any previously recorded blues artist had. Beginning at the exact moment when Big Bill Broonzy landed in Chicago, these women echoed the tent-performance and black-vaudeville styles that the thousands of black migrants then moving to New York, Chicago, Detroit, Cleveland, and St. Louis had grown to love back home. Perry Bradford understood that black audiences were quite familiar with the blues in 1920 when he recorded Mamie Smith, arguing that fourteen million African Americans in the United States would "buy records if recorded by one of their own" because those who were outside of the African American experience lacked the ability to interpret and convey the meanings of blues songs.[45] From this sentiment, then, race records—music recorded by African Americans for an African American commercial market—profoundly changed the American music industry and subsequently placed black music at the center of the country's musical landscape.

Just as blues emerged as an identifiable art form from various strains of black culture and geographic centers of black life, the United States became embroiled in one of the most transformative wars in human history, World War I, or the "the Great War." Broonzy's first opportunity to leave Arkansas or the United States itself came during World War I. Broonzy entered the United States Army in 1917. He received basic training at Camp Pike, Arkansas, then transported to Newport News, Virginia, and finally shipped off to Brest, France, as a member of the American Expeditionary Force (AEF). As a soldier of the Services of Supply stationed in France, Broonzy transformed himself into someone vastly different from the Arkansas sharecropper, country fiddler, and preacher he had been before the war, who "didn't want nobody tellin'" him how to live his life.[46] Between 1918 and 1919, Broonzy served in the U.S. Army, one of the 380,000 African Americans contributing to the nation's efforts in World War I.[47] Like many of his fellow black soldiers, Broonzy had witnessed both the horrors of war and the open racism that had followed the AEF from the United States to Europe, and he was forever changed by these experiences.[48]

Of course, the 160,000 African Americans stationed in Europe working in "supply companies" were forced to build roads, dig ditches, bury the dead, deliver mail, and construct camps, what Broonzy called the "dirty work" of the military.[49] Most black soldiers stationed with the Services of Supply worked in the same manner as southern gang laborers back home, in some cases for nearly sixteen hours a day.[50] As Broonzy remembered, some officers recognized skilled laborers among the black soldiers, but most believed that young black conscripts "didn't know anything else to do"; therefore, most of the members of the company "had that same old hard work [they] had at home."[51] In fact, most black conscripts were never intended for combat on the front lines, as many racist military staff and draft-board officials had concluded that black soldiers were unable to effectively serve in combat; this relegated almost all black soldiers to hard labor under the banner of making the world safe for democracy. In addition, black soldiers stationed in Europe faced harsh and cruel treatment from white soldiers and military police all too eager to remind African Americans of their subordinate status in a segregated military and to reinforce Jim Crow on foreign soil. Broonzy lived in strictly segregated barracks at camp, and black soldiers were forbidden to enter the white areas of the grounds. White officers believed that "the germs" from the black troops would infect the white-only areas, even though white soldiers were allowed to enter the black barracks and shoot craps. One lieutenant, whom Broonzy remembered as "tough," "didn't care what he said to a Negro or what happened. . . . He'd always put the hardest things he could on a Negro."[52] The black soldiers stationed in France learned quickly that white officers would "punish them for nothing," and life was especially difficult for those who "stood up for their rights."[53]

Despite the harsh realities for black soldiers in World War I, Broonzy's anecdotes of life in the camps of France often reflected a more multifaceted experience. He once recalled an incident involving a travel pass to town, six fellow black soldiers, twelve white soldiers, and a black cat. The superstitious black soldiers apparently had attempted to catch the cat in hopes of preventing a streak of bad luck in the middle of war-torn Europe, if the cat happened to cross their paths. So, as Broonzy told the story, the six men set out to chase the cat for nearly two hours, screaming, "don't let him cross," while the twelve white soldiers watched in befuddled amusement.[54] Broonzy and company finally caught the cat, returned it to the proper side of the street, and continued into town to grab a few drinks, as the white soldiers returned to base. "From then on," Broonzy remembered, every time black and white soldiers crossed paths in the camp, the white soldiers began laughing at all the black soldiers. After an extended period of time, the black soldiers in the camp took offense to the laughter, as they thought the whites were laughing because the soldiers "were black."[55] As a result, the black soldiers crossed the imaginary color line in the camp to confront their white comrades, prompting the executive officers to inquire what the escalating dustup was about. As a crowd of a thousand soldiers gathered, one of the dozen white soldiers explained the story of the six black troops and the black cat, creating uproarious laughter in the camp that even caused the commanding officers to chuckle. "After that day," Broonzy remembered, "the white soldiers would come over and play games with us, and for fourteen months, everybody laughed about the night we catched the black cat."[56]

An important part of Broonzy's race consciousness throughout his life was his ability to find humor and personal strength in difficult situations, often reflecting those sentiments in a quick turn of phrase or his next song. The story of the black cat is filled with racist overtones of life in the camps for black soldiers, but it also demonstrates Broonzy's emphasis on humor in what was surely a very difficult period for a young man who did not know where he was "more than a goat."[57] Broonzy's wartime experience caused a profound development in his maturity and consciousness. Broonzy once told Alan Lomax,

> You see, after I went into the Army and come out of the Army I couldn't stand that way. . . . Because when I went to the Army it was a dead cinch you had to keep clean in the Army. . . . Those people on levee camps they wear the same clothes or sleep in the same clothes. . . . But in the Army you had to keep yourself clean, and when I went into the Army I had gotten used to that, keeping clean, and then when I went back, they would still want to put me back in one of those places and I couldn't stand it any more, see? Cause I stayed in their two years and I got used to that. . . . And fact of the business, when I come back home they want to put me back in one of them camps or back one of them jobs like that, see? I couldn't stand that no more. I wanted to be clean, I wanted to be presentable and be around in public places and meet people and get along with people. . . . And that's why I say it opened my eyes, you know, and let me know that people could be human beings, not beasts.[58]

Like many of his fellow black soldiers, Broonzy had witnessed both the horrors of war and the open racism that had followed the AEF from the United States to Europe and back, and he was forever changed by these experiences.[59] But traveling across the Atlantic and living in Europe had fostered in him a sense of self-respect that military training often provides. By the war's end, the towering black intellectual W. E. B. Du Bois described how this shift in consciousness would be a recurring phenomenon among returning black veterans when he wrote, "They began to hate prejudice and discrimination as they had never hated it before. They began to realize its internal meaning and complications. Far from filling them with a desire to escape from their race and country, they were filled with a bitter, dogged determination never to give up the fight for Negro equality in America. . . . A new, radical Negro spirit has been born in France which leaves us older radicals far behind."[60] Long before Broonzy left for military service, a lifetime of humiliating public spectacles and uncomfortably close encounters with extrajudicial, racialized violence in the river bottoms of the Arkansas Delta had instilled an inescapable contempt for his ancestral home and profoundly shaped his race consciousness. Broonzy once explained that his own recognition of what Du Bois described as "the veil"[61] and "double consciousness"—the moment "from when he could remember" until he "could understand what [his] people was saying," when he realized that he was black in a fundamentally racist society—occurred from a series of conversations he had shared with his mother as a child about the inherent dangers of associating with white women.[62] But his experience as a veteran of the Great War removed that "veil," ultimately redefining how he viewed what his blackness, the Deep South, and American democracy might be.

Upon Broonzy's receiving his discharge from the U.S. Army at Camp Pike, near Little Rock, Arkansas, in 1919, he faced challenges to his newfound perspectives almost immediately. For many white Americans, the presence of black veterans in uniform returning to their homes across the country signified eminent danger to the power of Jim Crow. These returning service members "contributed to a volatile social, political, and economic climate," which spawned an enormous growth of clashes in racial violence and public lynchings.[63] In Arkansas, Broonzy stepped off the train wearing his clean, crisp uniform with pride and dignity. Immediately, like countless other black veterans, he received an embarrassing public berating from an old, white acquaintance for whom he had once worked. Later in life, Broonzy continued to view this moment as a major turning point. The white man's rancor was palpable: "I got off the train. . . . I met a white fellow that I was knowin' before I went to the Army. So he told me 'Listen boy, now you been in the Army?' I told him 'Yeah.' He says, 'How'd you like it?' I said, 'It's O.K.' He says, 'Well . . . you ain't in the Army now.' 'And those clothes you got there . . . take 'em home and get out of 'em and get you some overalls. Because there's no nigger gonna walk around here with no Uncle Sam's uniform on up and down the streets.'"[64] The white man continued to direct Broonzy toward the commissary, where he could buy overalls and immediately return to sharecropping's system of debt peonage. But the hardened and awakened veteran that Broonzy had become was no longer indifferent to what was happening. Indeed, African Americans throughout the United States were quickly learning that newly conscious black service personnel in uniform posed a real threat to the existing social order.

Immediately following the war, black newspapers across the country featured columns and editorials filled with outrage and disgust at white Americans' belief that "these Negroes who have been in the camps and across the seas will 'forget their places' . . . and be well to have to them get rid of the uniform."[65] It seems impossible to know if these instances of racial antagonism were surprising to returning veterans from the Deep South, such as Broonzy. What remains clear is that these public humiliations and threats of racial violence would not go unchallenged. As Broonzy later recalled, "That's why I didn't never stay in the South no more after I come outta the Army. . . . I couldn't stand that bossing around by anybody."[66] Once Broonzy's memories of black life in the Deep South forged with those from his recent participation in the AEF in Europe, he quickly developed perspectives on race in the United States that were very much in the New Negro vein.[67]

The historian Chad Williams has suggested that black veterans of World War I "embodied a 'reconstructed' Negro, radicalized at the levels of racial, gender, and political consciousness by the combination of war and the ferocity of white supremacy."[68] Broonzy knew that the life he led after the army forced him to relinquish control to the white overseer who managed his tenant farm; to his wife, Gertrude Embrey, who demanded that he improve their lot in life; and, most of all, to the U.S. government—the institution that asked him to fight and die abroad but refused to guarantee his rights at home. Broonzy knew quite well that black men in the South "never get to be men. . . . It's always boy until you get too old, then they called you uncle."[69] Broonzy once admitted that after returning home, his personal life would never be the same:

> Well my wife always, before I went into the Army, whatsoever she said went. An when-after I went into the Army and came out, well, then she wanted to do the same thing, you know. . . . Well I wouldn't stand for that, see? And the same things about a white man down there I had to work for. They'd try to tell me this and tell me that, and I didn't care no more about a white man than I did about a black man, see? And whensoever he tried to tell me something that I had to do, why, that's why we fell out.[70]

Broonzy further explained to Lomax that Gertrude had wanted him to leave farming and take up the difficult but lucrative work of an extra gang for railroad companies.[71] Of course, he knew that white employers, whether on tenant and sharecropping farms or on levee and railroad gangs, viewed black laborers' lives as having little or no value.[72]

All African Americans from the Deep South knew the dangers of working on levee camps, road crews, and extra railroad gangs, as any of these jobs were often conduits to southern prisons or death.[73] Broonzy's older brother James, for example, drowned in a horrific revetment accident while working on the Arkansas River in Pine Bluff. An April 14, 1919, piece in the *Pine Bluff Commercial* indicated that on April 10, an unidentified white male had fallen alongside of James, as the barge on which they were working suddenly listed and ejected both men into the Arkansas River. The anonymous white man was of course saved, but Bradley, "paralyzed with fear," could not accept the offered help and disappeared to the bottom of the river. Five days later, his body was discovered and identified as James Bradley and later buried near the family's home.[74] Once again, Broonzy was reminded of the disparaging world of the Jim Crow South, as his brother's life was sacrificed so that a white man's could be spared.

No evidence exists that conclusively reveals why Broonzy left Arkansas for Chicago. His growing New Negro consciousness, his disillusionment with his marriage, and the lifelong humiliations of the Jim Crow South, when combined with the death of his brother, may have pushed him over the edge. Broonzy later lamented,

> Well the main reason I left from home because I couldn't stand the way that the white man had been treating me. I was just dumb to the fact; I thought it was the right way to be treated. And when I found out it was the wrong way to be treated, I just wouldn't take that no more. . . . That's from me being in the Army. . . . And fact of the business, after I found out that was more of the world than just Arkansas . . . and other people living in other parts of the world and was doing a durn sight better than I was doin. . . . So I said "what the heck. . . . Down here a man ain't nothing no how."[75]

It also seems plausible that he became involved in a life-threatening altercation that forced him to run; but little evidence exists of any event of that nature, and he never discussed that possibility with anyone. The blues legend Riley "B. B." King, for example, left his Indianola, Mississippi, home in the middle of the night in 1945 after severely damaging the smokestack of the tractor he operated for a local plantation. Scared of violent retribution, he fled his wife and home for Memphis with a guitar and $2.50 in his pocket, never to return.[76] Both King and Broonzy would use their experiences of life in the Deep South as fodder for their songwriting for decades. Twenty years later, Broonzy depicted his emotions upon leaving home and the difficulties he faced in doing so in one of his most well-known songs, "Key to the Highway":

> I got the key to the highway
> And I'm billed out and bound to go
> I'm gonna leave here runnin'
> 'Cause walkin' is most too slow
>
> I'm goin' down on the border
> Now where I'm better known
> 'Cause woman you don't do nothin'
> But drive a good man 'way from home

Late at night in January 1921, hearing "a freight a coming," Big Bill Broonzy left Arkansas for good and "hoboed from there into St. Louis."[77] Broonzy found a job and worked for about one month, until he had saved enough money to continue on to Chicago.[78] On February 8, Broonzy arrived at the Illinois Central Station at 135 East Eleventh Place, more commonly known as the "Twelfth Street Station," perhaps arriving on Illinois Central Railroad's most famous locomotive, the *Panama Limited*, which traveled daily from St. Louis to Chicago.[79]

Broonzy quickly made Chicago's Black Belt his home. Several known Chicago addresses for Broonzy from 1930 to 1946 place him and his family throughout the city's South Side: on Washburne Avenue in 1930, on West Washington Boulevard in 1944, and on South Parkway in 1946 and at his death.[80]

In reality, Broonzy was but one out of the approximately twenty-nine million southerners who left the South for opportunities in the North, Midwest, and West during the Great Migrations of the twentieth century. A country fiddler from rural Arkansas with a fledgling New Negro sensibility, he arrived in Chicago at a critical moment in the city's history. Like tens of thousands of other southern migrants, he settled in Chicago with deep roots in his southern past but wanting desperately to move beyond its ponderous grasp. Quickly, the blues queens of the early blues craze transformed Chicago into one of the most important musical centers in the nation. Already an aspiring, part-time musician in the South, Broonzy immediately engaged with the ubiquitous and potent musical environment that still characterizes Chicago today. But before he could fully engage the city's vibrant culture, he first had to learn to navigate urban life amid a city fully engaged in its own New Negro Renaissance.

CHAPTER TWO

Carving Out a Home in the Promised Land

In the early 1950s, Big Bill Broonzy revealed a fascinating recollection of his worldview upon arriving in Chicago:

> In every place I go, all the people I meet of different races is glad to say and be from where they was born. But me, when anybody asks me if I'm from Mississippi, I'll say yes but I'm mad and don't like to talk about it, because I was born poor, had to work and do what the white man told me to do, a lot of my people were mobbed, lynched and beaten. The ones who owned something, the white man wanted his wife or his best horse, he had to give it up. For everything I raised on my farm, the white man was setting his price; he paid me what he wanted to give and I had to take it. So when I came North I tried to be like him. . . . So I straightened my hair, changed my way of talking and walking, always trying to do things like the white man so I wouldn't have to get back. . . . I came to the North and tried it. I tried everything I had seen him do, then I would go home and look in my looking glass and could still see Mississippi.[1]

Broonzy carried an enormous weight as a black, southern migrant looking to make a new home in Chicago. The preceding quotation reveals a man who had wrestled with the power and privilege of whiteness, the economic and social stranglehold of Jim Crow, and Chicago's great promise. In time, Chicago would provide a host of new opportunities for Broonzy, and he would gain fame and celebrity. The city granted Broonzy anonymity and allowed him to reinvent his own past and transform his image when necessary. Despite Alan Lomax's description of Broonzy as a "slum dweller" during his early years in Chicago, Broonzy was well equipped to negotiate a new life rooted in the city's New Negro Renaissance.[2] And yet these struggles to adapt were fundamental to his experience as a black migrant worker and aspiring blues musician. At the same time, Broonzy's life in Chicago highlights the impact of the New Negro Renaissance outside of Harlem and beyond the United States' boarders.[3]

The concept of the "New Negro" is as old as the black experience in the United States, popping up along a trajectory of moments in African American history, appearing as a descriptor in slavery, Reconstruction, the rise of

Jim Crow, the Great Depression, and even World War II. Pinpointing a solid and lasting definition of the New Negro proves difficult in a field that is currently "in formation."[4] Historical scholarship spanning decades has placed writers, artists, intellectuals, and activists at the nexus of the creation of a black cultural renaissance that lasted from the turn of the twentieth century until the middle of the Great Depression. This renaissance, so the argument went among later scholars of the movement, signaled the emergence of a "New Negro"—a cultural, political, and intellectual architect whose collective contributions to African American, and, more broadly, American, life would one day erode the debilitating stereotypes of African Americans that were so ingrained in the dominant narratives of American life. At the same time, the New Negro would prove to whites that the black experience in the United States—the contributions of the elite, in particular—deserved a place alongside mainstream (i.e., white) culture as an integral contribution to the fabric of American exceptionalism. This conception of the movement was defined in Alain Locke's *The New Negro: Voices of the Harlem Renaissance*, with its insistence that in "Harlem, Negro life" had "seiz[ed] upon its first chances for group expression and self-determination."[5]

But the New Negro concept can be more appropriately defined as "a moment in time," rather than a collection of individuals following the same intellectual trajectory.[6] It is now understood as a diasporic movement situated in a much broader geographic area. Central to this repositioning are the analytics of class, gender, sexuality, and place, which would, invariably, hold enormous sway over how and by what means a New Negro movement would play out. If black intellectuals in Harlem during the New Negro movement were advocating self-determination and cultural autonomy, black entrepreneurs, artists, politicians, and intellectuals in Chicago, for example, began construction of the Black Metropolis, communities in which ideals of a New Negro consciousness were openly contested within the city's producer and consumer cultures.[7] Under the watchful eye of whites, in both the public and private spaces of Chicago's Black Metropolis, intellectuals, musicians, artists, policy runners, factory workers, domestic laborers, community uplift organizations, military veterans, movie theater managers, and others wrestled daily with what the New Negro might mean for black political, economic, and cultural developments in what one scholar has described as black Chicago's "marketplace intellectual life."[8] Broonzy's migration to Chicago directly positioned him in an epicenter of black cultural and intellectual upheaval that would transform his worldview and make Chicago his home.

Broonzy chose Chicago as his final destination because the city was a logical destination for black migrants from Mississippi, Arkansas, and Louisiana, given the heavily trafficked railroad lines of the period. Like thousands of fellow black migrants, he had an established network of family and friends that eased his transition into urban life. As countless other relatives of black migrants did, Broonzy's brother Andrew J. Bradley greeted him upon his arrival. Andrew worked for the Pullman Company and lived with his wife at 4630 South Michigan Avenue.[9] Almost immediately, Andrew called a friend to help Broonzy find a job. These well-established social networks were important components of a migrant's journey: they often provided lodging, hot meals, opportunities to make employment connections, and a physical address that could serve as home base until migrants made their own arrangements.[10] When Broonzy arrived in Chicago, he found that he could participate in American life to an extent not possible in Arkansas.

By the turn of the twentieth century, Chicago had become the most important metropolis in the Midwest. The city had risen from the ashes of the great fires of 1871 and 1874 and the labor unrest of the following decade to stand as an exemplar of the United States' potential as an emerging global power. A rich mixture of working-class immigrants and migrants had settled into distinct communities, each of which contained a fascinating amalgam of ethnic and cultural backgrounds while simultaneously sharing "an orientation to 'localism.'"[11] These steel, garment, packinghouse, and manufacturing laborers often lived in tight-knit, ethnically segregated communities with names such as Packingtown, Old Immigrant, Avondale, Bridgeport, and Lincoln Square.[12]

From 1910 to 1990, some eight million blacks, twenty million whites, and one million southern-born Latinos left the South in the great upheaval known as the "Southern Diaspora."[13] The effect of their migration to Chicago was dramatic. Nearly fifty thousand African Americans migrated from the South to the North during World War I alone, and this trend continued well into the 1930s. According to the U.S. Census, the black population of Chicago increased from 44,103 in 1910 to 109,594 in 1920 (nearly 150 percent) and reached a total of 233,903 in 1930.[14]

Recent histories on the Great Migration offer complex explanations for why so many black (and white) southerners left the South during the late nineteenth and early twentieth centuries. By the last decade of the nineteenth century, some African Americans began leaving the rural South to seek jobs in a growing array of factory, service, and domestic industries in urban areas. Others chose to escape the terror of Jim Crow, which had triumphed in the region by 1890.[15] In the case of Chicago, African Americans were also drawn to the city's vibrant culture: the explosion of art, music, black entrepreneurship, and growing community vitality. This culture defined Chicago's own "Harlem," the South Side neighborhood known passionately as Bronzeville.

Beginning in 1916, the community's "fearless, sensationalist, and militant" newspaper, the *Chicago Defender*, urged black migrants to leave the South's racism for good, while simultaneously extolling the enormously expanding industrial boom of Chicago's manufacturing districts.[16] At the same time, however, the *Defender* described a community fully engaged with American modernity and one complete with unparalleled schools, churches, and leisure-time activities. With help from a subscriber base that reached about two hundred thousand by the 1920s, hundreds of thousands of black southerners began pouring into urban areas across the country.[17] By 1921, moreover, enormous webs of grassroots network "facilitators" also enticed many more black migrants.[18]

The boundaries of Bronzeville were the Chicago River on the north, Sixteenth Street on the south, the South Branch of the river on the west, and Lake Michigan on the east.[19] Within a decade, this neighborhood expanded south from downtown to Thirty-Ninth Street, and within the next fifteen years, it absorbed fifteen thousand more black new arrivals. This rapid growth in the city's black population created a lack of adequate housing and economic opportunity. Chicago was tough on many migrants, but most understood both its problems and its possibilities. The poet Langston Hughes summed it up with sharp wit and elegant style:

> Chicago is a town
> That sure do run on wheels.
> Runs so fast you don't know
> How good the ground feels.[20]

Yet racism was entrenched in Chicago when Broonzy arrived, creating enormous difficulties for black migrants forced to live in the city's segregated South and West Sides. The rapid expansion of African Americans in the Windy City from 1910 to 1919 culminated in a struggle for adequate housing and violent resistance by white residents. As blacks pushed east of State Street and south of Fifty-Fifth Street in search of better living conditions, whites began an aggressive campaign to buy formerly white-owned real estate, establish racially prohibitive homeowner organizations and clubs, or force blacks to retreat through measures of public humiliation and violence.

The hostilities and anger that whites unleashed against blacks often reached boiling points throughout the decade in public parks, playgrounds, schools, and beaches.

These events, when combined with the uneasy presence of returning black AEF veterans and the anti-immigrant, antilabor hysteria of the immediate postwar period, culminated in the great Chicago Race Riot of 1919. This dark chapter in Chicago's history left the city's working-class communities with thirty-eight dead, five hundred injured, $250,000 in property damage, and thousands homeless. Because of this racial violence, many Chicagoans concluded that the city did indeed have a "Negro" problem. The response was a series of investigations and studies, beginning with the Chicago Commission on Race Relations' 1922 sociological study *The Negro in Chicago* and continuing notably with the 1944 *Proceedings of the Mayor's Conference on Race Relations* from the City of Chicago's Mayor's Committee on Race Relations, and St. Clair Drake and Horace Cayton's *Black Metropolis* in 1945. Social scientists, politicians, community leaders, and concerned citizens wrestled with the issue of race relations in the Windy City for much of the twentieth century, and the process began at the very moment when Big Bill Broonzy arrived. Broonzy's adopted home in Bronzeville and the city's South Side lay at the heart of the investigations of and discussions in Chicago.[21]

Recognition of a "Negro Problem" did not alleviate Chicago's racism. By the end of the 1920s, the city remained almost completely segregated, with newly arriving African Americans increasingly restricted to the South Side. This small enclave housed nearly 90 percent of the black population in the city by 1920.[22] By 1930, the South Side Black Belt had moved south to Sixty-Seventh Street and east to Cottage Grove Avenue, and by 1950, it had pushed east toward Lake Michigan. As thousands of southern black migrants poured into the city's South Side, they were forced to expand their neighborhood in the face of racially restrictive covenants and racial violence.[23] Even in the face of such racism and violence, there were echoes of promise.

Like thousands of others, Broonzy had heard stories throughout the South about the promises of northern life and rumors of a "Land of Hope." In a 1946 interview, he discussed the clandestine circulation of the *Chicago Defender* and its impact on southern readers who longed for stories about black autonomy in the developing Black Metropolis.[24] In addition to the great hope of freedom and dignity were the economic opportunities in the booming metropolises of the North and Midwest. Labor recruiters for wartime industries revved up an enormous recruiting campaign that convinced millions of southerners of a seemingly endless supply of industrial jobs. Taken together with the severe limitations placed on European immigration at the onset of the war and the addition of over three million manufacturing jobs, cities such as St. Louis, Detroit, and Chicago became targets for young, mobile, black southerners eager to escape a rapidly shrinking agricultural economy in the South. The promise of decent wages combined with African Americans' growing disgruntlement with the Jim Crow South to make these industrial centers teem daily with new arrivals.

Although Chicago did not exhibit the open racism of the Arkansas and Mississippi River bottoms of Broonzy's youth, racism remained a great influence on his worldview after his move north. Surely this new urban environment had more to offer than the ubiquitous oppression of a life in the South as a black laborer. For one, African Americans partook in the various manufacturing industries then thriving throughout the city. On Broonzy's first job as a molder, he recognized that because blacks were barred from labor unions, whites would always receive higher pay for the same work.[25] He later recalled what happened while he was on another job as a welder: "[I] taught this young white guy to be a welder, and as soon as he learned to be a welder they fired me."[26] He had left Arkansas, in part, to avoid embarrassing racist confrontations, only to find that race also shaped life in the urban, industrialized North. He then worked at the Phoenix Foundry and the American Brake Shoe Company, "first as a molder's helper, then as a molder." In spite of these moments of race-driven marginalization, he eventually worked his way into a position at the Pullman Company.[27] Broonzy had settled into the "City of Big Shoulders" and seemed well on his way toward black middle-class respectability.

Black notions of respectability in turn-of-the-century Chicago embodied a number of critical elements of racial uplift ideology. At its core, racial uplift monitored public behavior in hopes of "turning the pejorative designation of race into a source of dignity and self-affirmation through an ideology of class differentiation, self-help, and interdependence."[28] Class differentiation mattered in the sense that elite and middle-class African Americans could, through displays of cultural capital and evidence of cultural production, persuade whites to be more sympathetic toward blacks. Proponents of racial uplift believed that expanding "bourgeois morality" could alleviate the racist stereotypes that whites held only if whites began to understand that many blacks espoused strong notions of class that were embedded in ideas of chastity and filial devotion.

Black Chicago had grown dramatically from 1880 to the first decade of the twentieth century.[29] The early settlers, African Americans, often of mixed ancestry, who moved to the city from the East Coast and Upper South following the Civil War and Reconstruction, had established a position within black Chicago's class structure that relied less on white definitions of wealth and more on ideas of "refinement" and "respectability" that carried over from the Victorian age.[30] The Victorian respectability politics espoused by the old African American elite relied on dichotomies of public and private life, and male patriarchy and female domesticity, and placed an emphasis on one's role as an active producer instead of a passive consumer in the marketplace. With these divisions in mind, the old elite inserted bourgeois conceptions of efficiency into superficial representations of "economic thrift, bodily restraint, and functional modesty in personal and community presentation."[31] With their close association with white businessmen, this old guard of the African American elite vigorously resisted the development of all-black institutions and businesses that operated exclusively in black neighborhoods. All-black institutions would both erode the status that white patronage had conferred on elite African Americans and also force these leaders to associate with fellow black citizens whom they saw as less refined. They were willing to accept residential segregation but only to preserve their own integrated social and economic life.

To outsiders, black Chicago represented a uniformly segregated mass. Beneath the surface, however, both older and developing ideologies between the old elite, the growing black bourgeoisie, and the ever-expanding black working class made Chicago's South Side home to competing visions over both class distinction and the future of black modernity. Because the wealthy old elite shared the same segregated space with newly arrived southern migrants, a complete realization of Victorian respectability became increasingly impossible.

From the beginning of the twentieth century to the peak of the migration, a new group of black leaders emerged within the city.[32] These new middle-class leaders increasingly looked to Chicago's black community for political and economic support and rejected older Victorian notions of industrial productivity and public presentation as tools for combating white supremacy. Instead, they relied on Chicago's commercialized leisure world as a place for "alternative forms of labor, routes toward upward mobility, and visions of the racial community."[33] Could southern migrants' drive and ambitions for higher wages and greater participation in American democracy represent the growth of a new working class, which might elevate African Americans to the status of a new proletariat?[34] Many black Chicago entrepreneurs, politicians, ministers, editors, musicians, and professionals believed so, as they transformed their community into one of the most important centers of black business and culture in the United States.

Robert Abbott, the founder and chief editor of the *Chicago Defender*, was one of the more famous members of this emergent middle-class leadership. Abbott used the weekly paper to broadcast throughout the United States (especially the South) the importance of Chicago as a hub of black urban life. As one of the most widely distributed black newspapers in the country, the *Defender* urged readers to see for themselves the strides that African Americans had made in Chicago.

Along the "Stroll," black Chicago's entertainment and business district, the growing black bourgeoisie and working classes found "alternative sources of labor and new kinds of leisure" that allowed for the growth of new "routes and rites of respectability."[35] Quickly, labels of "Old Settlers" and "New Settlers" began to merge and "became much less about when one arrived in Chicago" and much more about "one's relationship to ideas about industrialized labor and leisure as expressions of respectability."[36] In other words, the old elite, the growing black middle class, and new arrivals such as Broonzy espoused competing ideologies that spurred on heated debate over black Chicago "as a physical space and as an intellectual vision."[37] What really mattered was how all of these groups, forced to live in the same segregated area, defined and related to the growing consumer marketplace rooted in the city's vibrant world of leisure. Broonzy's migration to black Chicago had placed him in an epicenter of black cultural and intellectual upheaval that would transform his worldview, and he would make Chicago his home.

Perhaps the most complex dynamic of the Black Metropolis's race and class developments was the old leadership's open ambivalence about southern migrants' adherence to and/or disregard of prevalent social norms. As new southern migrants arrived in Chicago, they brought many old southern customs with them. Their public behavior—speech, dress, body language, manners, foodways, and etiquette—as well as their work ethic, living conditions, and child-rearing practices, were all points of criticism and concern for the city's established black leadership. Led by the Chicago branch of the National Urban League, Bronzeville's own *Defender*, and civic and social organizations such as the YMCA, black Chicago's leadership established dozens of programs "designed to help and pressure the newcomers to adjust" to an urban, northern, and industrial world that would "enhance the reputation of blacks in the lager (white) community."[38] The *Chicago Defender* revealed these social norms in its "A Few Do's and Don'ts" column, which acted as a guide for appropriate modes of public behavior, such as public sobriety, personal hygiene standards, dress, and interactions between the sexes and with authority figures.

For Broonzy, as for many black residents of Chicago, interracial encounters and the tension they often brought continued to figure prominently in daily life. Broonzy's interactions with whites were common, as he was forced to venture out of Chicago's South Side for most of his day jobs. The workplace, however, was not the only site of racially charged and embarrassing moments in Broonzy's new life. Two such moments explain much about his personality and strategies for navigating quotidian racism. One afternoon in the late 1940s on his way to meet his friend Studs Terkel, Broonzy was running late. He found Terkel waiting at their meeting spot, accompanied by an unfamiliar white man. When Terkel introduced the two men, Broonzy learned that the man was a state senator and a friend of Terkel's. The senator shot out quickly to Terkel, "So he's your boy, eh?" Before Terkel could attempt to diffuse the awkward situation, Broonzy fired right back with, "That's right. . . . He may not look it; but he's my father." With a nervous chuckle, the senator departed down the street with a "So long, boy," directed at Broonzy.[39]

The same incident in Arkansas would have undoubtedly ended with more than just an uneasy giggle. To finesse the uncomfortable situation, Terkel approached Broonzy to offer his apologies and consoling advice. "Studs turned to Bill and whatever he'd meant to say, didn't come out. For Bill was laughing. He was laughing loud enough to have it reach the senator, who was now near the end of the block."[40] Despite Broonzy's having lived in Chicago for over twenty years by the time this encounter took place, his race consciousness was shaped by his coming of age in the Jim Crow South. He had learned to approach racially tinged interactions with caution. In Chicago, African Americans more freely applied wit and humor to difficult race moments. But Broonzy knew that when traveling into the South (which he did often to see his mother), he had to curtail the sharp wit he used on Chicago's city streets. When outside Chicago, Broonzy's approach to confrontations with racism changed, further suggesting that Broonzy realized he could only give full rein to his urban race consciousness within the city.

The second moment concerns one of Broonzy's trips to see his mother in Little Rock. When Broonzy pulled into a service station just outside the city, the white attendant, surprised to see a black man driving a nice Cadillac, asked, "Whose car is this, boy?" Without batting an eye, Broonzy replied that it belonged to his "boss."[41] In Chicago, Broonzy and his peers would have been proud of his Cadillac and the hard-earned money he spent to purchase

Carving Out a Home in the Promised Land

the car. In the Jim Crow South, however, Broonzy knew that deference could prevent an episode of intimidation or overt physical violence.

Skin color, too, quickly became an important facet of Broonzy's expanding race consciousness in black Chicago. For many African Americans, and for Broonzy specifically, differences in complexion were a highly sensitive issue. He often noted that the nature of black relationships was based on skin color, a feature that could be critical for social interaction in both public and private spaces among African Americans in the North.[42] Variations in skin color were also important to most African Americans because a lighter complexion often meant preferential treatment by whites and wealthier blacks.[43] A hierarchy of skin color that privileged lighter complexions often placed urban African Americans in awkward situations with both light-skinned blacks and whites, who seemed to look down on darker African Americans. Within this social practice and its etiquette, darker African Americans such as Broonzy were particularly sensitive to the use of the word "nigger." In the South, the slur was so common that both whites and blacks of all hues used it freely. In the North, however, the use of the word was a violence-inducing social faux pas, especially if used by light-skinned blacks and whites in the presence of darker-skinned African Americans. Broonzy had learned very early in Chicago that "Northern Negroes don't like to be called nigger."[44]

Broonzy attempted to pass on this knowledge to a fellow black musician in 1939. Tommy McClennan, a blues artist whom Broonzy had scouted from Yazoo City, Mississippi, refused Broonzy's advice to remove the word "nigger" in one of his big hits, "Bottle Up 'n Go." In typical Broonzy fashion, he suggested that McClennan change the lyrics once they arrived in Chicago, from "the nigger and the white man" to "the big man and the little man," observing that the use of double entendre was more prudent and just as effective. Broonzy warned McClennan that northern blacks would take issue with the word and that continuing to use it in an urban environment might cause trouble. Sure enough, when he and McClennan were invited to a rent party filled with fellow blues musicians eager to hear the new sounds of Bluebird's most recent discovery, McClennan was asked to perform. Disregarding his friend's request, he sang the song for the audience, and both men were made to exit the party through the closest window.[45]

Broonzy's defiance of black Chicago's prevalent social norms also reveals important shifts of his new urbanism. From the moment he arrived in Chicago, Broonzy rejected the old elite definitions of respectability as he began participating in the city's expanding leisure culture. Of greatest concern to the black leaders invested in respectability was new migrants' apparent attraction to this vibrant culture and its nightlife. "Vice dens" of gambling, prostitution, drinking, illicit drugs, and "sinful music" were the focus of black middle-class criticism. Black leaders believed that this culture reinforced white fears about the black community and perpetuated white hostility toward southern migrants. Many of Chicago's black bourgeoisie thought this new generation of young black men and women was spending too much time in the city's cabarets, sporting dens, rent parties, dance halls, vaudeville houses, and movie theaters. Moreover, this embrace of nightlife challenged the black bourgeoisie's Victorian-derived ideals of a solid and viable working class.[46] This new commercialized leisure world signaled the emergence of a new ideology that revised ideas about respectability. And yet this world of vice, while driving black leadership in Chicago to reform its working class, was at the same time establishing important cultural currents for African Americans in Bronzeville. Essentially, these new migrants embraced this vibrant leisure world that promoted new racial identities and challenged established stereotypes of migrant behavior.

This generational shift within black Chicago had an enormous impact on Big Bill Broonzy.[47] This new world provided spaces in which African Americans could advance economically while simultaneously displaying pride in their community. Black men and women traded in the dirty coveralls and dusty work dresses they wore in the long hours in Chicago's labor and domestic industries for the latest risqué fashions as they frequented Chicago's nightlife destinations.

This new class could still advance the race by presenting and adhering to public principles that focused on labor pursuits and modes of behavior that defied white notions of black inferiority. After work, however, aspiring black migrants such as Broonzy began frequenting the rent parties, vaudeville theaters, and recording studios that had become centers of self-expression and sites for identity-forming cultural production within black Chicago.

For the next three decades, Broonzy recorded hundreds of blues songs for labels such as Paramount, Gennett, Champion, ARC, Vocalion, Okeh, American, Perfect, Bluebird, Victor, Decca, and many others across the country and around the world. And the names of the musicians he performed and recorded with along the way—Black Bob, Charlie Jackson, Sonny Boy Williamson, Tampa Red, Washboard Sam, Memphis Slim, Lil Green—were legends of Chicago's blues pantheon.[48] As a laborer by day and musician by night, Broonzy navigated the social and cultural spheres of black Chicago's fluid class lines with ease. He traversed a path that gave life and vitality to the New Negro movement in Chicago. More important, by engaging in illegal drinking, gambling, sexually explicit behavior, music, dancing, laughing, and performing and recording with friends and fellow musicians, Broonzy became part of black Chicago's embrace of modernity.[49]

Broonzy openly challenged community ideologies that defined migrant stereotypes, including race, class, gender, and sexuality. Big Bill admitted that when he arrived in Chicago in the 1920s, he would try anything to change his image and style in hopes of gaining respect outside of the racial stereotypes that defined black behavior in both the North and South. At the center of Broonzy's challenges was his outward appearance. To change his look, Broonzy bought a Cadillac, a hundred-dollar suit, a forty-dollar hat, and forty-dollar shoes; straightened his hair; changed the way he walked and talked; and altered the way he played guitar and sang songs. He also deliberately dated white women.[50] Broonzy was big, handsome, and impeccably dressed, and nearly all of his publicity photos show a polished and sophisticated performer.

Sobriety and temperance were aspects of respectability ideology that Broonzy and others openly defied. Many of his life stories and anecdotes in Chicago, New York, and Europe involve an almost continuous consumption of alcohol. One could argue that a bottle of whiskey became as central to Broonzy's "Big Bill" persona as his guitar was. Whether fishing with friends, hanging out at rent parties, barrel houses, and juke joints, or passing out drunk with Sonny Boy Williamson at Schorling Park watching the Negro League hero Satchel Paige pitch against the Chicago American Giants, Broonzy enjoyed a drink. He was often paid for performances, appearances, and contests with alcohol.[51] As a regular street performer on Maxwell Street's open-air market, where musicians, patrons, and passersby could purchase anything from used household wares to stolen weapons and illegal narcotics,[52] Broonzy may also have been an occasional marijuana user. He once reflected, "I found out that in all the five bands I've been the leader of, that a tea smoker is not nosy and don't forget his music and isn't hard to get along with and he always wants to try to learn something new and to improve old songs. A musician who drinks too much, won't listen to his leader and the way he plays tonight he'll play in a different key tomorrow night or start an argument or won't play at all."[53] Here Broonzy reveals a fascinating and telling assessment of his personal approach to prevalent social norms. Even as a big drinker, Broonzy recognized alcohol's effects on professional musicianship by suggesting that marijuana was an acceptable alternative to overconsumption of intoxicating liquors. Many of his colleagues, including Albert

Brand, Leroy Carr, Tommy McClennan, Blind Blake, and Sonny Boy Williamson, suffered alcohol-fueled deaths, whether through alcoholism or alcohol-fueled violence.[54]

Broonzy's own ideas concerning gender in Chicago's Black Metropolis also provide a fascinating insight into the changes in notions of sexuality among African Americans during the early twentieth century. Broonzy challenged the established social norms of black masculinity on the one hand and whites' belief in black promiscuity and immorality on the other. His own sense of masculinity stemmed from two separate elements. First, his race consciousness and his experiences in the South had taught him about the frequently hypocritical, racialized sexual mores of southern white men and the subsequent emasculation of black men that often lay at the center of southern racism. Second, by being branded as a "boy" or "uncle," black men such as Broonzy had to face the often-humiliating double standard of southern white men's own interracial sexual activities. A white man in the South might threaten to kill a black man for even hinting at a sexual advance toward a white woman, even while the white man has an affair with a black mistress.[55] Broonzy understood this dynamic quite well: "You take there is a negro woman down there that's nice-lookin . . . and they wants a negro man for their husband. But the white man want her. So now for her to live and her family to get along alright and to be satisfied down there and keep whatsoever their family's got, like a home or they got a little property or something like that around there you know. Well now this white man, if he want the Negro woman, then whoensoever this Negro that's got her, he gotta give her up."[56] The coupling of Broonzy's own racial pride with his sense of masculinity had begun long before his arrival in Chicago.

Broonzy and other migrants of the period, immersed within Chicago's vibrant black community, witnessed important changes in black sexuality that only the environment of the city could provide. The tensions created by the black migrant experience were gripping and exciting to both the blues musicians—men and women—who pioneered the music and to those who chose to participate in its consumer marketplace. As one scholar has noted, of all these new tensions, "none were stronger than those around sex."[57] In cities across the North and South, migration generated highly visible and novel social formations: rooming houses full of unattached black women (at the turn of the century, black women formed the majority of black migrants fleeing the South) and vibrant communities of black lesbians and gay men. The most striking representatives of those groups—the sexually unfettered, independent black woman; the visibly effeminate, "freakish" gay man—aroused tensions over female autonomy, familial authority, and the boundaries of "normal" manhood that echoed through interwar black culture.[58]

The overt sexuality of the interwar blues period defined many of Broonzy's most popular numbers: songs such as "Horny Frog Blues," "I Want My Hand on It," and "Flat Foot Susie with Her Flat Yes, Yes" helped to construct his modern, urban persona. To be clear, this process was one of give-and-take. Often, the sexuality of his urbane persona clashed with that of the southerner who held the utmost respect for a mother who had taught him important lessons about respect for the opposite sex and the dangers of interactions with white women. But soon he realized that, in the city, once he "got rid of one," he always had "another one in sight."[59]

Broonzy demonstrated throughout his life an often-contradictory attitude toward women that further reveals the fluidity of Broonzy's amalgamation of Old Settler and New Settler perspectives. Although he traveled frequently for both work and his music, he always tried to respect and take care of the women who depended on him. Perhaps the most constant female presence in his life was his mother, who died in 1957 at the age of 102. Mettie Belcher remained a strong influence on Broonzy until her death: "I was the kind of a boy that I was crazy 'bout my mother, I always was."[60] The only man Broonzy ever threatened to kill had called his mother a "damn liar" because she claimed he had stolen two of her chickens. Broonzy demanded an apology, and with the help of a lever-action Winchester rifle, he fired four shots at the man, as the thief ran for his life. In 1939, after years of keeping up his regular visits to his mother, Broonzy bought her a house in Arkansas with the money he had earned as a foundry laborer.[61]

Even as an itinerant blues performer moving from town to town, Broonzy typically provided financial support to help his wives maintain a solid domestic life for themselves and their children. In 1941, he traveled for nearly two months with Lil' Green's Traveling Road Show, making approximately $50 a week. Of that fifty dollars, Broonzy sent his wife whatever he had left over from road expenses, which usually amounted to $10 or $15. From 1944 to 1945, he often appeared at Harlem's Apollo Theater and Greenwich Village's Café Society, making $250 and $165 a week, respectively. Each week, he sent his third and then-current wife, Rosie, $50 to help her make ends meet.[62]

On the other hand, Broonzy was not opposed to his wives working to contribute to the family. Records indicate that Rosie worked for the Pullman Company's Chicago North Yard in 1944 and 1945, cleaning cars for 66¢ an hour.[63] Broonzy's respect for women extended beyond his personal relationships. He admired the artistry of many women blues singers and worked with a number of them, including Ma Rainey, Ida Cox, Bessie Smith, Mamie Smith, Memphis Minnie, Georgia White, and Hazel Scott.[64] Of all his female blues colleagues, he spoke the most reverently of "Memphis" Minnie Douglas. To Broonzy, Douglas's guitar virtuosity was unparalleled; he believed she could "pick a guitar and sing as good as any man" he had ever heard.[65] He once faced Douglas in a blues contest on his birthday in 1933. With a crowded house looking down, Broonzy played two songs, much to the delight of an audience that cheered and clapped for nearly ten minutes. The house fell silent as Douglas took the stage, as the predominantly male audience and judges' panel had never heard her perform. But Douglas awed the crowd with her guitar skill and vocal delivery, ultimately winning the contest and Broonzy's respect for the remainder of his life.[66]

Broonzy was never openly aggressive with women on Chicago's city streets, and he often criticized men who sexually harassed women in public or coveted another man's wife or girlfriend. Moreover, he insisted to Alan Lomax that he was always slow with women and was never inclined to sleep around. Too often he had witnessed what happened when his friends had "bothered the other man's woman" and insisted that he was never flirtatious with unacquainted women.[67]

Although Broonzy's accounts reflect established norms such as family devotion and respect for the opposite sex, he was promiscuous. In his autobiography, he revealed that he wished to be remembered by history as happy when drinking whiskey and partying with women. To be sure, he certainly had relationships with many women, as did his fellow bluesmen. He was married at least three times. He married his first wife, Gertrude Embrey, in 1914, but by 1930, he had a second wife, named Annie.[68] Broonzy told jazz journalists in the late 1940s that he married "a creole woman" named Rose from Houston, Texas, in 1941 after two weeks of romance. The marriage lasted until 1947.[69] At his death ten years later, he was married to yet another, a woman named Rosie, who at the time was believed to be the woman whom he had married in 1941. But "Rosie" was actually another Rose: Rose Lawson, whom he had married in Chicago.[70] Broonzy's opinions on monogamy, moreover, suggest that he understood the reality and power of seduction, and if his partner was "sneakin out," he never worried about it as long as she did not make it obvious. Quite bluntly, as long as Broonzy "got service," he seemed little concerned about his wife's or girlfriend's transgressions.[71] These assertions reveal Broonzy as a man who both assimilated and challenged traditional community fears about black promiscuity, infidelity, and immorality. Although married throughout most of his adult life, he had many lovers, held ambivalent views on the nature of monogamy, and may have been a serial polygamist.[72] Rather than fully espouse established norms of respectability concerning gender and sexuality, he chose to uphold only specific elements addressing family and kinship while forgoing those addressing promiscuity and monogamy.

Broonzy's complex and at times contradictory stance toward the older social norms of African American life is indicative of the significant cultural negotiations taking place in black Chicago during the 1920s and 1930s, as well as Broonzy's transformation into a New Negro. These historical shifts provide a lens through which to view the "lived history" of blues entertainers such as Broonzy. Like the tens of thousands of southern black migrants who came to northern centers of industry with burgeoning black communities, Big Bill Broonzy was forced to navigate a new way of life that both challenged and reaffirmed prevalent customs of race, class, and gender. By investigating Broonzy's relationship to respectability, his life and experiences as a southern migrant, urban laborer, blues pioneer, and husband and lover become tools for reaching a deeper understanding of black Chicago, urbanization, and race pride, while challenging the parameters of blues music history more broadly.

CHAPTER THREE

Southern Migrant Blues
Lee Bradley and the Black Metropolis

In 1927, Big Bill Broonzy first met Althea Dickerson at J. Mayo "Ink" Williams's recording studio on State Street in Bronzeville. Broonzy's polite and affable interaction with Dickerson became one of the most important of his life. Two years earlier, "Willie" Broonzy (as he was then known) from Arkansas had met William Henry "Papa Charlie" Jackson, who had recorded for Williams. Papa Charlie, a minstrelsy and medicine-show veteran, immediately recognized Broonzy's instinctive but raw talents and began teaching the younger, aspiring Broonzy how to "start . . . and make chords" on the guitar.[1] With encouragement from Jackson, Broonzy entered the recording office and was instantly greeted by the office's secretary, Althea Dickerson. Nervously, Broonzy and his partner, John Thomas, recorded two songs for one of the largest and most important labels for recorded blues during the period. After the session ended, Dickerson turned to Broonzy and asked him his name. Broonzy remembered, "I told her 'William Lee Conley Broonzy' and she said, 'For Christ's sake, we can't get all that on the label.' She said she'd think of a name for me and later on when she wanted me for something, she said, 'Come over here, Big Boy.' That gave her the idea to call me Big Bill and that's the way I've been known ever since."[2] With one short quip, Althea Dickerson shaped a component of Broonzy's personality and evolving style that remained with him forever. Even as his thirty-year career experienced its many inventions and reinventions, Broonzy always clung to this moment. For the rest of his life, all who knew him called him Big Bill. Whether he was recording in a Chicago studio or frequenting rent parties along the Stroll, Big Bill traded licks with some of the most important blues musicians. These moments transformed "Willie" into "Big Bill."

As Broonzy took on black Chicago and its emerging commercialized leisure world, he was exposed to dozens of talented male blues performers, such as Arthur "Blind" Blake, Papa Charlie Jackson, Blind Lemon Jefferson, and "a hundred . . . different guys" who were music pioneers involved in the city's rent-party and recording cultures. These individuals introduced Broonzy to the rich culture of the black vernacular music that had originated in the South from which Broonzy had been sheltered. Broonzy had made his first forays into music as a country fiddler in Arkansas, where he had played for segregated weekend picnics. Slowly, this consumer marketplace seduced Broonzy as he transformed his life as a southern laborer—who happened to be a country fiddler—into an urban blues guitarist/singer, who worked a day job to supplement his passion for music.[3]

The emergence of a vibrant consumer marketplace rooted in commercialized leisure represented a new alternative to the backbreaking physical labor of both the sharecropping South and northern centers of industry. Broonzy's music career in black Chicago negates the "popular notion of a typical prewar blues artist, . . . [the] ragged guitarist wandering the dirt roads of the Deep South." Rather, through Broonzy, the blues emerges as cultural by-product of the "savvy, urban, smartly dressed" black men and women who "dominated the market, . . . set the trends" for the blues of the New Negro Renaissance era and catapulted black communities such as Bronzeville into the modern age.[4]

Even after the abolition of slavery, physical labor defined black contributions to the United States, as African Americans living in the countryside and cities from as far south as the Mississippi Delta and as far north as Boston were forced to work within each respective region's industries, often subject to discriminatory hiring practices, humiliating working conditions, low wages, debt peonage, poor treatment, and violence. Yet when African Americans such as Big Bill Broonzy left work, they were free to participate in autonomous cultural practices beyond the watchful eyes of white men. Collective dancing, drinking, music-making, and religious and civic activities led to community and individual development based around their time *away* from their labor. In effect, the blues singer documented this experience through song, transforming the audiences' experiences of sadness, frustration, and fear into something communal, filled with wit, desire, intelligence, humor, and passion.[5] As the blues found a home in Chicago, this new blues culture defined Chicago's Black Belt and its ever-expanding intellectual life. In short, blues audiences and entertainers shared a collectivized experience that transformed the traditional distinction between performer and audience into a mutually participatory group. In a sense, blues performers were artists engaging a consumer and commercial culture that echoed modern aesthetic forms that rejected Jim Crow, embraced personal pleasure, and confirmed that the black mind and body were more than tools for labor.[6]

Perhaps the strongest reason that Broonzy migrated to Chicago was the fact that the Windy City was rapidly becoming a music town.[7] By the turn of the twentieth century, Chicago had become an important incubator for black music culture that included blues, vaudeville, ragtime, martial music, dance bands, and minstrel acts. It had transformed private parties, cabarets, movie theaters, and roadhouses into important centers for self-expression and cultural production. Moreover, this explosion of Chicago's interest in the nation's musical heritage reflected a larger popular-music craze in the United States that gave birth to the codified and commodified production of popular music.

In 1904, Emile Berliner revolutionized the nascent music recording industry with his development of the double-sided 78 rpm disc, which was more durable and easier to produce than Thomas Edison's industry standard cylinders. After years of dogged competition—including legal battles—between sound recording engineers Berliner, Edison, and Eldridge Johnson, the Victor Talking Machine Company emerged in the 1910s as the dominant force behind the phonograph. Johnson, a recording pioneer and founder of Victor, and his biggest rival, the Columbia Phonograph Company, dreamed that one day the phonograph would enter the homes of all Americans and become an important part of their daily lives. To fulfill that dream, Victor and Columbia revolutionized the phonograph in scope and design by transforming the aesthetic of the once-chintzy and toy-like players into finely crafted devices. Owning a phonograph became a sign of modernity and affluence, and buying phonograph records became a national phenomenon through the 1910s and 1920s.[8]

Beginning in the 1910s, American popular music experienced rapid and significant changes, many of which deeply influenced Broonzy.[9] With this craze came an evolution in technology dedicated to record production, arenas for musical performance, and the dissemination of popular music across the nation. By 1921, sales of sound recordings of music actually surpassed those of sheet music at the very same time that the first commercial radio stations began to emerge. Moreover, in 1926, the National Broadcasting Company launched the first networked radio station and pioneered electronic recording technology. Gradually, these methods replaced the difficult and quirky techniques of acoustic recording. Facilitating all of these advances in popular-music production was the incredible growth of the country's railroad system and the trade it enabled. Music culture, from Tin Pan Alley songs to sheet music and vaudeville shows, traveled anywhere these rail lines stopped, forming networks for performance and the dissemination of all types of music accouterments, from instruments to recorded music.[10]

At the dawn of the recording industry, the New York–based manufacturers of phonographs also controlled record production and talent recruiting. But soon a number of new record labels helped place Chicago on the map as a center for the burgeoning industry. Recognizing the immense commercial possibility in records created and recorded by African Americans and targeted to black audiences, white-owned record companies such as Okeh (operated by the Otto Heinemann Phonograph Supply Company), Paramount (owned by the Wisconsin Chair Company), Vocalion (run by the Aeolian Company), and Columbia (of the Columbia Phonograph Company) immediately launched an intense wave of "race record" production. The eventual target market for these "race records" was both the established black bourgeoisie and newly arriving migrants, as these labels and their subsidiaries distributed bulk sales to local entrepreneurs who both marketed them in black newspapers and sold them out of South Side storefronts to patrons eager for new sounds. From 1924 to 1928, the *Chicago Defender* was rife with advertisements informing customers "where to buy Okeh records" at stores and locales across the city, including various piano, phonograph repair, and music shops on South State Street in Bronzeville.[11]

By the time Broonzy stepped off the Twelfth Street Station platform, Chicago had embraced the nation's flowering "dance craze," burgeoning commercial recording industry, and love of jazz. Many black Chicagoans, moreover, lauded the important cultural production coming from their communities as a reflection of the new business entrepreneurialism and the "unmistakable transformation" of black art into industry.[12] In time, Broonzy's artistry would contribute to the transformation of the blues as a genre of black pop from its vaudeville and southern roots to the distinct jazz-tinged urban sound established in Chicago.

Bronzeville spawned dozens of performance clubs, cabarets, cafés, and dance halls where this culture could grow roots. Beginning with the Pekin Theater in 1904, black Chicago's music scene gave birth to black- and white-operated clubs along South State Street. Between 1915 and 1930, this flowering entertainment district stretched from the Twenty-Second Street block all the way south to Forty-Eighth Street. Both the east and west sides of State Street housed dozens of clubs, "black and tan" cabarets, theaters, saloons, gardens, and inns. This sea of clubs—bearing such names as the Savoy Bar, the Monogram Theater, Dreamland Café, the Plantation Café, Sunset Café, and the Red Mill—were sandwiched between the Local 208 musicians union, Dave Peyton's Music Shop, Clarence Williams Music Publishing, and the *Chicago Defender*. The "Stroll" pulsated with an unrivaled music culture that transformed every migrant's cultural expectations.[13]

This vibrant scene was just a few short blocks from the Mecca Flats at the 3000 block of South State Street. Sometimes for a day, a week, or a month, the Mecca Flats were home to some of the most important blues and jazz artists of the era and aided in the development of Chicago's jazz culture. The housing project's open-air atrium stood as a cornerstone of black life in Chicago. One can hardly imagine the incredible music pulsating from the rent-party and speakeasy events held within those hallowed walls.[14] In fact, Big Bill never mentioned the Mecca Flats by name, though he certainly was familiar with its thriving scene.[15]

Throughout the 1920s, Chicago replaced New Orleans as the nation's epicenter for jazz. Many of New Orleans's greatest jazz artists—Joe Oliver, Louis Armstrong, Jelly Roll Morton, Earl Hines—had migrated there in the 1910s. From 1915 to 1930, some Chicago clubs catered to white and black jazz enthusiasts looking to dance to "black jazz, white jazz, hot jazz, New Orleans jazz" or "Dixieland jazz."[16] What later would be described as the nexus of Chicago jazz, the South Side Stroll, was home to the vaudeville and stage-show acts identified in Chicago at the time as cabaret and dance-hall music. Chicago cabaret and dance-hall music—or Chicago jazz—differed from traditional New Orleans jazz in that it integrated the music of minstrel shows, traveling tent circuses, and medicine shows with European-influenced classical music, producing a hybridized mixture of "blues, marching band tunes, social dance music, popular songs, and ragtime."[17] In fact, the types of music then identified and sold on record as blues came from the vaudeville and cabaret clubs and were performed by the classic female blues singers, who were often accompanied by the city's increasing number of jazz and classically trained musicians.[18]

Wherever jazz grew as a musical idiom—New Orleans, Chicago, New York—the blues always made its presence known. Faint echoes of the Chicago blues that Broonzy was to pioneer in the 1930s could be heard, however, far beyond the walls of the vibrant music clubs on the Stroll in Bronzeville. A focus solely on the cabaret and dance-hall performance culture would not tell the complete story of Broonzy or other black migrant musicians' experiences in Chicago. Alongside the cutthroat world of the performance circuit stood an informal world of street performing, rent parties, and buffet-flat culture that was critical for the career development of dozens of the city's most famous musicians from the 1920s to the 1950s.

In 1925, still a dedicated fiddle player, Big Bill Broonzy bought his first guitar for $1.50 at Maxwell Street's famous open-air market.[19] With the help of his new acquaintances, he spent about a year polishing his guitar chops among some of the city's best and brightest blues talents in one the city's oldest and most fascinating bazaars.[20] Maxwell Street Market emerged in the second half of the nineteenth century in Chicago's old immigrant neighborhood, around the intersections of Thirteenth and Halsted Streets. Originally developed by eastern European and Jewish immigrants, by 1912 Maxwell Street was home to thousands of recently arrived migrants wishing to peddle their wares in the city's only officially designated, open-air market. The bazaar was legendary for having almost any conceivable item for sale at a negotiable price. As one scholar has noted, "a typical month saw more than one million dollars change hands in the street," and the "atmosphere was pure Chicago: hard hustle tempered with flamboyance and enthusiasm."[21]

By the 1920s, recently arrived southern African Americans began erecting street-side stands to purvey their own goods, as they had done in the open markets of the South, where tobacco, cotton, cattle, timber, and grain were sold. Of course, for decades, European immigrants tempered the atmosphere with songs and shouts of their respective old worlds, in an attempt to compete for the attractions of potential buyers. As scores of black migrants landed in Chicago's expanding migrant neighborhoods, they, too began looking to profit from the market's lucrative exchange, bringing with them their rich musical heritage then emanating from the black South.[22] The romanticized, rural blues of the South—the song of the guitar-accompanied, itinerant plough hand—found a home on Maxwell Street. The sheer number of black bluesmen who made their start on Maxwell Street from the 1920s to 1940s, including Bill Broonzy, is staggering. Dozens and dozens of recently arrived migrants flooded the seven-day-a-week street fair, performing for change, scouting better instruments, looking to meet other players, and hoping to catch their big break.[23]

The flood of migrants along the Stroll also increased the demand for spaces of leisure within Bronzeville. This rapid demand for entertainment and leisure space affected the city's ability to grant entertainment licenses. Resourceful black residents, however, established a vital network of rent parties "above storefronts and in private apartment buildings," which served as alternative spaces for leisure that easily complemented the licensed establishments along the Stroll.[24]

Rent parties served as clever alternatives to public spaces for leisure. On nearly every Saturday night—as well as other nights of the week—throughout the 1920s until the end of Prohibition in 1933, multiple rent parties could be found up and down the Stroll in Chicago. Hundreds of freshly paid young men and women would "stroll the Avenue" looking for "some flat with a red, pink or blue light in the window" and hear "the plunk of a tin-panny piano" pulsating in the night air.[25] More often than not, however, folks within the community might be handed a ticket from a friend or neighbor, advertising the address and the event with witty phrases such as, "There'll be brown skin mamas / High yallers too / And if you ain't got nothing to do / Come on up to ROY and SADIE'S 228 West 126st Sat. Night, May 12th / There'll be plenty of pig feet An lots of gin / Jus ring the bell An come on in" or "Save your tears for a rainy day, / We are giving a party where you can play / With red-hot mammas and too bad She-bas / Who wear their dresses above their knees / And mess around with whom they please."[26]

A host of patrons, including tourists, Pullman porters, elevator operators, and household domestics, would explore the building and be greeted by a hostess, who would gregariously introduce new clientele to other guests, including the house band and a few select "small time pimps and madames."[27] For as little as twenty-five cents, patrons could "partake freely of the fried chicken, pork chops, pigs feet, and potato salad," as well as fried fish, collard greens, chitterlings, dirty rice, and gumbo. Thirsty customers could wash down their plates with homemade corn liquor or bathtub gin, available "in the kitchen or at a makeshift bar in the hallway."[28] The hostess would then make room for dancers by clearing the floor of nearly every stitch of furniture, leaving only a small space for musicians to squeeze around a piano. The pioneering black intellectuals and poets Langston Hughes and Arna Bontemps recalled frequenting many rent-party flats: "Where God knows who lived—because the guests seldom did—where the piano would be augmented by a guitar, or an old clarinet, or somebody with a pair of drums walking in off the street. And where awful bootleg whisky and good fried fish or steaming chitterlings were sold at very low prices. And the dancing and singing and impromptu entertaining went on until dawn came in at the windows."[29] Many Saturday evenings raged until Sunday morning, as young musicians such as Broonzy—in a dapper suit, sharp fedora, and polished shoes—mingled with more popular entertainers of the period, including Bessie Smith, Ma Rainey, Ida Cox, Blind Lemon Jefferson, and Arthur "Blind Blake." When Broonzy first met Blind Lemon Jefferson in late 1925 or early 1926, the latter was already a star in the South. Broonzy recalled their introduction at a rent party in Chicago, when Jefferson was in town to record for Paramount Records.[30] At that first encounter, Jefferson apparently taught Broonzy about tuning the guitar's strings and offered lessons on, as Broonzy put it, "how to get along with the guitar" and "the different names of the strings and the different things on it."[31] From that moment forward, Broonzy remembered Jefferson as a "good fella . . . and a swell fella to meet."[32]

Moreover, performing at rent parties next to more anonymous musicians with such names as "Late Kidd Morgan," "Kid Professor, Father of the Piano," "Blind Johnny," and "Skinny at the Trap" provided a template for Broonzy's transformation into "Big Bill."[33] Within these walls, Big Bill began his transition from country fiddler to blues singer and guitarist. Much of his early repertoire, such as "House Rent Stomp," "Gonna Tear It on Down," "Big Bill Blues," "I Can't Be Satisfied," "Skoodle Do Do," "Tadpole Blues," were inspired by and performed and polished at rent parties throughout black Chicago. In fact, his motivation for the song "Just a Dream" stemmed from his interaction with a patron at a rent party:

> One night there was this girl at a house [rent] party where I was playing. At a certain moment I was in the kitchen having a glass of moonshine whisky and I talked to this girl. "When I get off from playing tonight I'm going to take you home with me." "Take who home?" she asked. "Yes," I said. "I'm gonna take you home with me tonight." "That's just a dream you've got on your mind," the girl answered, "and you can get it off because my husband is coming after me at twelve o'clock sharp." That's how I got the idea to write that song, "Just a Dream."[34]

Years later, nearly all Chicago blues musicians who had experienced this vibrant underworld of buffet-flat and rent-party culture affectionately reflected and reminisced about it. Within this world, musicians learned and honed their craft, established crucial musical networks, and developed identities away from work. From the 1920s to the 1950s, as national touring acts visited Chicago for performances at the Savoy, the Regal, and the Club De'Lisa or to record in the city's recording studios, they often appeared somewhere within the city at parties that lasted all night.[35] These artists enjoyed this world of illegal liquor, prostitution, and down-home cooking. At the same time, they helped to develop new generations of musicians who would follow their lead in challenging prevailing stereotypes of respectability, vice, and leisure culture. Broonzy often reflected on house rent parties and their importance to black musicians and community fellowship:

> In 1920, I came to Chicago and the people there asked me to come to their house. Some of them had known me at home and knew I could play and sing the blues. So I went to their houses and they had fried chicken and pig feet and chittlins for seventy-five cents a plate, and if you could play and sing you got all the eats and drinks for free. So I went every Saturday night, and I named one of my guitar solos the *Saturday Night Rub*. I named it like that because that's all they was doing while I was playing. A man and a woman would join up out on the floor and rub their bellies together and stomp and say to me: "Play the thing, old boy." . . . All of them was from some part of the South and had come to Chicago to better their living. Of course I did too, but I would go back every time I got enough money to get a ticket. And those people started to give parties and some Saturday nights they would make enough to pay the rent, and so they started to call them "house rent parties," because they sold chicken, pig feet, home brew, chittlins, moonshine whiskey. The musicians didn't have to buy nothing and would get a chance to meet some nice looking women and girls, too.[36]

Chicago's house rent parties and buffet flats helped collectivize the experience of migrants. The historian Davarian Baldwin has argued that "buffet flats and rent parties with their soul food dinners and small fees served as alternative sites of cultural production, leisure and labor on the stroll."[37] As blues celebrities such as Bessie Smith and Ma Rainey traveled to Chicago to record or perform, they often appeared at informal settings, where aspiring musicians such as Broonzy watched with amazement.

It also was in these spaces that Broonzy could build a reputation as a capable up-and-coming musician. He began honing his skills and developing his style by asking questions about guitar technique and studying the approaches of many of the country's most popular artists. He was able to jam at the feet of and emulate black recording celebrities such as Bessie Smith, Blind Lemon Jefferson, and Blind Blake. In addition, he and his contemporaries developed a measure of local celebrity within a distinct culture based on notions of black autonomy. In effect, the gambling houses, rent parties, vaudeville theaters, cabarets, and dance halls that made up Bronzeville's public and private spaces became centers of self-expression, personal ambitions, and desires. Engaged in illegal drinking, gambling, sexually taboo behavior, music, dancing, laughing, and relaxing, Broonzy was involved in well-worn and new cultural practices that enabled the development of an identity beyond the realm of traditional labor. Moreover, these informal settings provided alternative forms of entertainment that were cheaper than the jazz clubs on the Stroll and featured local blues musicians who carried forward the musical style of southern juke joints and barrelhouses.[38] More importantly, these bluesmen and women were creating a world that directly challenged ideas about the dangers of the Black Metropolis's nightlife.

During the late 1920s and early 1930s, Broonzy reinvented both his public identity and his music at rent parties as a celebrated musician leading the audience in a momentary embrace with modernity and black urban life, one song at a time. His switch from fiddle to guitar and his wearing nice suits were deliberate acts of revision; he also began to craft a repertoire that catered directly to black migrant audiences from all over the South and their love of buffet-flat and rent-party culture. This pattern of carefully crafted revision and reinvention carried forward into the future and helped make blues one of the most popular music genres of the twentieth century.

At the very moment when Big Bill Broonzy began to refashion himself from a sharecropping fiddler into a blues-guitar-picking New Negro, the "race record" industry ballooned in size and popularity. By the mid-1920s, the recording industry had become big business. Though raw statistics are difficult to determine, record sales reached upward of 140 million units—worth $106 million in sales—by 1921, with race records representing roughly 5 percent of that total. Okeh launched two campaigns, in February and June 1926, intended to announce "a new northern urban era of black enterprise in the record business."[39] Okeh and its successors helped launch the careers of many important musicians looking to perform and record in an emerging race-records market. And yet the race-records industry represented everything that was difficult, unethical, and unscrupulous within Chicago's developing blues culture. Owned and operated by white entrepreneurs who often held ties to East Coast elite business interests or the criminal underworld, recording companies took advantage of black performers at nearly every opportunity.[40] Unfair contracts offering little to no compensation were commonplace, and cutthroat competition led to artistic thievery and contested agency for aspiring musicians. White-owned recording companies' interests in Chicago music culture exemplified community notions about white patronage in the world of black business, while simultaneously challenging the viability of a completely autonomous black business culture.[41]

This situation created a path that provided Broonzy and others with opportunities to develop new musical identities and forms of celebrity. Most musicians of the period were willing to suffer the vile practices of the blues-record industry just to see their name on a record and hear the ephemeral magic of their blues preserved on disc. Although self-contained, the music business seemed quite willing to exploit newly arrived migrants eager to participate in new consumer markets.

Yet a homegrown, Chicago-based sector of the recording industry was undeniably emerging. During the 1910s, Paramount Records established a reputation as the most important Chicago label with the most popular talent. In 1918, the Wisconsin Chair Company from Grafton, Wisconsin, invested its resources in its own line of records under the Paramount label. As the Great Migration rapidly developed, the Wisconsin Chair Company quickly recognized the potential commercial market. In the summer of 1922, in order to compete with local labels, Paramount launched one of the most important race-record lines in American music history. The gamble was a big one because at the time, recording any black music was basically a novelty. Yet the aspiring label's largest risk was its hiring of one who was to become one of the most important figures in race records from the 1920s to the 1940s and a shining example of a Chicago New Negro: Jay Mayo "Ink" Williams.[42]

Born in Jefferson County, Arkansas, in 1894, Williams and his mother migrated to Illinois in 1901, after Williams's father was gunned down in a melee at the Pine Bluff, Arkansas, train station. Coming of age roughly two hundred miles from Chicago in nearby Monmouth, Williams received a public education and excelled in academics and sports. After school, Williams attended Brown University at roughly the same time Broonzy toiled overseas as a member of the AEF. Williams made his mark at Brown as a football and track star, graduating in 1921 with a degree in philosophy. After graduation, he initially returned home to his mother and soon made Chicago his home. He joined the roster of the Hammond Pros, of the National Football League (NFL), becoming one of the first black athletes to a star as an end for the nascent league. As a professional athlete, Williams also wrote a sports column for the *Chicago Whip* and bootlegged bathtub gin to the Grand Terrace jazz club on Thirty-Fifth and Calumet Streets in the heart of Bronzeville.[43]

But athletics and bootleg liquor were not Williams's only passions. His mother had reared him on the powerful and poetic sounds of the blues and instilled in him "the heretical belief that the blues represented an important aspect of his racial heritage."[44] Fortunately for Williams, one of his Alpha Fi

Alpha fraternity brothers from Brown offered him a job as a collecting agent for the only black owned and operated record label in the country, Harlem's Black Swan Records. Williams recognized that the label suffered from a lack of specialization in a rapidly expanding market and argued that "if they'd stuck with blues they would have been more successful."[45] When Black Swan collapsed, Paramount purchased the defunct label's collection of master recordings, prompting Williams to aggressively pursue a position for the Wisconsin Chair Company's recording subsidiary. Rather than hire Williams outright, Paramount chose instead to make him a manager in its newly created satellite publishing division, Chicago Music. As a manager for Chicago Music, Williams was responsible for "arranging to have songs scored for publication and registering them with the copyright division of the Library of Congress."[46]

Through the creation of Chicago Music, Williams received payment for all of the royalties generated by his stable of artists, which he could then share with his artists at his discretion.[47] Like most recording companies of the era, Paramount frequently took advantage of blues musicians' naiveté concerning copyright laws. One blues scholar has suggested that most of Williams's talent, including stalwarts Blind Blake and Blind Lemon Jefferson, probably never received any money in royalties and were more than likely paid with flat sums and bottles of whiskey.[48] In time, this process accumulated a small fortune for Williams and left novice recording artists—including Broonzy—frustrated and skeptical of the music business for decades.

When Broonzy stepped into the studio for his first recording date, he was unaware of most of the machinations of the race-records industry. One of Broonzy's primary mentors, Papa Charlie Jackson, had already recorded for Paramount, and Broonzy was crafting a style as a self-accompanied solo blues performer patterned on Jackson. Born in New Orleans around 1890, Jackson had migrated to Chicago in the early 1920s and emerged as a virtuosic banjo-playing street musician. A gifted ragtime and jazz player, Jackson represented the older vaudeville and minstrel traditions when he recorded his first blues for Paramount in Chicago and appeared in the *Defender* as the only "man living who sings, self-accompanied, for blues records."[49] Papa Charlie Jackson and those who followed—such as Blind Lemon Jefferson, Arthur "Blind" Blake, and Tommy Johnson[50]—were setting the standard for a new generation of blues musicians such as Broonzy by molding a rich mixture of expectations and stylistic approaches parleyed between musicians, consumers, and producers for the blues and its industry.

Underneath the growing popularity of the self-accompanied, down-home bluesman lurked a recording-business secret agenda that sought to erode the image of wealthy, urbane black musicians such as Bessie Smith or Ma Rainey, whose record sales alone made them incredibly potent cultural icons of black modernity. Frightened record-company executives put off by the sophisticated image of the vaudeville blues queens were the driving force behind this agenda. These savvy, assertive performers were totally incongruent with white listeners' romanticized notions of southern authenticity and reductive understandings of the musical styles of southern black musicians. In a sense, as one historian has noted, the "power politics between music and industrial control, community standards, and black musical innovation" highlight the contestations between black artists and white record companies over the direction of the race-record industry.[51] The "down-home" music craze was part of a much broader interest in the "folk" as a reaction to the strong forces opposed to the black cultural renaissance of the Jazz Age. Broonzy entered the recording industry, then, at the very moment when white interest in black blues as a sellable commodity began altering its marketability by subversively steering blues marketing strategies away from imagery highlighting urbane blackness and sexuality and toward the racialized romantic ideal of the seemingly ubiquitous country blues musician.[52]

Broonzy met Charlie Jackson in 1924, when the latter found out that Broonzy could carry a tune on a fiddle. Jackson introduced him to a new kind of blues, and as Broonzy remembered, "[Jackson] first got me started on guitar and showed me how to make chords. . . . Charlie was a well known recording artist at the time and he got me to go to Mayo Williams who was working for Paramount."[53] After Broonzy practiced with his fellow rent-party and street musician John Thomas, he decided to cash in Papa Charlie's incredible favor. Broonzy knew that record executives wanted down-home music, and he was ready to provide it.

Yet an eruption in the world of recorded blues made Broonzy's initial attempt at recording uneventful but fascinating. In 1926, two artists driven by the industry's emphasis on down-home styles created a tidal wave of interest in a new self-accompanied, male-centric blues and serve as a major inspiration for Broonzy. These were the Texas street musician and guitar virtuoso Blind Lemon Jefferson and the Florida-Georgia finger-picking guitarist Arthur "Blind" Blake. Both musicians were extremely important in Broonzy's transformation from rural country fiddler to urban pop musician, since Broonzy based his own expectations of how successful he might eventually become on the examples of Jefferson and Blake. His relationship with them demonstrates that, much like his time learning from Jerry Belcher and See-See Rider, Broonzy specifically sought out musicians who knew the music he wished to learn. From 1926 to 1929, Blind Lemon Jefferson recorded one hundred songs, fifty of which were commercially released. This body of work made him the most commercially successful early solo male blues artist. During the same period, Blake recorded eighty songs for Paramount Records and became the successor to Jefferson's early breakthrough.

Although both men were guitar-accompanied performers, Jefferson's style was starkly different from Blake's: Jefferson's recordings stick almost exclusively to the twelve-bar blues form, while Blake's style was centered on the vaudeville and ragtime style of Papa Charlie Jackson and the classic female blues singers. With regard to picking-hand attack, Jefferson's and Blake's styles stood quite far apart. Blake became a master of transposing what was essentially piano music (ragtime) onto the fret board of the guitar, using all ten of his fingers to do so. Blake's picking technique featured an extremely challenging and highly unusual style of strumming (one Broonzy eventually learned to emulate), in which he raked his thumb over the two lowest strings, striking two highly syncopated bass notes instead of one. At the same time, Blake used his other fingers to pick out the midrange and treble notes of the melody, creating a bombastic and full sound that made a lasting impression on a novice such as Broonzy. In contrast, photographs show Jefferson using a thumb plectrum, thereby using his thumb and forefinger to pick alternating single-note, melodic lines in between his chordal strumming patterns. Occasionally, Jefferson would bend a note or two and add other rhythmic effects. Blake's and Jefferson's styles both had an enormous impact on Broonzy's approach to the guitar.

Blind Lemon Jefferson offered Broonzy a template for shaping his persona as a solo male blues performer; Jefferson tutored and encouraged Broonzy as the younger musician tried to gain entry into Chicago's blues world. They shared a somewhat similar path to the blues. As Broonzy had in Arkansas, Jefferson began his music career at rural picnics and weekend dances in East Texas farming communities. As his popularity grew, the guitar wizard began performing on street corners and in the brothels and bordellos of Galveston and Dallas, where he could get better tips. Jefferson mastered a wide-ranging repertoire in the songster tradition and quickly established himself in the South as one of the blues' most important artists, often traveling to perform or record in Oklahoma, the Mississippi Delta, Georgia, Virginia, and, most notably, Chicago.[54]

Broonzy first met Blind Blake at Paramount Records on State Street, describing Blake as the "jolliest fellow you've ever seen in your life, to be a blind man." Broonzy recalled,

> I had a dollar and a half guitar. So me and him was talking and he ask me how long I had been playing the guitar and so I told him about a couple of years. So he asked me to let him see the guitar and he sat down and showed me a lot of things on there. . . . He was one of the best guitar pickers that I ever seen in my life. I never seen a man that take his natural fingers, no picks no nothing, and just his natural fingers and pick a guitar, never seen a man pick that much guitar. . . . I've seen him sit down and take a guitar, just an ordinary straight guitar, and just play: and I've seen him make a guitar sound like every instrument in the band, saxophone, trombone, coronets, . . . clarinets, bass fiddles, pianos, drums and all that.[55]

Blake, too, had grown up an itinerant rural and urban street musician. By the mid-1920s, traveling around the Midwest and the Southeast, he frequented Chicago, where he rented a flat at Thirty-First Street and Cottage Grove Avenue. On Mondays, Blake's flat became a rehearsal space for South Side rent parties where guitarists such as Broonzy showed up to "drink moonshine and trade songs."[56]

Broonzy expected that meeting artists such as Jackson, Jefferson, and Blake would pay off in the form of either musical knowledge or insight into the politics of Chicago's music industry. With endorsements from veterans such as Papa Charlie Jackson and Blind Lemon Jefferson, Broonzy gained enough credibility to walk through the door of Chicago's rapidly expanding recording industry.[57] The first door he entered was Paramount Records' State Street office in 1926. Broonzy had been practicing his guitar licks and blues lines for over a year in hopes that he, like his newfound musician friends, might record for Paramount. Yet when he and his friend the guitarist and vocalist John Thomas arrived at Williams's office and began playing for the usual crowd gathered there, Williams advised Broonzy that he was not ready and that he needed to continue practicing. Williams then scrapped the cuts that Broonzy and Thomas had performed, which included songs Broonzy later rerecorded for Paramount, such as "Big Bill Blues," "House Rent Stomp," and "Tod Pail Blues." As Broonzy later discovered, Williams secretly gave one of the takes, a Broonzy original titled "Gonna Tear It Down," to the Chicago musician Barbecue Bob.[58] Broonzy remembered that "Barbecue Bob was a guitar player, a pretty good one at the time, and so he gave it to Barbecue Bob and called it 'Tear it Down.'"[59] Broonzy admitted that, at the time of his first recordings, several musicians in Chicago were better guitarists, singers, and performers. He was aware that Paramount and Williams had a habit of recording musicians' songs, scrapping the takes, and giving the songs to "better" musicians whose instrumentation and vocal phrasings might sell records more readily.[60]

Broonzy returned to the studio again in November 1927, yielding much more successful results. But he was again given a lesson in the unprincipled world of the recording business. Following an initial session that proved unsuccessful, Broonzy and John Thomas recorded their first Paramount title, "Big Bill Blues" and "House Rent Stomp," under the name "Big Bill and Thomps."[61] This early recording showcases the influence that more successful solo male blues performers such as Charlie Jackson and Lemon Jefferson had on novices such as Broonzy and Thomas. The first song, "House Rent Stomp" reveals elements of the ragtime style popularized in the early 1900s and more recently by Papa Charlie Jackson. This upbeat dance number offers a fine ragging interplay of two guitars and an interlocutor (Thomas) instructing listeners and musicians alike on how to enjoy the song's vibrant aesthetic. Most likely written and performed at numerous rent parties, "House Rent Stomp" serves as a tribute to the rent parties that had such an impact on Broonzy's nascent career. The B-side, "Big Bill Blues," is in contrast slow and melancholy, with Broonzy delivering field-holler-influenced vocals over a duo guitar texture between him and Thomas. Thomas plays an elegant melody over Broonzy's slightly out-of-tune rhythm part and echoes the sound of the increasingly popular country blues sound of the period with its acoustic-guitar-based, improvised, twelve-bar melodic AAB structure, slow tempo, and emphasis on powerful vocal expression. In some ways, both songs reveal a hybridization of the styles of Jackson, Johnson, and Jefferson.

By the late summer of 1928, Paramount began advertising the 78 containing "Big Bill Blues" and "House Rent Stomp" in the *Chicago Defender*, alongside the recordings of such luminaries as Ida Cox, Ma Rainey, Papa Charlie Jackson, Blind Blake, and Blind Lemon Jefferson.[62] Broonzy's reputation as a rising blues star was cemented when his name appeared prominently next to famous blues musicians in the largest circulating black newspaper in the country. But this experience also taught him something about the music business that he would never forget. Broonzy explained,

> Me and Thomas was sitting down, talking about what we had to do to make a record. They had my head in a horn of some kind and I had to pull my head out of the horn to read the words and back in to sing. And they had Thomas put on a pillar about two feet high and they kept on telling us to play like we would if we was at home or at a party, and they kept on telling us to relax and giving us moonshine whiskey—and I got drunk. I went to sleep after the recording and when I woke up, on the way home, John Thomas told me that I had signed some paper. I told him I hadn't. . . . And sure enough there the paper was, signed with ink. "You've let them make you drunk," Thomas said, "and you've signed our rights away."[63]

When Broonzy was asked what he made off his first record, he simply replied, "Well, he [Williams] didn't pay me anything."[64]

Broonzy did not receive a dime in royalties for recordings until 1939, more than ten years after he began recording. In 1928, Broonzy was neither comfortable nor talented enough to record and perform as a solo artist, inevitably enlisting the help of his friend to shout and play the guitar with him. The recordings were poor in quality and sales but were good enough for him to be invited back to Paramount to record more material, including the 1928 recording of "Down in the Basement Blues" and a commentary on black poverty titled "Starvation Blues."[65] Over the next thirty years, Broonzy's recorded work as leader and sideman amounted to over four hundred songs. An enormous part of his experience as a bluesman was rooted in his mistrust of the industry and those who operated it, including Ink Williams.

Williams's account of the incident, however, provides the perspective of a producer doing his best to navigate the challenging world of blues musicians. Paramount had found in Williams a Bronzeville insider with connections to the city's ever-expanding leisure world. His "manager" position with Chicago Music was essentially that of a clerk, but he quickly transformed the job, assuming the responsibilities of artist and repertoire (A&R) agent and record producer. Williams proved savvy and aggressive in his pursuit of new talent, and he recorded many of the early blues greats, including Ma Rainey, Papa Charlie Jackson, Ida Cox, Blind Lemon Jefferson, and Blind Blake.[66]

Williams understood the developments the recording industry underwent in the 1920s and used that knowledge to his advantage. For example, following the 1909 Copyright Act, composers organized themselves within the American Society of Composers, Authors, and Publishers (ASCAP) in order to guarantee their rights of ownership of published music. Musicians also relied on the recently developed American Federation of Musicians. But neither group allowed African Americans to become members.[67] Williams's practice of holding the copyright to all Chicago Music recordings and collecting all royalties was a deliberate circumvention of the demands of ASCAP, enabled by the organization's habit of excluding black artists. Williams also knew that African Americans wanted to hear the blues. The country blues fad that occurred following the seminal recordings of rural blues artists such as Son House, Charley Patton, Blind Blake, and Blind Lemon Jefferson solidified the existence of a national market for black male blues that quickly surpassed the popularity of the classic female singers. Ultimately, these events proved that the scene was ripe for a new generation of naïve, southern migrant musicians. The early recording industry structured its business so as to exploit many of its most gifted talents.

Williams, to his credit, expanded the leisure world that many black Chicagoans equally loved and feared. Immediately upon beginning his job with Paramount, Williams faced aggressively self-promoting, upstart musicians whom he "trusted about as much as [he] could throw an elephant."[68] He recalled musicians—both men and women—who continually attempted to befriend him and take advantage of his status to obtain free drinks and meals or the chance to record for the only race-record talent scout in Chicago. Williams found the South Side underworld too dangerously exploitative for his increasingly bourgeois sensibilities. Williams later recalled that the blues were everywhere in Chicago in the mid-1920s. He observed that "there was more talent than any company could handle" and admitted that he "could have missed a whole hell of a lot of good singers because there were more artists than places to put 'em."[69]

Ink Williams's State Street office stood at the center of the Stroll, where from Friday night to Monday morning, his neighborhood looked "like an Easter parade, or promenade down the boardwalk in Atlantic City."[70] Given his experience, he expected benefits from his recording endeavors and for his discovery of blues talent. Ink Williams's interactions with Broonzy were extremely important in shaping Broonzy's methods of managing the Chicago recording industry's expectations; the relationship was also crucial in advancing Broonzy's career. Broonzy gained the much-needed "street credit" of a musician who had recorded for the most popular blues label of the period. Even if his Paramount recordings sold poorly and were musically and sonically unremarkable, the label's name was enough to boost Broonzy's reputation. Working with the industry also prepared him for the ruthless and unscrupulous business practices in the world of black popular music.

Even more importantly, Broonzy's relationship to the power dynamics of the recording industry presents a window into his personality. As a young man in his twenties, he could avert his problems with authority in Arkansas by catching the first train out of town and hoboing his way to Chicago. In his forties and fifties, however, he simply accepted unfair treatment from the white-operated recording industry. The tension between the personal agency that pushed him out of the South and the professional accommodation that led to the exploitation of his talents reveals an important factor in the connotations that racism and urbanism held for Broonzy. When asked why he was not more assertive in his demand for royalties, he explained that he was often told untruths about the number of his sales, even though he could hear his records on phonograph machines throughout his neighborhood and beyond. As always, his reasons for not challenging those who had taken advantage of him were more personal and in a way philosophical rather than financially pragmatic:

> I really don't want to have no connections with a man that I got to fight him and raise sand to try and get anything out of him for what I've done. Until I started in running in this music business, I had never lived around no people that would kill they own brother, like, for a lousy dollar or would rob they own family for a few nickels. I'd always been around people that they making a little something, they'll give you something, too. So, well, these guys would give me just enough to sort of live on and, by me being the way I am, I just let it go.[71]

Perhaps, like many other black migrants, Broonzy employed the deference he had learned in the Jim Crow South in his new surroundings. Rather than confront the merciless recording business head-on, Broonzy seemed much more comfortable weathering these betrayals and maintaining his artistic integrity. He preferred to just "let it go."

Broonzy had learned to play the guitar, sing, and record in the popular style of the "down-home" self-accompanied male blues performer, a musical world wholly different from his country fiddler roots. By cultivating critical relationships within Chicago's recording industry and the city's informal house-rent-party circuit, Big Bill Broonzy transformed himself from a sharecropping country musician into a solo male blues performer. Broonzy in his twenties was nowhere near the caliber of performer he was to become, but as a songwriter, he was beginning to make significant strides. Broonzy's songwriting had earned him enough attention to propel his career in a direction that reflected the blues' generic transition from its vaudeville and stage-show beginnings to urban pop.

Yet Broonzy's associations with blues luminaries such as Blind Lemon Jefferson provided him with concrete, tangible examples of the promise of the city's expanding world of leisure. He had learned at a young age the potential of celebrated musicianship. As Broonzy and his contemporaries forged these elements—celebrity, community, leisure time, the commercial marketplace, and shifting black consciousness—into Chicago's blues culture, they expanded the possibilities of black intellectual and artistic life in the United States. A laborer by day and musician by night, Broonzy helped to create new components of the Black Metropolis, the New Negro Renaissance, and black intellectual life, and he helped open a new world for the thousands of African Americans who followed him. His transformation into a black urban pop celebrity occurred through meeting one of Chicago's most important pre-war blues-industry stalwarts: the white music publisher and talent scout Lester Melrose.

CHAPTER FOUR

The Rise of Big Bill

In 1928, Big Bill Broonzy met Lester Melrose while recording for Paramount and Gennett Records and established one of the most important relationships of his career. Melrose, a white Illinois native and former record salesman, emerged in the 1930s as a leading force in the scouting, production, and publication of Chicago's blues scene. In effect, Broonzy became Melrose's most important musician in what became a long-standing, formulaic approach to recording the Chicago sound. In return, Melrose helped make Broonzy a black pop music celebrity. Broonzy remembered, "In 1928, I met Mr. Lester Melrose. I was a grocery boy and he told me to come to his office. So I did and I carried my guitar with me. Him and his buddy Herman took me to the studios and I made four songs for them: *Date With and Angel Blues, The Walking Blues, Big Bill Blues No. 2*, and *House Rent Stomp No 2*."[1]

Within two years, Melrose, Broonzy, the gospel giant Thomas Dorsey, Arthur Pettis, Frank Bradswell, and Mozelle Alderson "all piled into a Ford and drove" to New York to record for the American Recording Company, ultimately linking Chicago's incipient urban blues music with the East Coast's recording industry. For the next two decades, Broonzy and his contemporaries crisscrossed the continent, taking their developing sounds to any record company or recording venue that would have them.[2] From 1936 to 1951, Lester Melrose recorded "at least 90 percent of all rhythm-and-blues talent for RCA Victor and Columbia Records."[3] Yet, as much as Melrose helped develop Chicago's blues culture during the interwar years, Big Bill Broonzy helped make Lester Melrose. Just as Broonzy, Melrose, and their cadre of Chicago blues talent began carving out sonic space for Chicago's urban blues sounds throughout the United States, a new wave of black migrants and studio musicians transformed Broonzy's career again, forcing him to engage with new sounds and a new audience. But before these developments could take root, the Great Depression drastically reshaped the recording industry. Big Bill Broonzy became a major part of its rebirth. Through Broonzy's relationship with Melrose, Broonzy's career erupted, as he became a blues celebrity and seasoned performer of urban blues and one of the most successful recording artists of the 1930s. Broonzy's knowledge of the expectations of the white-brokered music industry helped sustain this successful period of

Broonzy promotional photo, ca. late 1920s–early 1930s. Courtesy of the Frank Driggs Collection at Jazz at Lincoln Center.

his career. With one exception, Tampa Red, Bill Broonzy became the most popularly recorded artist in blues from 1930 to 1942, recording over two hundred sides for record labels across the nation as a solo artist and hundreds more as an accompanist.[4]

The 1929 stock-market crash and the subsequent collapse of the American economy devastated black Chicago. From July to August 1930, every bank in Bronzeville collapsed. Thousands of black fortunes, earned over three decades of establishing one of the most important African American communities in the country, vanished into thin air. Long-standing black domestics across the city were sent to the bread lines. Black factory workers, both skilled and unskilled, faced the first wave of termination in every industry. South Side white-collar professionals turned to the illegal world of the numbers racket, known in Chicago as "policy," to make ends meet or sought help from municipal, civil service, or federal employment agencies. By 1931, nearly half of black Chicago's citizens of working age faced unemployment. The community's first response "was a deep sense of panic, followed by unorganized demonstrations of frantic mobs."[5] Bronzeville quickly forged a powerful political response, launching the "Spend Your Money Where You Can Work Campaign," which essentially forced white-owned businesses within the South Side to hire African Americans instead of unemployed whites. But the National Recovery Act helped maintain discriminatory hiring practices across Chicago, ensuring that black Chicagoans' experiences throughout those "lean years" were the hardest among the city's nonwhite ethnicities.[6]

The end of the 1920s ushered in dramatic change in the South Side landscape for jazz, performance halls, and recording companies. By 1928, many of Chicago's most visible and prominent jazz musicians had moved from Bronzeville to Harlem, New York, to initiate the next stylistic developments in jazz. Decades of perceived immorality and licentiousness within the Stroll, moreover, drove segregationists and reformers to intimidate entrepreneurs with threats of Prohibition enforcement and police raids. The Plantation Café at 338 East Thirty-Fifth Street, for example, made headlines after it was forced to close for one year after many people had "witnessed" open "set-up" violations of the "prohibition act."[7] What reformers could not accomplish, the Great Depression achieved, as many former patrons stopped spending their dwindling earnings in South Side clubs, keeping what little they had for subsistence.[8]

Times were also bleak for the recording industry: "For nearly three years after the stockmarket crash, the record business lay shattered, its sales figures plummeting and many recording firms sliding into bankruptcy. Only 6 million records were sold in the United States in 1932, about 6 percent of total record sales for 1927. The production of phonographs dropped from 987,000 to 40,000, or 96 percent."[9] Ink Williams left Paramount to form his record label Black Patti, which ultimately failed in the debilitating economic climate. In the early 1930s, Williams left the record business altogether to coach football at Morehouse College, but he made a successful return in 1934 to work for Decca Records. With Williams's departure and the onset of financial collapse, Paramount stopped recording in 1932 and closed its doors in 1935. Its rival Gennett was likewise defunct by the mid-1930s. By 1926, Okeh Records had sold its rights to Columbia. Columbia barely scraped through the first half of the Depression and was bought in 1934 by a newly conglomerated label, the American Recording Company, which had begun consolidating many smaller labels in 1929.[10]

In some ways, the Great Depression defined Big Bill Broonzy's career. After his successful duet recordings with John Thomas, Broonzy recorded as a solo performer for at least thirteen different sessions from 1930 to 1932 under pseudonyms such as Sammy Sampson, Big Bill Johnson, and Big Bill and His Jug Busters; these sessions resulted in over forty sides issued by record labels across the country. As an accompanist on guitar during the same period for artists such as Georgia Tom Dorsey, Mozelle Alderson, and Frank Braswell, Broonzy contributed to nineteen sessions that produced sixty or more sides for the same labels. His collaborations with Georgia Tom Dorsey, moreover, helped ignite a major shift in recorded blues style away from the solo, male, rural blues performer to a cosmopolitan style in which solo or duo vocalists sang clever twelve- and eight-bar forms with the nonchalant confidence of a barroom crooner.[11] Georgia Tom Dorsey, born Thomas A. Dorsey in rural Georgia in 1899, migrated from Atlanta to Chicago around 1916 as an adequate but ordinary pianist with a background in the house parties, bordellos, and buffet flats of Atlanta's all-black neighborhood around Decatur Street. In Chicago, Dorsey continued his work in rent parties along the Stroll, but he also began formal music studies at the Chicago School of Composition and Arranging. He quickly established a reputation as a gifted blues player, earning enough acclaim to work with Ink Williams as a songwriter for the Chicago Music Publishing Company. By 1924, Ma Rainey had invited Dorsey to join and lead her touring vaudeville band. But the most important collaboration for Georgia Tom (and Big Bill) happened at Ink Williams's State Street studio in 1928, and it fundamentally changed the nature of the blues.[12]

While touring with Ma Rainey in the late 1920s, Dorsey met a talented and spirited young guitarist from Florida who had cut his teeth as a teenager on the southern theater circuit. Tampa Red, born Hudson Whittaker in rural Georgia in 1908, landed in Chicago sometime during the mid-1920s, looking to partake in the rich musical ferment of Bronzeville. Like Broonzy, Tampa Red gained a reputation as a street musician and house-party performer, while supporting himself during the day as a laborer. Of Tampa Red's good nature, Big Bill remembered twenty years later, "Tampa Red, anybody in the world can get along with Tampa Red. You know what I mean. Because he's a fellow that practically anything a person do with him, if he don't like it he won't know it anyway, see. He'd walk off and go home or something, see. Fact of the business, he got a good wife and a good home in Chicago, and I never know him to be in an argument with a man in my life and I been knowing him ever since 1928."[13] By the 1930s, Tampa Red and his wife, Frances, were living at 3432 South State Street in the heart of the South Side, earning their livings as a "recorder" for a recording company and a cleaner for the steel cleaning industry, respectively.[14] More important, Tampa Red was arguably the most gifted guitarist of the early era of recorded blues, wielding razor-sharp virtuosity on slide guitar that was simply unmatched at that point.[15] In 1928, Tampa Red and Georgia Tom collaborated on the most important recording of the next two decades, a slick ragtime-influenced blues with bawdry lyrics and an upbeat rhythm called "Tight Like That." By 1929, the guitar and piano duo of Whittaker and Dorsey sparked its own craze. By the 1930s, Dorsey, like Whittaker, had made enough money as a recording artist and performer to own his own home and list his occupation as a musician and composer.[16] The *Chicago Defender* reported the song's success in the fall of 1929, citing the remarkable sale of over five hundred thousand copies of the side and arguing that "everybody has heard 'Tight Like That' and everybody has danced to it."[17] This new style, known as "hokum blues," moreover, became the tawdry urban party music that dominated the recording industry and blues music until World War II.

Hokum blues ensembles "were made up of guitars, piano, bass, drums, trumpet, saxophone, and occasionally a washboard" and provided "an upbeat, happy-go-lucky sound, closer to" minstrelsy and vaudeville musical shows than to Broonzy's country blues.[18] Chicago's South Side and its rent-party circuits became the undisputed home of hokum blues throughout the 1920s and 1930s. Immediately following the success of Whittaker and Dorsey, Big Bill Broonzy became an irreplaceable cog in the hokum blues machine and what eventually came to be identified as "Chicago blues." In 1930 and 1931, Broonzy and Dorsey collaborated on dozens of hokum blues numbers under the banners of Georgia Tom, the Hokum Boys, and the Famous Hokum Boys, with song titles such as "Papa's Getting Hot," "The Duck's Yas Yas Yas," "Barrel House Rag," "That Stuff I Got," and "What's That I Smell."[19]

By 1934, Georgia Tom Dorsey had quit blues recording altogether and was in the process of formulating the genre of gospel music with the help of the singer Mahalia Jackson.[20] Dorsey recalled, "In 1932 I got a job directing this choir down there at . . . Pilgrim Baptist Church. I hung on with the blues fellows—tried to hang on with 'em for a year or two, but they was goin down so fast."[21] By leaving the world of Chicago blues, Dorsey made room for Tampa Red and Big Bill Broonzy to help usher in a transformation of Chicago's blues music scene. Additionally, the shift of jazz's center of gravity to New York enabled the conditions that allowed Tampa Red, Big Bill Broonzy, and Lester Melrose to remold Chicago into a blues town.

Broonzy was working as a laborer in a foundry and as a part-time grocery boy when he met Melrose.[22] Broonzy had gained some experience recording with Paramount but was not quite ready to record as a solo artist as, according to one scholar, the quality of his records was almost as poor as their sales.[23] Nevertheless, Broonzy had established a solid-enough reputation as a songwriter and accompanist that Melrose sought him out. Broonzy needed a spark to ignite his career—some type of agent that might catapult his celebrity to new heights. Lester Melrose had already experienced success in Chicago's music scene, publishing jazz compositions by greats such as Joe "King" Oliver and Jelly Roll Morton out of his Cottage Grove music store. Broonzy and Melrose immediately recognized each other's potential and invested expectations in the relationship.

Born in 1892 in rural Richland County, Illinois, Melrose moved to Chicago in 1912 to begin work at Marshall Field's department store. In 1914, he opened his own grocery store in Bronzeville at the corner of South Vincennes and Thirty-Seventh Streets, where he worked for four years before he was forced to sell the store after receiving his draft notice. In August 1918, Melrose moved from France as a member of the AEF to the dangerous World War I front lines. The following summer, he returned to Chicago, picking up jobs where available and biding his time. His big break came in 1922, when he and his brother Walter opened a small music store at 6309 Cottage Grove Avenue, offering a "full stock of pop sheet music, piano rolls, small musical instruments, and records."[24] As Bronzeville's music culture exploded in the 1920s, the Melrose Bros. music company grew right along with it, moving across the street in 1923 to 6318 Cottage Grove Avenue into a larger space, where the brothers began distributing pop records from every major label—Emerson, Gennett, Victor, Columbia, Brunswick, Okeh, Paramount. As a result, local South Side musicians began to inquire about making records on the labels the store was then soliciting.

The Melrose brothers backed into the music publishing business by chance, as jazz luminaries such as Joe "King" Oliver and Jelly Roll Morton showed up at the music store looking to use the Melrose brothers' connections to the music recording and publishing industry to promote their compositions, ultimately placing the Melrose name on the South Side Chicago music map. By 1926, Lester Melrose had sold his stake in the music store and publishing business to strike out on his own as a talent scout and record company agent, signifying a major shift in the music industry from sheet-music production to recorded music.[25]

From the late 1920s through the 1940s, Lester Melrose held more influence over Chicago's blues music than perhaps any other individual artist or promoter did. The list of artists who worked for Melrose is vast and includes a who's who of Chicago's early greats: Tampa Red, Memphis Minnie, Georgia Tom, Washboard Sam, Big Joe Williams, and, of course, Big Bill Broonzy.[26]

Broonzy's relationship with Melrose helped him to develop into one of the most important figures in Chicago blues. He began recording with Melrose for Gennett Records in 1930 under the pseudonym "Big Bill Johnson."[27] Recording a series of his own compositions in the self-accompanied male-blues-artist style, including "Can't Be Satisfied," "Skoodle Do Do," and "Tadpole Blues." These recordings demonstrate growth in Broonzy's musicianship, as his vocal delivery sounds more confident and relaxed. A closer listen, however, exposes a similarity to the smooth inflection and deliveries of Leroy Carr and Lonnie Johnson. But the beginning of Melrose and Broonzy's working relationship occurred at a critical point in the history of American music. As the recording industry began to recover from the Great Depression's devastation in the early 1930s, important developments within American musical culture had begun to change the black pop music landscape. The repeal of Prohibition and the emergence of the jukebox profoundly changed the musical world in which Broonzy worked: "The New Deal brought a new lease on life to the record business. The repeal of Prohibition revitalized the nightclubs and saloons of urban America. Simultaneously, the demand for popular records was stimulated by a new technical innovation, the jukebox, which began to supplant live music in bars and clubs.... By 1939, there were 255,000 jukeboxes in operation using 13 million disks."[28] The audiences of newly established saloons and bars were hungry for the sounds of developing urban blues styles, especially those coming out of Chicago. The rent-party circuit was also affected by the repeal of Prohibition: Chicago's South Side saw the development of legendary blues clubs in the 1930s, pushing the once-private world of blues-drenched buffet-flat parties into the public world of the beer and dance halls of the 1930s. These clubs became landmark venues for the performance of Chicago blues. This network of performance venues—South Side clubs such as the Three Deuces on North State Street, the Boulevard Lounge and Square's

The Rise of Big Bill 75

at 931 West Fifty-First Street, the 35th and State Club, the Club Georgia at Forty-Fifth and State Streets, George Wood's Tempo Tap at Thirty-First Street and Indiana Avenue, and the White Elephant at 528 West Forty-Third Street—marked the dawning of an identifiable Chicago blues scene. In this community, Broonzy became a star, ultimately revealing "how notions of race community in the broadest sense register change for black folk, as much as establish the resilience of their identities."[29]

Though blues popularized by the classic female blues singers of the early recording era had not yet disappeared, the emerging urban blues sound became increasingly popular throughout the 1930s. The days of expensive ventures into the South with mobile recording equipment to record local blues talent were over. Many of the South's best and brightest, moreover, had left the region during the Depression, and a considerable number found their way to Chicago. New tastes, new record labels, new performance venues, and a large pool of incredibly gifted talent coalesced in Chicago to create of one of the most vibrant and important music cultures in twentieth-century American history.

Under these auspices, Lester Melrose and Big Bill Broonzy were becoming a powerful combination within the Black Metropolis's blues community. Melrose held expectations for his own vision of Chicago blues markets, and Big Bill Broonzy was to play an integral part—but on his own terms. Through Melrose, Broonzy met lifelong friends and musical companions who together built Chicago's distinct blues sound block by block. These blues greats included Memphis Minnie, John Lee "Sonny Boy" Williamson, Memphis Slim, Black Bob, Sleepy John Estes, Big Maceo Merriweather, Jazz Gillum, Arthur "Big Boy" Crudup, Roosevelt Sykes, Joe Williams, Bumble Bee Slim, Walter Davis, and many others.[30] Together they became critical to the development and maintenance of Broonzy's career, and they should be recognized as *the* pioneers of Chicago blues. Broonzy and these architects collaborated on many of Broonzy's most popular songs, including "Keep Your Hands Off Her," "Horny Frog," "Trucking Little Woman," "Hit the Right Lick," "Key to the Highway," and "Night Watchmen Blues."

By 1932, Broonzy's vocal delivery and guitar skills had far surpassed his work from just a few years earlier. On such songs as the 1932 hit "Long Tall Mama," his signature thump-and-rake over the bass strings is already present, as are his forefinger-picked melodic runs on the treble strings. As early as 1932—a few years before the great explosion of swing music—Broonzy was beginning to "ride the back of the horse," placing the bass notes just behind the beat to give his music a distinctly "swung" rhythmic feel. His

From left to right: John Lee "Sonny Boy" Williamson, Walter Davis, and Big Bill Broonzy, ca. 1939. These three were critical in the development of the Chicago blues sound. Courtesy of the Frank Driggs Collection at Jazz at Lincoln Center.

vocal style matured as he began singing more from his diaphragm rather than through his nasal passages. This resulted in a powerfully smooth and extraordinarily versatile baritone voice that could cut across any ensemble during recording sessions of the period. Broonzy's guitar technique and his commanding baritone became one of the most potent combinations in blues.

In 1934, Broonzy's recordings as an individual performer began to wane, as Melrose, recognizing Broonzy's raw talent, persuaded him to perform with accompaniment. Essentially, each of these two Chicago blues pioneers forged his career successes and identity by fulfilling the expectations of the other. Broonzy expected that Melrose's extensive experience within Chicago's music business and his connections with record companies would provide guidance for Broonzy's own associations with black popular music. Melrose anticipated that Broonzy's songwriting, affable personality, dogged persistence, and clear talent would serve as a critical component for realizing his vision of the blues genre. The poor sales of Broonzy's solo records were also motivation for Melrose's decision to record Broonzy with ensembles.

The duo recorded on at least two dozen occasions from 1932 to 1937.[31] Most of the musicians Melrose used appeared on one another's recordings, often as instrumentalists or credited as songwriters, a practice that helped create a recognizable sound in the realm of black pop music. Broonzy and his close friend Washboard Sam were two of Melrose's most prolific songwriters and critical for the development of Melrose's brand of blues. Melrose expected this stable of talented musicians to fulfill his vision by creating what one scholar has called the "Bluebird beat."[32] Bluebird, the race-record subsidiary of RCA Victor, had emerged out of the bleak Depression-era music scene to become synonymous with a polished and urbane sound of jazz-tinged blues and featured Melrose's handpicked cadre of musicians. Just as Ink Williams had, Lester Melrose expected to get rich from his "brand" of black pop music, and Chicago's urban blues sensation Big Bill Broonzy was a key contributor to that brand.

Melrose, leaning on his music production roots, paid small sums for original compositions by his talented group of musicians and copyrighted all songs under his own name. Not only did this ensure that he would receive all royalties for Bluebird songs, but it also helped keep his artists active, productive, and, most important, creative.[33] Melrose's production philosophy created the "hokum" that shed the blues' country roots by adding jazz instrumentation and swinging beats in hopes of appealing to a wider audience, signaling the artistic roots of what was to become the third stage of Broonzy's career—the professional urban blues pioneer.

This period of Broonzy's long career highlights extremely important developments within the country's expanding commercial music landscape. White music entrepreneurs such as Melrose were quite successful in brokering record deals and dictating style for black recording artists immediately following the Great Depression. But the Second Great Migration, which occurred between 1940 and 1970, brought even more southerners to cities in the North, Midwest, and West than had the first wave, and once again cities such as Chicago quickly became recognizably southern. The combination of new audiences and artists, along with smaller recording labels, began to incubate

Broonzy promotional photo, ca. mid-1930s. Courtesy of the Frank Driggs Collection at Jazz at Lincoln Center.

new styles with more frequency than record promoters such as Melrose and larger corporate labels RCA Victor and Columbia could compete with. Blues in the South during the 1940s—the blues these southern migrants were willing to buy—were quite different from the polished sounds pulsating from northern and midwestern urban areas that Broonzy had helped pioneer.

Complicating this picture further, a complete reorganization of the music business on the basis of radio play, jukeboxes, record sales, and expanding membership in musicians' unions remapped the nation's recording industry. The segregated but vital Chicago Local 208 chapter of the American Federation of Musicians, established in 1902 and centered at 3934 State Street, had grown to nine hundred members by the start of the 1940s. The union survived the epic collapse of Chicago's music scene during the Great Depression, steadily increasing its membership numbers by 50 percent between 1929 and 1940 despite facing ever-increasing discrimination by the Local 10, an all-white union. In 1939, Broonzy made the decision to become a member, a choice he remained proud of until his death.[34] By the time the United States entered World War II, the union "prevailed upon many clubs to follow a union only hiring policy with musicians," while simultaneously "extending its influence" on the reorganized recording industry.[35]

The industry's expectations were different after 1940, as recording became the dominant way of forming one's reputation and securing financial success as a musician. Before the reorganization of the industry in 1940, recordings were a supplement to live performances. Broonzy and many of his contemporaries expected to land significant stage work because of their recording experience. But their identities, reputations, and finances were enhanced onstage night after night in performance. After 1940, even the least experienced blues musicians were potentially one hit record away from stardom. Personas were created overnight, and live performances were often relegated to supporting acts for a musician's latest hit.[36] This shift in the economy of the U.S. music industry transformed Broonzy's fortunes, jolting him from unbridled success into nearly abject obscurity. Broonzy's experience during this shift offers an interesting window into the broader travails of musicians.

By negotiating Melrose's vision for a new urban blues sound, Broonzy had transformed himself from a solo male blues shouter in the Blind Lemon Jefferson mold into a smoothed-over, almost jazz-like, blues crooner. His vocal phrasings became relaxed, carefully phrased, and more confident, while his guitar accompaniment remained a subtle companion to various accompanists' pulsating piano rhythms. In effect, Broonzy's work with Melrose suggests that he had begun to view vocal style and inflection as more important or perhaps aesthetically superior to the frequently dissonant and polyrhythmic guitar style and vocal phrasing that dominated the Mississippi Delta and East Texas sounds. He was transforming his professional style and image in the same way he had transformed his consciousness in black Chicago back in the early 1920s. Over the course of the 1930s, Broonzy became "Big Bill"—perhaps the most important blues artist of the era, lending songwriting, vocal performance, and guitar accompaniment to hundreds upon hundreds of recordings. Broonzy expected Chicago's continually evolving blues music culture and industry to recognize his ongoing relevance to Chicago's urban blues sound. He was becoming a leader within this community and an important architect of the city's evolving blues sound. Indeed, the blues were changing into a more urban sound that featured ensembles that included piano, guitar, harmonica, the occasional woodwind, and drums, a precursor to the swing, jump blues, and boogie-woogie craze of the early 1940s, but relying less and less on hokum's bawdy lyrical content and expression. His 1938 classic "It's a Low Down Dirty Shame" exemplifies this incredibly potent sound, with Broonzy on vocals, a teenage George Barnes on electric guitar, Blind John Davis on piano, and Bill Osborn on tenor saxophone. With this combination of instrumentation and approach, Broonzy's swinging blues and smooth urban style began moving closer to the rhythm and blues that was to become extremely popular in the 1940s. The lyrics, too, seem to shift from overt and humorous sexual innuendo to the melancholia created by Broonzy's relationship to a woman he could not trust. Broonzy continued to be aware that successfully engaging Chicago's music business meant recognizing the expectations of those who held power within that world. Even if fulfilling these expectations did not produce immediate financial gains, it did help build strong reputations for performers and songwriters within the black pop music world.

As Broonzy came into his own as an urban blues musician, his songwriting became increasingly prolific and sophisticated, covering in his lyrics a wide array of topics including politics, racism, relationships, city life, agriculture, industrial labor, the Great Depression, natural disasters, religion, alcohol, migration, and World War II. This wide-ranging repertoire helped further establish his popularity and solidify his reputation as "Big Bill." As new migrants arrived in Chicago during the 1940s, many recognized Broonzy as the leader of Chicago's blues community.[37] In a 1946 letter to his friend Alan Lomax, Broonzy explained how both his transformation into "Big Bill" and his own understanding of the music business had paid off.[38] As a black pop artist throughout the 1930s and into the 1940s, Broonzy appeared and recorded all over the country, often crisscrossing from Chicago to New York. He had recorded for various record labels including Paramount, Black Pattie, Vocalion, Perfect, and Gennett and on the ten subsidiaries of RCA Victor.[39] The letter further lists over thirty-five artists with whom he had once worked over his long career.

Throughout most of the prewar period, Broonzy continued to perform in many of the clubs and bars that emerged from the repeal of Prohibition, further establishing his persona as "Big Bill." Clubs and theaters such as Ruby Lee Gatewood's Tavern, the 1410 Club, the Regal Theatre, and the 8th Street Theatre in Chicago and Town Hall, the Apollo Theater, and Café Society in New York were the sites of some of Broonzy's best gigs and hosted many of the country's best blues and jazz talents. Some of these clubs featured performers for five to six hours at a time.[40]

The dominance of urban blues in Broonzy's recordings from the 1930s and 1940s should not suggest that he had abandoned his country blues roots. National and local Chicago blues audiences held expectations of their own, outside those fostered by the recording industry. One of these expectations was country blues, and Broonzy continued to perform in the rural style during this period in clubs, theaters, and parties in self-accompanied or guitar-piano arrangements. In 1938 and 1939, for example, he appeared in John Hammond's New York-based productions "From Spirituals to Swing," a "concert of Negro music sponsored by the leftist New Masses."[41] Playing to a nearly all-white audience, Broonzy, a polished urban blues veteran, wore coveralls and his first pair of "store-bought shoes" as he played, according to Hammond, the South's latest blues straight from the fields of Arkansas.[42] Broonzy's public performance of "Just a Dream," the first song he performed during his two-year run at "From Spirituals to Swing," symbolizes an important moment in American music and memory. Broonzy first recorded "Just a Dream" for Vocalion Records in February 1939 with Joshua Altheimer on piano, just a few months after his big break at "From Spirituals to Swing." Altheimer's piano provides the central rhythmic and melodic accompaniment on which Broonzy offers a confident and strong vocal performance evoking the sound of a veteran recording artist. His guitar playing is low in the mix but demonstrates his skills as a rhythm and lead guitarist, alternating between solid rhythmic chording and impressive countermelodic lead runs with the piano. The signs of the guitar master he was to become are present but not yet fully developed.

At Carnegie Hall, Broonzy performed the song accompanied by Albert Ammons; Broonzy played the role of the in-between-gigs farm hand with "naïve 'down home' charm," according to a review at the time.[43] His first public performance of "Just a Dream" helped the blues gain a more prominent standing in the American folk-life experience. Broonzy performed for perhaps the largest audience of his long career, and in so doing, he became a lens through which to view the shifting grounds of American racial formation and its association to culture. The poetic but nonlinear lyrics of "Just a Dream" echo with the protean pain of a lifetime of unrecognized hopes and unfulfilled promises from black life in both the South and Chicago:

> It was a dream, just a dream I had on my mind
> It was a dream, just a dream I had on my mind
> And when I woke up, not a thing could I find
>
> I dreamed I went out with an angel, and had a good time
> I dreamed I was satisfied, and nothin' to worry my mind
> But it was just a dream, just a dream I had on my mind,
> And when I woke up, baby, not an angel could I find
>
> I dreamed I played policy, and played the horses too
> I dreamed I win so much money, I didn't know what to do
> But it was just a dream, just a dream I had on my mind!
> Now, and when I woke up, not a penny could I find
>
> Dreamed I was in the White House, sittin' in the president's chair
> I dreamed he's shaking my hand, and he said "Bill, I'm so glad you're here"
> But that was just a dream, Lord, a dream I had on my mind
> And when I woke up, baby, not a chair there could I find
>
> I dreamed I got married, and started me a family
> I dreamed I had ten children, and they all looked just like me
> But that was just a dream, Lord, what a dream I had on my mind
> Now, and when I woke up, baby, not a child there looked like mine[44]

The references to the numbers racket and horseracing, for example, highlight Bronzeville's vibrant gambling culture and Broonzy's association with the high-risk, high-reward stakes of policy that might leave unfortunate southern migrants penniless or catapult the lucky few to new economic heights. Moreover, the stanza featuring an imagined visit to the White House symbolizes his belief in the importance of egalitarian politics in the face of the stark reality that he and his community were completely disfranchised. The final stanza perhaps reflects Broonzy's hope and eventual disappointment in coming from a large family but never having one of his own. It is plausible that Broonzy may have fathered several children across the United States and Europe, but those who have explored his biography have discovered only one son, living in Amsterdam, Netherlands. Taken together then, the themes of economic insecurity, political disfranchisement, and Jim Crow America's attempts at destabilizing black family life in the United States reflect both past and continuing inequalities within the African American experience in the United States. Broonzy tapped this root in "Just a Dream" and continued to express these themes in his music until his death. Broonzy's expression of the "Blues Model of Individualism" and his lifting of the veil entailed employing his music as a weapon against racism in the United States.[45]

Lester Melrose shared Broonzy's continued interest in the country blues of the Mississippi Delta and often expected Broonzy to scout popular talent from the South. In the late 1930s, Melrose desperately wanted to record the Mississippi bluesman Tommy McClennan, whose distinct style, Melrose believed, would sell readily on the Bluebird label. Broonzy understood all too well how a northern white man engaging African Americans from the Mississippi Delta would be perceived by local farm and plantation bosses. He suggested that Melrose should find "a Negro out of town" to talk to McClennan in hopes of avoiding any confrontation. Disregarding Broonzy's warning and knowledge of black labor systems in the South, Melrose traveled to Mississippi himself, only to flee Yazoo City for his life, leaving behind his car and money for McClennan to travel to Chicago. Broonzy recalled, "I told you they don't like a white man from the North out on their farm or anywhere they have five or six hundred Negroes working. I told you might get hurt or killed on one of those farms or camps." Melrose replied, "Get hurt, get hurt, hell, they nearly killed me, and they would have done it if I hadn't run like hell." Melrose never again visited the South after the McClennan incident, enlisting Broonzy for scouting trips, arguing that he would "certainly never go down there again!"[46]

Broonzy's fulfillment of Melrose's musical expectations evolved throughout the 1930s in a manner that reflected the evolution of the blues genre. Both men had survived the Depression-era collapse of the recording industry to create a style of urban-tinged, black pop blues that made one of them rich and provided the other with an incredibly potent celebrity within Chicago's blues community. The 1940s, however, presented new challenges for Broonzy and his expectations of Chicago's blues and its culture by forcing the last stage of his musical development. A new generation of younger musicians was augmenting the modes and pathways of recorded blues, adding increased sophistication to the composition and recording process. The development of the black pop sound of the late thirties and the early forties with swing bands, boogie-woogie, and jump blues led to a merger of jazz big bands into the blues realm, essentially meshing both worlds. Jazz, moreover, was slowly becoming the measure of how the blues was understood.[47] Indeed, in 1939, Broonzy appeared with the jazz pioneers Benny Goodman and Louis Armstrong in the feature film *Swingin' the Dream*.[48]

Between the middle of 1942 and the beginning of 1945, Broonzy's recording opportunities disappeared, in large part because of the recording strike of the period. Moreover, although Broonzy was technically still a Columbia Records artist under contract with Lester Melrose, his professional relationship with Melrose had come to a close. Looking to keep his body of recorded work fresh and varied, Broonzy began recording with ensembles that provided a contrast to Melrose's formulaic sound. In early 1945, Broonzy joined the tenor saxophonist and arranger Don Byas and his swing quartet to record for New York's Hub Records under the name "Little Sam and the Don Byas Quartet."[49] Among the four songs recorded at the session was a new version of Broonzy's hit song "Just a Dream" in an arrangement for vocals, guitar, tenor saxophone, piano, bass, and drums. Taken at a moderately slow tempo, the 1945 recording captures Broonzy's powerfully emotive voice supported by interwoven melodic background figures by the guitar, saxophone, and piano. A close listening reveals the ways in which Broonzy's new arrangement of the song had slowly evolved from its Chicago blues roots and into the increasingly popular rhythm-and-blues style of the period. Broonzy later took a stab at the jump blues sound in a 1947 recording for Columbia of his "Big Bill's Boogie," featuring the typical jump blues ensemble of boogie-woogie piano, saxophone, upright bass, drums, and rhythm guitar. In 1949, Big Bill and His Fat Four recorded a handful of takes for Mercury Records, including a rhythm-and-blues number called "I Love My Whiskey" with Broonzy on electric guitar and vocals, backed by an alto sax, piano, bass, and drums. The recording's acoustic and artistic quality and the arrangement, including Broonzy's astonishing electric guitar lead runs, capture his evolving style and sounds eerily similar to the sound of the rising rhythm-and-blues star Aaron "T-Bone" Walker.

Broonzy's live performances from the immediate postwar period also reflected how broader changes in musical style manifested themselves in his recorded output. According to the *New York Amsterdam News*, from early June 1945, New York's Harlem awaited the arrival of the jazz saxophonist and

Broonzy with the jazz singer Rosetta Howard, 1947.
Courtesy of the Frank Driggs Collection at Jazz at
Lincoln Center.

arranger Teddy McRae's fine new swing band, whose singer, "Big Bill," stood as one of "the most popular male singers in the country." Broonzy was scheduled for his first appearance at New York's famed Apollo Theater, and he was heralded by the newspaper as "the nearest approach that the theatre yet had to Bessie Smith," even suggesting that his recordings were "America's best selling blues records."[50] At this point, Broonzy had performed with many of the nation's top jazz bandleaders and musicians, who had often crossed over into blues. These included Benny Goodman, Count Basie, Eddie Vinson, Bunk Johnson, Fats Waller, Fletcher Henderson, and Lionel Hampton.[51]

As much as Broonzy tried to stay modern and up to date, his carefully fashioned celebrity did not quite mesh with the changing blues landscape of the immediate post-World War II era.[52] Indeed, he had conformed to the expectations of black pop hit makers and their targeted audiences by moving away from his Delta and country blues roots. He had learned to alter his vocal delivery and tonal approach, even though he believed this was moving away from the power and raw passion of the blues of the late 1920s and early 1930s.[53] He had grown quite comfortable being known among his peers and the industry as "Big Bill" from Chicago. And he had even learned to perform and record in ensembles with as many as five other musicians. Nevertheless, Broonzy reflected on this change ruefully. "You know they tell me now? These young boys playing this here bebop? They tell me blues is old-fogeyism. They done give it all up. It don't rate in these modernist times. And they mean it! Don't you try comin in one of those joints on the South Side and singin one of those down-home Arkansas blues. Man they'll beat you to death."[54] For Broonzy, the recording and performance culture within this new generation of black musicians was changing for the worse. In the studio, younger musicians, a generation that Alan Lomax called "half-educated," began taking control of recording culture.[55] Broonzy was especially concerned about this new generation's reliance on written music. For over a decade, a central component of Broonzy's "Big Bill" personality relied on the knowledge that he could walk into the studio, rehearse a few memorized numbers with his accompaniment, and make a record just on the reputation of his name alone. By the mid-1940s, however, the process had become much more complicated.

> Nowadays you walk in a studio without no music for the different instruments and they tell you they don't know what to play—they will say that and yet those same guys wouldn't have been eatin around here for a few years ago if they couldn't play the blues by ear. . . . Pete Johnson, Albert Ammons, Count Basie—all of um—they wasn't nothin but barrelhouse blues players a few years ago, playin all night with nothin in the world in front of um but a big drink of whiskey. Now they tell me they can't play blues if it ain't wrote down.[56]

With increasing frequency, Big Bill became immersed within the country's jazz world, and although it welcomed him, he never quite felt comfortable there. Harlem's Hollywood Music Shop, located at 384 West 125th Street, marketed Broonzy's recordings as part of its "New & Best Selling" jazz records collection in the *New York Amsterdam News*.[57] In 1946, Art Hodes, a jazz pianist and the editor of the jazz music magazine the *Jazz Record*, edited the first major biographical piece about Broonzy, "Baby I Done Got Wise," written by Broonzy himself. The national wire from the *Chicago Defender* picked up a story in which Broonzy had joined a "star-studded" music revue featuring "artists from all the leading shows and night clubs in New York" for the 1947 Human Welfare Festival. Broonzy and host of others lent entertainment support for the Southern Conference for Human Welfare festival so that the event's proceeds "might be used down South to fight against Jim Crow and bigotry."[58]

Despite the warm reception from New York's jazz press, Broonzy's inability to read music proved frustrating in a world of fluent and trained jazz musicians. By the mid-1940s, Big Bill Broonzy was one of the most recorded and respected musicians in blues history, but when he entered the studio, he was often forced to alter his playing and personal style to fit with a younger group of extremely professional musicians who were not quite familiar with the rhythmic eccentricity, improvised lyrics, and nontonal harmonic asides that defined Broonzy's music. European scales, arrangements, transcriptions, and rehearsal—all elements that clashed with Broonzy's musical abilities and past experiences in the business—were supplanting and challenging the commanding improvisation and whimsical guitar and vocal deliveries that had shaped his "Big Bill" persona. "You got to be so perfect . . . the blues ain't no pleasure no more. You're always in a strain, worrying if you gonna make a bad chord. What make me so hot is those guys telling me they can't play nothin. They don't know but one move in the blues and when they through with that, they done. That's why all these records sound so much alike. You can't tell when one leaves off and the next one start, if it wasn't for the nickels dropping in the Rockolas."[59] Broonzy felt that this formulaic recipe and the professional musicians who created it were taking the blues in a direction that did not wholly fit his style.

To a certain degree, Broonzy was simply reacting to the changing landscape of the recording industry. For nearly six months following the Japanese bombing of Pearl Harbor, the American Federation of Musicians and its 140,000 members initiated an all-out ban on commercial recording in response to the recent reorganization of the American music industry.[60] Alliances between the recording industry and radio and jukebox companies presented significant challenges for the traditional role of a musicians' union interested in recovering lost revenue from royalties forfeited to radio stations and jukeboxes. By 1940, the radio had become an increasingly dominant force in home entertainment. Radio targeted specific demographic groups, including European and Hispanic immigrants and southern and northern African Americans, as well as whites. Radio programs featuring a wide array of music and acts were emerging in every city in the country.[61] The creation of Broadcast Music Incorporated (BMI) in 1940 established a point of contact between radio stations and owners of publishing rights held by ASCAP and the American Federation of Musicians (AFM). These intercessions, in turn, led to a weakening of both musicians' unions—AFM and BMI.[62]

Compounding these events was the explosion of jukebox production from the mid-1930s into the 1940s. The number of jukeboxes manufactured increased dramatically from twenty-five thousand units in 1934 to five hundred thousand in 1940, with the three leading manufacturers, Wurlitzer, Rockola, and Seeburg, all based in the Midwest. Purveyors and purchasers of jukeboxes held their own ideas about music and artist royalties as well. Essentially, the jukebox allowed club and bar owners to provide house music for pocket change, without having to deal with the higher prices and volatility of live musicians. More important, the jukebox and the radio concretized the power that both industries held within the popular music business, as records bought by jukebox owners constituted over 50 percent of all record sales in 1938.[63]

In response, the AFM organized an all-out strike against the recording industry that lasted for two years, from 1942 to 1944, until new contracts were written. No AFM artist commercially recorded during this period. Significant changes in the recording industry, then, were altering musicians' professional approach to recording. With the popular-music industry nearly crippled, the AFM and its leadership appeared in news outlets across the country as traitorous villains with little concern for public morale. Outside pressure from Senate investigations and an antitrust lawsuit held very little sway over the union's dogged determination. As the United States ended its first full year of participation in World War II, prospects for morale-boosting cultural production in the form of recorded popular music seemed grim.[64] These changes culminated in a complete restructuring of the music industry in Chicago. One scholar has argued that "throughout the 1940s and afterward, musicians and producers revised the meaning of blues in Chicago—not only through focus on the urban context, but also a more professional understanding of black music, which encouraged artists to view their cultural work in more material terms."[65]

Lester Melrose, with his affiliations with RCA Victor and Columbia Records, was at the height of his power during this period of reorganization. His ability to integrate other contemporary music forms into recorded blues ensured new studio musicians were constantly on hand, many of whom were trained jazz musicians. This studio sound and its nuances drastically affected what Broonzy could expect when he participated in a recording date. Following the end of the recording strike in 1944, Broonzy's recording output decreased tremendously. Whereas he had twice recorded in ten different sessions or more in 1938 and 1939, he recorded three times in 1945, once in 1946, three times in 1947, and only twice in 1949.[66]

When recording resumed, independent record labels began to emerge in Chicago's blues community. These labels were eager to capitalize on the city's rapidly expanding migrant population and newly arrived musicians. Before the strike, RCA Victor, Columbia, and Brunswick Vocalion, all national labels, dominated the black pop market. By the early 1940s, Broonzy had recorded for subsidiaries of all three labels. Melrose had maintained tight control over Chicago's RCA Victor and Columbia recordings through his own vision of a studio sound, essentially creating the model that many emerging independent labels would follow when he immediately signed all of Chicago's established talent.

The absorption of the Chicago blues vanguards by Melrose and his associated labels left the city's emerging smaller recording companies to scramble for new talent and new blues personalities. This next generation of southern migrants became the catalysts for a completely new Chicago sound. Featured in this group of young talent are some of the most legendary names in Chicago blues: Little Walter Jacobs, Johnny Williams, Jimmy Rogers, Otis Spann, Johnny Shines, Sunnyland Slim, and, of course, Muddy Waters.[67] Beginning in 1945 and continuing through the rest of the decade, a series of independent labels emerged in Chicago, including Rhumboogie, Hy-Tone, Sunbeam, Tempo-tone, Old Swingmaster, Miracle, Regal, and Atlantic.[68] Many of these labels expected to recruit Chicago blues veterans by churning out the same formulaic, multi-instrumental blues pioneered by Melrose's artists and the Bluebird sound. Instead, most of Chicago's big-name talent— Tampa Red, Big Bill Broonzy, Big Maceo Merriweather, Memphis Minnie Douglas, Washboard Sam, Arthur "Big Boy" Crudup, and John Lee "Sonny Boy" Williamson — immediately signed with Melrose following the end of strike, ensuring that their contracts would remain under the major labels RCA Victor and Columbia. Broonzy, Melrose, and many other Chicago blues veterans held outdated expectations for a business and a genre that had reorganized around new sets of standards involving new musicians and styles that centered on radio and jukebox play.

As World War II came to a close, Big Bill Broonzy had lived and experienced professional musicianship and all it entailed in Chicago for twenty-five years. He had participated in the first wave of the Great Migrations that had brought the blues to Chicago from the South, and he was a key player in establishing the blues as a substantial form of black popular music with a national market and audience. The blues, as a genre, had evolved from its vaudeville and country roots to become urban, slick, sophisticated, and central to an ever-expanding consumer marketplace. The leading recording labels featuring veteran artists such as Broonzy and Tampa Red of the World War II era continued to rely on the formulaic studio sound that emerged out of the 1930s. They paid scant attention to the changing expectations of black audiences.

The Mississippi Delta sound was still prevalent in the Deep South, a phenomenon exemplified by Alan Lomax's 1941 Library of Congress field recordings of young McKinley Morganfield, better known as Muddy Waters.[69] To the west in Helena, Arkansas, KFFA radio was blasting its daily radio program *King Biscuit Time* featuring Delta artists Rice "Sonny Boy Williamson" Miller, Robert Lockwood Jr., and Willie "Joe" Wilkins.[70] KWEM and WDIA in Memphis, Tennessee, also began airing live blues shows and radio programs that electrified the Delta blues tradition. These stations featured future stars B. B. King, Bobby Blue Bland, Rufus Thomas, Rice Miller, Chester "Howlin' Wolf" Burnett, and Hubert Sumlin. All of these younger musicians had cut their teeth on the records of urban artists such as Broonzy.[71]

As southern migrants poured into Chicago during the second wave of the Great Migrations, it is hardly surprising that this rougher, edgier, electrified Delta blues would follow them. This is what these migrants had heard on the radio, in juke joints, and in barrelhouses throughout the South during the period, and this is the sound that Muddy Waters mastered in Chicago. This new generation had returned to the "down-home" style of the Mississippi Delta but played it louder and faster. They crafted a grittier, louder, and rawer sound than the urban blues ensembles of which "Big Bill" was king.[72] To be clear, Broonzy and others had amplified the guitar as early as 1940 to combat the noisy and rowdy clubs and bars in Chicago.[73] But the sounds emerging out of the South in the 1940s were wholly different—more percussive, driving, and virtuosic. They shed the jazz-tinged instrumentation—namely, the piano and brass horns—that Broonzy and Melrose had pioneered for stripped-down electrified blues, with new arrangements featuring double bass, drums, electric guitar, and amplified harmonica. Musicians such as Muddy Waters, Howlin' Wolf, and Willie Dixon, and their expectations of Chicago's music industry, further confirmed the Windy City as home to the blues.

To be sure, Broonzy was an inspiration to these up-and-coming musicians,[74] but they would challenge Broonzy's role as a leading figure of Chicago's blues. Yet in 1948, when Muddy Waters recorded his breakthrough hit "Can't Be Satisfied," Broonzy was older than Waters, and younger audiences and musicians began viewing Broonzy as a vanguard of a dying tradition. Jazz enthusiasts and folklorists commented on Broonzy's dwindling influence as they watched him perform his "country ways" in the late 1940s and early 1950s as younger audience members "walked out on him." Even Muddy Waters admitted to giving intermission spots to Broonzy, essentially recognizing that he had "displaced" Broonzy and older bluesmen in the late 1940s.[75]

While Broonzy's reputation grew as a leader of Chicago blues culture in the 1930s and '40s, he stood as an authoritative voice for dozens of fledging musicians, ultimately playing an assertive role in the development of Chicago blues. Many people in the music business—especially Melrose—took advantage of Broonzy throughout his career on a multitude of levels, and only later in life did he challenge these abuses. Conversely, as an authoritative figure within Chicago's blues culture, his warmth, leadership, and devotion to the blues' younger generations were critical for up-and-coming blues musicians. Many younger bluesmen and women viewed him as a father figure and a harbinger of an expanding blues landscape. Broonzy helped guide the early careers of recently arrived musicians, offering sage advice and coordinating important introductions. In Big Bill Broonzy, these musicians found a generous and affable veteran of the Chicago scene who knew the appropriate individuals within the city's club circuit as well as the city's evolving recording-company market and its transformation from an art form into an industry.[76]

The list of aspiring artists who benefited from Broonzy's warmth and generosity is immense: Muddy Waters, Homesick James, J. B. Lenoir, Tommy McClennan, Johnny Williams, Floyd Jones, Georgia Tom Dorsey, Little Walter, Eddie Boyd, Jimmy Rogers, Washboard Sam, and Memphis Slim all cited Broonzy as an influence. J. B. Lenoir suggested that Broonzy treated him "like a son."[77] Georgia Tom Dorsey remembered Big Bill was always having "a good attitude" and "jolly," once claiming that he had never seen Broonzy mad.[78] The Clarksdale, Mississippi, bluesman turned Chicago migrant Eddie Boyd met Broonzy through a family acquaintance, and Broonzy guided Boyd through his discovery of the city. Boyd recalled that upon his migration in the early 1940s, he "spent a lot of time with Big Bill," and Broonzy always shared "information." Boyd proclaimed that Broonzy was "never a selfish type of guy."[79] As an authoritative figure for young and upcoming blues artists, then, Broonzy was nothing less than a stalwart, and like other New Settlers of the era, he ushered many young migrants into the city's rapidly developing leisure world. Yet, rather than lead this new talent astray in the same manner he had experienced at times, he helped guide them through what could be a difficult transition for aspiring migrant musicians.

Perhaps Broonzy's greatest impact was on one of the most celebrated figures in all of blues culture, Muddy Waters. Nearly every time the two musicians crossed paths, Broonzy offered praise and kind suggestions, a smile, and friendship. Waters recalled,

> Big Bill, that's the nicest guy I ever met in my life. He really say I had it. I guess he was the cause of me going over to England the first time you know. . . . Big Bill was my mainline man. He was one of the greatest in the business. . . . I met some real good cool people like Big Bill, now. He was big name but cool. And I got acquainted with him, and every time he'd see me, he had swap some words for me, or say something's funny, you know. He wasn't the head-tall man, done like this, walk in a place lookin' all over everybody in there.[80]

Like Broonzy, Waters was a Delta sharecropper. Born in 1913, Waters came of age on Stovall Plantation, near Clarksdale, Mississippi. By age ten, he had learned the harmonica; at thirteen, he had acquired enough skill to play community gatherings. Waters's style is notable in that it developed at the very moment when post–World War II southern blues traditions were forming and broadcast across the South on radio stations such as KFFA, out of Helena, Arkansas.[81] Muddy, however, discovered influences from both local musicians and 78 rpm phonographs from a neighbor's Victrola and, eventually, one owned by his grandmother. He bought his first guitar at age seventeen, absorbing recorded sounds from Blind Lemon Jefferson, Blind Blake, Barbecue Bob, Roosevelt Sikes, Memphis Minnie Douglas, Tampa Red, and Lonnie Johnson. At the same time, local Delta guitarists such as Charley Patton, Son House, and Robert Johnson equally influenced his approach to the instrument. By the time he reached adulthood, Waters had become a well-known sharecropper, musician, bootlegger, fur trader, proprietor of a local juke joint, and all-around hustler. Mostly, Waters remained in and around his Delta country home and family. Things changed one day in August 1941, when John W. Work III and Alan Lomax arrived at his doorstep from, respectively, Fisk University and the Library of Congress, looking to record Delta blues musicians. During the summers of 1941 and '42, Waters made his first recordings for what became known as *Muddy Waters: The Complete Plantation Recordings: The Historic 1941-42 Library of Congress Field Recordings*. The following year, disillusioned with plantation life and ready to try his hand at a recording career, Waters left Mississippi for Chicago, never to return.[82]

Broonzy was critical to Muddy Waters's becoming a household name in Chicago and in Europe, telling many people, "You ain't heard nothing to you

John Lee "Sonny Boy" Williamson and Big Bill Broonzy, ca. early 1940s. Notice Broonzy holding an early-model Gibson L-4 archtop with a removable electric pickup. This could have been the electric guitar Muddy Waters mentioned when he first met Big Bill. Waters had never seen an electric guitar before. Courtesy of the Frank Driggs Collection at Jazz at Lincoln Center.

hear that young boy from Mississippi."[83] Warmly and openly, he mentored Waters in the music business and on stylistic nuances that affected Waters's transition from an acoustic, Delta blues player into to an urbane, electrified dynamo. Broonzy was the very first musician Waters had ever seen play an electric guitar. Broonzy informed Waters that his "little acoustic wouldn't work" in the raucous taverns, clubs, and bars of Chicago's South Side.[84] Affably and graciously, he introduced Waters to everyone he could, including record-company talent scouts, suggesting, "All as I can do, introduce you to a company. . . . If the company don't like you, that mean it's just the same thing."[85] Just as Broonzy helped Waters become the undisputed champion of Chicago blues in the 1950s, Broonzy, who had experienced a lifetime of disappointment within the music industry, began taking a more assertive role in his career.

Although younger musicians respected Broonzy's stature—no one had more positive and sentimental remembrances of Broonzy than Waters—many of Chicago's young blues musicians and audiences believed he was antiquated, if not redundant. Broonzy and Melrose had updated the southern blues of the 1920s by synthesizing jazz and blues elements into a fresh urban sound, experimenting with various instrument arrangements and demonstrating the pervasive impact a few individuals could have on evolving musical styles. But by 1948, Muddy Waters and Chess Records were redefining blues culture and its industry in Chicago. Leonard and Philip Chess—the brothers who owned and ran Chess Records—proved the savvy of small independent labels that had gambled on the changing landscape within blues culture and its audience, a gamble that more established labels and veteran promoters such as Melrose had avoided.[86] At the end of the 1940s, Broonzy's prospects as a professional musician appeared bleak. Faced with both a changing audience and an evolving recording industry, Big Bill Broonzy, one of the most experienced and seasoned blues artists in the country, had few options. In 1949, he recorded twice, cutting eight tracks for Mercury Records in Chicago.[87]

CHAPTER FIVE

I Come for to Sing

By 1950, even though Broonzy's recording opportunities had disappeared, he still had a regular performing gig at Moore's Lounge, a small tavern off Cottage Grove Avenue.[1] Among generations of participants in Chicago's blues world, the man known affectionately as "Big Bill" was a household name and an identifiable mentor for up-and-coming musicians in Chicago. Yet by 1950, he had virtually disappeared. Had his remaining friends in Chicago—Tampa Red, Muddy Waters, J. B. Lenoir, Lonnie Johnson, Little Walter Jacobs, and others—gone looking for him in the city, they would not have found him. Big Bill Broonzy had moved to Ames, Iowa, to take a job as a custodian at Iowa State College.[2]

How one of Chicago's blues pioneers, who had lived in Chicago for thirty years, ended up as a janitor in a solidly rural midwestern college town can only be explained by an examination of the protean nature of Broonzy's career. By 1948, Chicago folk-music-revival pioneers Louis "Studs" Terkel and Win Stracke had established a touring folk music revue, initially sponsored by the Renaissance Society at the University of Chicago and featuring a handful of local folk musicians performing English ballads, traditional folk arrangements, and country blues.[3] The "I Come for to Sing" tour became a popular traveling folk revue, narrated by Terkel and featuring music by Broonzy, Stracke, and Larry Lane, that traveled around the country visiting college campuses, often crossing paths with Pete Seeger and the Weavers.[4] Broonzy was still traveling and performing, but he had exchanged the smoky, alcohol-fueled clubs in the black blues circuit for the serene environs of midwestern college campuses. One of the performance venues on the 1949 tour was Iowa State College.

A part of Broonzy's relocation to Ames and engagement with the custodial arts is rooted in the evolving landscape of the Windy City's music scene. The blues, its audiences, and its recording industry, all elements he had helped pioneer in Chicago, no longer recognized the validity of his craft. Broonzy clung to older ideas and expectations of the music world in Chicago, when in actuality that world had expanded in new directions. By this point, Broonzy had nearly abandoned his music career, and he expected that his recording opportunities were over. Quite simply, unlike dozens, if not hundreds, of blues artists of the era, Broonzy had lasted long enough in the business to witness a transitional phase in the music industry and the evolution of the blues as a genre.

The second and larger part of the story, though, is that Broonzy, ever crafty and always willing to perform, began engaging a new audience by slowly reinventing his celebrity persona through new opportunities within a separate music culture. Broonzy did not land janitorial work at a midwestern agricultural college because of his reputation as a laborer. To Iowa State, he was a music legend whose career as an unmatched blues talent with over 260 recordings lent credence and prestige to the college. He was a popular entertainer from Chicago, the closest major metropolitan area, who was extremely affable and always willing to share his music. In essence, he was a campus treasure, a hidden gem that made the college special for students, staff, and faculty.[5] Ten years earlier, the same white, collegiate crowd probably would have never entered the all-black clubs and bars in Chicago where "Big Bill" and his blues were king. So how did a black pop music entertainer from Bronzeville become a folk music hero to white, university intellectuals and students? Quite simply, he did what he had always done: he transformed his public personality and his music to fit the expectations of his new audience, a community of academic folklorists, record collectors, music scholars, and college students who were awakening to the importance of the black musical tradition. Broonzy entered the last stage of his career transformation by becoming "Big Bill Broonzy, folk singer." Although he would forcibly erode the big-city, black-pop celebrity image of "Big Bill," his fame would reach new heights as a result of this last phase and firmly shape his legacy long after his death.

Of course, Broonzy's move to Iowa can be seen in the context of a larger shift in American vernacular music. Beginning in the 1930s, a folk music "revival" had emerged in the United States involving numerous white "folk" aficionados and trained folklorists taking a keen interest in white and black vernacular music. From roughly 1930 to 1970, an important transformation took place within American music culture that scholars are beginning to define as an inherently problematic social movement.[6] Stemming from the tense age of New Deal America and extending into the turbulent years of the postwar United States, a folk music revival began that "brought public folklorists, cultural preservationists, scholars, musicians, political activists, musical entrepreneurs, and folk music fans together" in hopes of capturing, collecting, popularizing, and disseminating a type of American vernacular music.[7] For this budding social movement, blues, gospel, work songs, protest songs, train songs, cowboy music, Appalachian balladry, old-time, and hillbilly were all fair game as evidence that "folk music" lived at the heart of an American consciousness or identity and beyond the commercial music landscape. Modernization, in the form of rapid urbanization and industrialization but, more specifically, the commercialization of American music, heightened the prevalent awareness among folklorists of the need to capture a disappearing folk music tradition. Early song-collecting luminaries—such as Carl Sandburg, Cecil Sharp, John Lomax, Bascom Lamar Lunsford, Dorothy Scarborough, and Robert Winslow Gordon—set out across all corners of the country to capture the "authentic" sounds of a fading musical past.[8] The federal government became interested in this process as well, opening the Library of Congress's Archive of American Folk Song in 1928 and running the New Deal's Works Progress Administration's Joint Committee on Folk Art throughout the 1930s. With these developments taken together, a conservative institutional (academic and governmental) interest rooted in the preservation of the nation's folk music past grew rapidly throughout the 1930s, witnessed by the beginnings of folk music festivals up and down the East Coast.[9]

If this folk music revival stemmed from the curiosities and concerns of white, academically trained, East Coast collectors, it also found a home within the vibrant left-leaning political landscape of the period. Commercialized music throughout the 1920s had, for the most part, existed as a novel pastime and rarely exposed more radical political currents of such an uneasy age. The Great Depression brought with it a revitalization of the labor movement in the United States, as many poor and broken Americans found labor organizations and their associations with socialism and communism an attractive alternative to the seeming collapse of industrial capitalism. Throughout the 1930s, then, folk musicians such as Woody Guthrie and Aunt Mollie Jackson and collectors such as Charles Seeger signified the presence of a much more liberal—and radical, in some cases—association with folk music, which throughout the 1940s gave rise to younger folk luminaries such as Pete Seeger, Burl Ives, Alan Lomax, Lead Belly, Josh White, Tony Kraber, Moses Asch, and Michael Loring. At the same time, the Left engaged in creating radio programs, integrated clubs, and live concerts, including Alan Lomax's *Back Where I Come From*, Greenwich Village's Café Society, and John Hammond's "From Spirituals to Swing" at Carnegie Hall. As war broke out in 1941, many of the nation's folk troubadours—Seeger, Guthrie, Lomax, Ives, White—joined the war effort in some capacity. But their work had launched momentum forward toward an emerging folk music revival.[10] This revival, moreover, pursued and eventually achieved a mass popularization of folk music in the United States through mass media in ways the Old Left could not have imagined. Nonetheless, the revival also exposed problems within the New Left's multiculturalism.

In most cases, running through the fabric of the folk music movement in the United States, from its inception at the turn of the twentieth century across the great revival into the 1970s, was the thread of American racism. Early folk song collectors, from Cecil Sharp to John Lomax to Howard Odum, expressed an often antagonistic worldview of the importance and legacy of black contributions to American vernacular music, especially in their relationship to English balladry. Collectively, while their investigations and expressions of early folk music documented what they perceived as an isolated, eroding tradition, these pioneers were far more successful in their attempts to demonstrate black folk musicians as naturally inferior and untouched by modernity in ways that vindicated folklorists' own expertise as collectors, while at the same time reaffirming their whiteness and middle-class status.[11] Even when folklorists and other stewards of memory during the revival took the chance to express their increasingly progressive political and social ideas, these manifestations often led to white expressions and imagery projected onto black music culture that seemed incongruent with black vernacular traditions. These folklorists, including Alan Lomax, who helped Broonzy reinvigorate his career in the 1950s, remained "trapped" in their "cultural perception of blackness" while their "white cultural assumptions . . . remain[ed] part of the academic construction of African Americans as folk," even as they extolled parts of black culture and artistry as representatives of the revival. In other words, as these agents aided Broonzy in the reinvention of his career, they also failed to see that the rich vernacular music traditions evinced in his enormous repertoire were anything but separate and monolithic in their relationship to whiteness.[12] Broonzy's work with Lester Melrose highlights this concept, in that Melrose's influence over the sounds and styles of black pop music coming out of Chicago in the 1930s and '40s was enormous. Yet folklorists, eager to transform Broonzy into a herald of the folk, assisted in the erosion of public memory of Broonzy's black pop days in order to make him more "authentic." Nevertheless, central to Broonzy's reinvention and to his place in the history of the folk music revival is the story of the folk music pioneers John and Alan Lomax.

Beginning in the 1930s, John Lomax and his son Alan had great influence over the collection, study, and dissemination of vernacular music. This influence lasted nearly sixty years. The Texan John Lomax took quasi-control of the Archive of American Folk Song in 1933, succeeding the avid field collector Robert Winslow Gordon. For the remainder of the decade, the Lomaxes crisscrossed the country searching on "remote cotton plantations, cowboy ranches, lumber camps," and "segregated southern prisons" for traditional folk songs that they believed still existed in these areas.[13] Critical to their research was the driving belief that the United States had produced its own vibrant folk music culture, outside the influence of the European traditions transplanted from the Old World. This culture, they argued, was still very alive throughout the country.[14]

In 1933, as Broonzy championed Chicago's blues scene, the Lomaxes' uncovered one of their grandest discoveries: a forty-four-year-old inmate at Louisiana's Angola Penitentiary named Huddie Ledbetter. Ledbetter, or "Lead Belly," as he was affectionately known, was a gifted black guitarist and vocalist serving a hard-labor sentence for murder. Born in 1888 in Louisiana, he was only five years older than Broonzy. Lead Belly and Broonzy were similar in their command of song repertoires, their instrumental virtuosity, and their desire to employ music as a tool for black advocacy in Jim Crow America. To the Lomaxes, Lead Belly was a crowning jewel; his repertoire and skill set were large, diverse, and masterly. More importantly, Lead Belly represented a critical component of the Lomaxes' folklore ethos: he was living proof that "America did have a folk song heritage independent of Britain."[15]

The significance of Lead Belly's "discovery" for Broonzy's career transition cannot be underestimated. The Lomaxes' true genius and their most significant contribution to the study of American vernacular music was the importance they placed on individual artists. One scholar has suggested, "By dispensing with the secondhand interpreters and foregrounding the rural musicians who created the folk music, the Lomaxes added a new source of authenticity—the performers themselves. Purity was now attributed not just to specific folk songs . . . but to the folk figures who sang them."[16] With Lead Belly, the Lomaxes publicized their find with fanatical zeal to college campuses, concert and lecture halls, recording companies, and media outlets up and down the East Coast. To the Lomaxes, Lead Belly was exotic; he was a black ex-convict with an ear-to-ear scar on his throat, a savage, "a killer," and as John Lomax once alleged, "a nigger to the core of his being."[17]

Even if much of what the Lomaxes advertised was untrue, the juxtaposition of the pure and the profane in Ledbetter's life was the exact paradigm they used to market their "discovery." Broonzy was introduced to this community in 1938 in the same manner. On that December night in New York, he was no longer "Big Bill" from Chicago. Instead, the audience was introduced to a shy and frightened sharecropper who had, according to the concert's promotional materials, spent a lifetime singing to his livestock.[18] The creation of this dialectic in folk music culture not only garnered the fascinated attention of whites within and without the country's folklore community but ensured that folk artists, including Broonzy, henceforward, would be viewed in much the same way. Ultimately, the Lomaxes had created a new cult—the cult of folk authenticity—that wholly rested on these ideals.

The cult of authenticity had a profound effect on the career of Big Bill Broonzy. From 1938, at the "From Spirituals to Swing" show, through the rest of his life, especially from 1946 until his death in 1958, Broonzy explored the United States' and Europe's folk and jazz music world. Like Lead Belly, he was marketed as a vanguard of a disappearing tradition and often advertised as someone wholly different from who he truly was. What set Broonzy apart from Lead Belly within the folk cult of authenticity were the conditions under which these two musicians were discovered. When the Lomaxes first discovered Lead Belly, he perfectly embodied the kind of musical figure they sought: a prisoner in a hard-labor penitentiary who knew dozens of folk songs that the Lomaxes had searched for.[19] Broonzy, however, was something different.

By the time Alan Lomax first recognized Broonzy's potential, Broonzy had been celebrated in black Chicago's recording and performance cultures for over a decade. He had participated in at least fifty-eight recording sessions as a lead performer and dozens more as a guitarist.[20] He had worked his way through many record labels and their subsidiaries in the Midwest, specifically Chicago, but going as far east as New York City. He had rubbed elbows, performed, and/or recorded with some of the most influential black musicians in the country. Photographs of Broonzy during the 1930s, moreover, depict a handsome man: poised, dressed to the nines in fedoras and wing-tipped shoes, with broad shoulders, a shining guitar, and a wide smile. While Lead Belly represented John Lomax's ideas about the pure folk, to Alan Lomax, Broonzy represented a completely new idea of the figure of the authentic black folk musician that rested more on genre than repertoire.

Folklorists and music promoters such as Alan Lomax (and John Hammond as well) were drawn to Broonzy's recorded work from the 1920s and early 1930s as a solo male blues performer in the Blind Lemon Jefferson mold. To folklorists, Broonzy was, in effect, a representative of the "primitive blues singer" popularized in the late 1920s.[21] Broonzy and early contemporaries' race recordings helped define the early blues industry, which had marketed these individuals as proponents of a specific genre of black music. The historian Karl Miller has suggested that most record companies demanded that black musicians record material that could easily be defined within the industry's "conceptions of black music."[22] The market had prescribed and constructed the genre that Lomax understood Broonzy to be a part of. The recording market had not defined Lead Belly, however, whose vast repertoire moved well beyond the blues when the Lomaxes discovered him. Lead Belly had been exposed to all types of American vernacular music and could play almost anything he heard, in the tradition of southern songsters who had not yet been limited by the recording industry's perceived notions of genre. The Lomaxes tried their best to restrict Lead Belly to a specific song list that they understood as folk so that they could market him as their find of the century to a growing audience of like-minded scholars. Broonzy was a folk treasure because of his work in early recorded blues, whereas Lead Belly was a representative of the folk because of his vast repertoire.

The white folk music community was not interested in the urbane, jazz-influenced "Big Bill" that had defined Broonzy's initial success in Chicago, in the same way that the folk revivalists were not interested in Lead Belly's take on Gene Autry.[23] Core members of the growing folk music revival, including Alan Lomax and John Hammond, knew that Broonzy had experience in the rural, country blues genre of Son House, and the man Broonzy had replaced at "From Spirituals to Swing," Robert Johnson. Broonzy was presented at the concert as a vanguard of the "country blues" genre that explained how white folk enthusiasts intended to preserve the heritage of black music.

As the latter stages of Broonzy's career demonstrate, the blues as a genre, especially in the male, self-accompanied country style, was becoming a critical component of the folk and a genre created by both intellectual communities and record companies. Just as Lead Belly, under the stewardship of the Lomaxes, was often forced to perform in his prison uniform or coveralls and a bandanna, the folk community depicted Broonzy as someone completely different from the black Chicago celebrity known as "Big Bill." For many architects of the folk revival, Broonzy represented the same otherness that the Lomaxes advertised in Lead Belly: naïve, poor, and rural. Lead Belly had been portrayed early on as an anomaly: a violent and rapacious vanguard of a timeless American folk music tradition. As was the case with Broonzy, many of those who knew Lead Belly beyond his public persona described his mannerisms and disposition as genteel and aristocratic.

In considering the folk community, Broonzy recognized that a commercially successful and "pure" folk image could coexist as part of the revival as long as his style was both rooted in the blues genre and contained within the narrow confines of the folklore community. Broonzy's mastery of country blues styles and traditional arrangements, most of which were rooted in the rural, black traditions coveted by folklorists, demonstrates that commercially successful, externally constructed genres such as the country blues could become the folk. Broonzy understood this because of his experience of navigating changing trends in the music business, and he utilized this knowledge to manage and fulfill the expectations of his new audience and its attendant industry.

Broonzy had considered the 1938 Carnegie Hall show as his "first big chance" to cross over. When he appeared again in Hammond's second "From Spirituals to Swing" concert the following year, he was booked for a week at Café Society.[24] Café Society, a progressive nightclub in the heart of New York's Greenwich Village, was the first nightclub in the United States to openly feature black artists in front of completely integrated audiences. The club quickly became a symbol of pride and hope for black musicians wishing to cross over to integrated audiences. Opened in 1938, the club featured many famous jazz and blues acts and frequently showcased talent from Hammond's Carnegie Hall shows.[25] Essentially, Hammond introduced Broonzy to many East Coast folk music entrepreneurs, including Alan Lomax. In 1939, Alan Lomax was in charge of systematically documenting race-record catalogues for all of the major record labels, including Columbia. At this point, Hammond was working for Columbia as a promoter and talent scout. Hammond, apparently, introduced Lomax to Robert Johnson's early Columbia recordings, leading Lomax to conclude that the deceased Johnson rivaled Blind Lemon Jefferson in skill and mastery. By the late 1930s, Lomax and Hammond were close associates.[26]

Seven years later, Broonzy cemented his reputation as a representative of black folk music when he headlined Alan Lomax's *The Midnight Special at Town Hall* series, presented by People's Songs, Inc. In 1946, Broonzy was living in New York, appearing at New York nightspots such as the Apollo Theater, Town Hall, Village Vanguard, and Café Society.[27] His only recording session of the year for Columbia Records and its subsidiaries produced four songs, including the hits "I Can't Write" and "What Can I Do," which feature Broonzy's vocals and guitar with a backing ensemble of piano, trumpet, saxophone, bass, and drums. He had arrived in New York in June the year before and at this point was corresponding with Alan Lomax.[28] Joe Glaser, a notoriously uncouth manager who had once steered the careers of jazz greats Louis Armstrong and Billie Holiday, had coordinated Broonzy's work in New York up to this point.[29] Whether Broonzy first met Lomax in New York remains unclear. Broonzy may well have met Lomax at the "From Spirituals to Swing" concert, as Lomax attended the grand event that December in 1938.[30] In any case, Alan Lomax suggested that by 1946 he had spent "a lot of time with Big Bill Broonzy . . . in Chicago in a rented single room."[31] As Ink Williams, Lester Melrose, and John Hammond all had, Lomax held expectations of how he could direct Broonzy's music, how he could shape Broonzy's celebrity persona, and what their relationship might produce.

By the early 1940s, Lomax was deeply entrenched in New York's socialist political and labor-union culture. This culture was beginning to mesh with the emerging folk music revival embodied by the creation of New York's Almanac House and its more organized successor, People's Songs.[32] Even the "From Spirituals to Swing" concert was backed by the magazine the *New Masses*, a communist-affiliated publication. Popular artists, including Lead Belly, Woody Guthrie, Burl Ives, Josh White, and Aunt Molly Jackson, immersed themselves in a world that coupled commercialization and politicization with the black and white, rural southern music they loved. But Broonzy remained suspect of this growing interest in the blues as a form of American folklore. In an exchange with Alan Lomax, Broonzy explained his understanding of "folk" music in a firm and direct manner.

> LOMAX: But you're having trouble in America with your own people, Bill, singing the real blues. You tell me you can't make a living [anymore] singing the blues, and I don't understand it because everybody likes folk music nowadays.
>
> BROONZY: Well, yes, yes, yes, they like it. That's true. Folk music. But that ain't the blues. They name it. . . . There's people that call it folk blues, folk songs. Because it's the Negro people that saying it's the blues, same as they used the [Negro] spirituals as folk songs, see. The thing about it is, the reason why the Negro that's from Mississippi that knows the blues that I'm singing he's ashamed of it when he hear it because he doesn't want the people to know that he's from Mississippi, why the people had said that he was treated so bad and was abused and pushed around and done so bad. He doesn't want the people to know he is even from Mississippi and Georgia and Alabama and Arkansas and Missouri and Texas and places.
>
> LOMAX: Why doesn't he want them to know for?
>
> BROONZY: 'Cause he doesn't want the people to know he's been pushed around in his lifetime. He wanna let people know that he's a great

man and maybe he's got a little money, he's got an automobile and he's got a home, he bought a home in Chicago, or maybe he's got a home in Detroit or California or a home someplace in the North or in the places where Jim Crow is not so bad. . . . So if they hear this guy singing the blues, he know this guy is singing the real thing.[33]

Broonzy seemed opposed to the romanticized way Lomax was then trying to portray blues music and culture. In effect, Broonzy was looking forward while Lomax was looking back. As Broonzy was becoming a vanguard of the folk, he understood quite well that the blues he had helped pioneer in Chicago had allowed for the development of his celebrity and a new black consciousness rooted in the consumer marketplace, the New Negro Renaissance in Chicago, and a profound engagement with modernity. Broonzy felt that the old country and rural blues too often reminded folks of unending moments of hardship, humiliation, and struggle in the Jim Crow South.

Maybe Broonzy was beginning to echo sentiments he had heard about his own music and the way in which it made a new generation of musicians and migrants confront a past they were ready to leave behind. On this, Broonzy lamented,

> Some Negroes tell me that the old style of blues is carrying Negroes back to the horse-and-buggy days and back to slavery—and who wants to be reminded of slavery?—and some will say this ain't slavery no more, so why don't you learn to play something else? I just tell them I can't play nothing else and they say to me: "You should learn, go and take lessons and learn to play real music." Then I will ask them: "Ain't the blues real music?" All they can and will say to me: "Not the way you play and sing about mules, cotton, corn, levee camps, and gang songs. Them days, Big Bill, is gone forever."[34]

Nevertheless, within this emerging folk culture, struggling musicians such as Broonzy were presented with opportunities to perform and record in support of social issues ranging from class struggle to labor organization. Folklorists desperately wanted to hear Broonzy "sing about mules, cotton, corn, levee camps, and gang songs" precisely because those elements of folk life were, in their minds, disappearing. Experienced and talented musicians lent a significant element of popularity to folk music's growing culture, and for someone such as Broonzy, whose career and style were transforming, moving toward the "folk" offered chances for greater notoriety. The historian Ronald Cohen has argued that by 1946, with these reciprocal expectations in place and with the help of music-recording insiders and folk promoters such as Moe Asch and Alan Lomax, "everything was in place for the coming folk music revival."[35] By the fall of 1946, Broonzy had appeared in at least one People's Songs New York hootenanny, a suitably titled "Union Hoot," and headlined Lomax's *The Midnight Special at Town Hall* series on November 9 with fellow black-music luminaries Pete Johnson, Sonny Terry, Brownie McGhee, and Sidney Bechet.[36]

On March 1, 1947, Broonzy again returned to Lomax's *Midnight Special* series with his Chicago friends the blues giants Peter "Memphis Slim" Chapman and John Lee "Sonny Boy" Williamson. According to Lomax, that night the three men "tore down the house at Town Hall, discovering that their Delta music was appreciated by an audience they never knew about."[37] Of course, by the late 1940s, Broonzy had played for many white audiences, and while these three musicians' styles featured country blues accents, the music was not in the vein of the blues of Son House or Skip James.

On March 3, 1947, Broonzy, Williamson, and Chatman followed Alan Lomax into Decca Records' New York City recording studio to make *Blues in the Mississippi Night*, which stands as one of the most candid and important commentaries on racism ever recorded in the United States. Lomax, with his own Presto disc recorder, initiated an oral interview unlike any other that he or the three blues greats had ever participated in. With booze, musical instruments, and cigarettes on hand, these four legendary Americans documented in song and spoken word a fascinating, culturally vibrant, yet horrific world of black life in the American South. Lomax recalled, "They explored the cause of this in the stringent poverty of black rural life. They recalled life in the Mississippi work camps, where the penitentiary stood at the end of the road, waiting to receive the rebellious. Finally, they came to the enormities of the lynch system that threatened anyone who defied its rules."[38] For over two hours, the four men engaged in a candid and probing conversation on numerous issues related to black southern life under the firm grasp of Jim Crow. At the top of the conversational list were these three blues greats' descriptions of the blues and its origins. Initially, they cautiously conceded to Lomax's romantic ideas about the blues, agreeing at least in part to the genre's roots in the poverty, racism, inequality, debt peonage, and lack of opportunity indigenous to most blacks across the South. Each man poignantly expressed the notion that "you have to have the blues to play the blues" and that trouble with both women and money was often the launching point for the next great blues song. All three agreed, moreover, that sharecropping, levee-camp extra gangs, and coerced prison gang labor were exactly the types of systems that could produce anxiety and melancholia among poor, rural African Americans who had been cheated out of their hard earnings, had witnessed community members publicly humiliated, had been incarcerated for the slightest infraction, and had watched as their family members disappeared. Many African Americans, of course, had absolved themselves of these indignities by attending church services several times throughout the week, and for Broonzy, Williamson, and Chatman, the blues fostered the same "spiritual" exaltation as the black church. As the conversation continued, however, the three musicians expanded their definition of the blues.

Broonzy had worked in the aforementioned labor systems many times throughout his life, including "levee camps, extra gangs, road camps, . . . rock camps and rock quarries." He even lived within the unhealthy and disgusting conditions of the levee and railroad extra gang camps, where men "slept in the same clothes they worked in." The blues reflected the struggle of black people in the South to find their own humanity in a sordid and grim environment. For Broonzy, "the blues was from the heart, and whensoever you hear fellows singing, . . . he's expressing his feeling about how he felt": "I've known guys who wanted to cuss out the boss, and he was afraid to go up to his face and tell 'em what he wanted to tell 'em, and I've heard him sing these things." As the plot thickened, then, Chatman retorted, "Well, Bill, I don't want to cut you off, um, but I mean, that's my idea of the blues. I think blues is mostly revenge." Broonzy quickly interrupted with, "Yeah, that's what I'm trying to get to." For these men, the blues was a means of exercising one's relationship to humanity—a point Lomax did not understand at the time. In effect, the music was more than just a passive reflection of black working-class life within the denigrating and inhumane world of the Jim Crow South, where white labor bosses expressed "kill a nigger, hire another, . . . kill a mule, I'll have to *buy* another" as a measure of the value of black southerners.[39]

Broonzy, Chatman, and Williamson had lived in labor camps and witnessed their colleagues whipped by "cat-o-nine-tails," drop dead from shear exhaustion, cheated out of money because of their illiteracy, coerced into dangerous, life-threatening tasks, trapped by debt peonage, and threatened by prison or death if they dared argue against any of these humiliating and dehumanizing infractions. The blues in this context represented "unorganized, often spontaneous battles with authority," which highlight the "inventive and diverse struggles" within black working-class life and politics.[40]

Clearly, much of these anecdotes reveal the particular folk-collecting interests of Alan Lomax, who by 1947 had combed the country's river bottoms, gang labor camps, prisons, plantations, and small farms in search of "authentic" folk music. Lomax, himself, can be heard prodding the story along into directions pertaining to taboo subjects such as lynching and coerced-labor prison camps. And even though Broonzy was from Arkansas and Williamson and Chatman hailed from Tennessee, Lomax ensured that only the roughest and darkest of all states in the Deep South, Mississippi, could provide a stage for such indescribable events. Lomax had essentially captured on disc the reflections of three black men who were fully aware of racism's stronghold on the United States and dared discuss it openly with a white man.

These recordings also reflect Lomax's ideas about the importance of the folk and its black music heritage to the country's understanding of social issues. For the *Blues in the Mississippi Night* sessions, Broonzy offered a hint of what would become his trademark folk celebrity style when he performed self-accompanied for the first time on record his controversial "Black, Brown and White" for Alan Lomax. Broonzy later recorded the song in Europe in 1951 as a commentary on racism in the United States. As the conversation intensified, Broonzy, Williamson, and Chatman delivered anecdotal evidence that even Lomax must have been surprised to hear—that "spontaneous" battles against Jim Crow could be found across the South in many forms and in many places.

The three men described several archetypal African American figures and the manner in which each fought the South's powerfully entrenched racism. The first, "the table-walkers," exhibited the types of behavior associated with the bad-man trope, "the merciless toughs and killers confronting and generally vanquishing their adversaries without hesitation."[41] To Broonzy and Chatman, the bad man was well aware that he would take "a whuppin from the boss" just for stealing food, having a .45 revolver in hand, from his fellow gang laborers because "he was tired of the way he'd been living and the kind of food he'd been eating." This type of scene would have most assuredly drawn the ire of the gang boss, whose punitive measure would have been a public beating for the entire gang to witness. In retaliation, however, the "table-walker" would pick himself up, get right back to work, "and kill one of his buddies!" For the bad man, revenge was best served to those who were powerless to protest, because if the bad man was one of the best workers, he could "kill anybody . . . in those days."[42]

Another derivative of the bad man, what Broonzy and Chatman described as the "crazy nigger," embodied both the inhumanities of the South's system of terror and African Americans' willingness to "speak up for their rights" and die for that cause without fear. These were the men and women who were not "afraid of white people" and "actually talked backed," instilling a fear in whites that they "might ruin the other Negroes" and "make them crazy enough to talk back." To drive this point home, Broonzy opened up about his personal life, painfully reflecting on the lynching of an uncle who refused a white boss's demand that would have forced the uncle's pregnant wife out into the fields. Broonzy described his uncle as an intelligent, hardworking southerner who "could figure as good as a white man," who "had a better education than some of them, and they would go to him for advice." After beating the white man off his horse and running him off the property, his uncle was eventually hanged by a mob of fifty or sixty, but not before "he shot four or five!" Twelve other members of his mother's family were murdered, Broonzy further explained, over a white man's lust for a black woman in the family who refused his advances and married her black lover. The result destroyed the lives of an enormous web of Langdale, Arkansas, blacks and left Broonzy with the powerful lesson that "if you try to fight back, it's not just you they're gonna get. . . . It's anybody in your family."[43]

The final bad-man trope that Broonzy and company described to Lomax, the "bad seed," stood as perhaps the most dangerous to the entire Jim Crow system. The "bad seed," otherwise known as a "smart Negro," was the man who "ruined the rest of the Negroes, by opening their eyes and telling them things they don't know." Broonzy recalled that smart blacks would obtain a copy of the *Chicago Defender* and share its meaning and messages among the poor, illiterate masses of the rural South. With a lookout man at the ready, deep-Delta African Americans absorbed the information and opinions conveyed in the country's leading black newspaper and were ready to incinerate the evidence, if suspected, in a nearby stove. If white southerners had caught the bad seed in the midst of spreading his knowledge, they certainly would have called him a "bad nigger" and probably would have "killed him."[44] Some Broonzy scholars have hinted that these and other "tales . . . owed as much to Mark Twain as they did to Richard Wright."[45] Others have suggested that Broonzy may have forced a higher standard of truthfulness into the conversation documented on *Blues in the Mississippi Night*. At stake here is the merging of Broonzy's experience as an African American living in the Jim Crow South with the consciousness of the expanding folk music revival in the United States. These interviews may have been embellished and exaggerated, but the "discrepancy between fact and memory ultimately enhances the value" of such an important oral testimony, in which these three blues pioneers attempted to make sense of important historical events and their relationship to blues music.[46]

Alan Lomax, "in particular, had consciously shaped the repertoires and aesthetic sensibilities of Ives, Seeger, White and numerous others," including Big Bill Broonzy.[47] Lomax was not the only folk music promoter who understood the important relationship between the blues, Jim Crow segregation, and racial politics. John Hammond's strong connections within New York's club scene had helped establish the career of the folk luminary Josh White.[48] Broonzy fulfilled white folklorists' expectations of the country blues as a subset of the folk; he was a veteran of the Chicago recording scene, he had sold thousands of records, his repertoire was large, and he was warm, charming, and much less volatile than Lead Belly or Josh White. With a little help and polish from the stewards of the growing folk music revival, he could become a different kind of celebrity—one defined by and created for whites. For at least twelve years before he left for Ames, Broonzy had performed and kept company with stewards of the white folk music revival in New York. His skillful handling of John Hammond's and Alan Lomax's expectations, moreover, was extremely important for his transformation from black pop artist to folk music hero. Like the legendary See See Rider from Arkansas, and Ink Williams and Lester Melrose in Chicago's recording industry, Hammond and Lomax held positions of power within a world that could usher in a new phase of Broonzy's waning career. Broonzy was smart and ambitious enough that he easily recognized their potential as agents in the expansion of his career.

Meanwhile, in Chicago, the growing folk music scene was finding a distinct home of its own in the Midwest. People's Songs founders Pete Seeger and Lee Hays visited Chicago in September 1946 to speak at a Congress of Industrial Organizations Political Action Committee (CIO-PAC) labor-school rally in hopes of establishing a local People's Songs chapter. In November of the previous year, People's Songs had held hootenannies in Los Angeles and had established a loyal following on the West Coast. This signified that the combination of music, labor organization, and leftist politics was a potent mix of interests for many Americans from coast to coast. By October 1947, People's Songs' impressive growth led to the coordination of its first national convention, appropriately titled "Sing Out America," at Hull House in Chicago, featuring Guthrie, Lomax, Seeger, and the local Chicago folk icon Win Stracke.[49]

Two members of People's Songs' Chicago chapter, Studs Terkel and Win Stracke, were incredibly important for Broonzy's transformation from black pop musician to folk music hero. They were critical to People's Songs' growth in the Windy City as they helped Raeburn Flerlage, the chapter's chief organizer, coordinate local house parties and hootenannies featuring performances by Lead Belly, Josh White, Woody Guthrie, and, of course, Big Bill Broonzy.[50] As Chicagoans familiar with the city's rich blues culture, they knew of Broonzy's long history as a blues giant. Moreover, they were two of Broonzy's closest friends during the latter stages of his career and even served as pallbearers at his funeral.[51] Like all of the other figures Broonzy worked with during his lifelong project of reinvention, they, too, held specific expectations of Broonzy, and he of them.

Stracke and Terkel shared many similarities. Both were the sons of European immigrant families and had moved to Chicago as boys. Both were deeply involved in Chicago's radio, television, and theater communities. The two had first met while working for the Chicago Repertory Group, a progressive theater troupe that often supported prounion and prolabor politics. Stracke rose to fame as Uncle Win, the host of the nationally syndicated children's television programs *Animal Playtime* and *Time for Uncle Win*, featured on NBC. Before Terkel landed the 98.7 WFMT program that made him famous and a folk music icon, he had also dabbled in Chicago-area television as the host of *Stud's Place*, an unscripted, improvisational television drama centered at a local diner and featuring numerous guests, including Stracke. Stracke and Terkel had served in the armed forces during World War II, and both men held lifelong loves for American vernacular music. Both were quite familiar with Broonzy and Chicago blues, and both men were blacklisted for their prolabor activities during the height of the anticommunist fervor created by the House Un-American Activities Committee (HUAC) in the 1950s.[52]

Big Bill Broonzy had already met Pete Seeger and Lee Hays when Seeger and Hays had visited Chicago to establish a local People's Songs chapter, and Stracke and Terkel were perfect candidates to lead a Chicago chapter. Their experiences in radio and television allowed access to media outlets that could promote the organization's message. They also knew many locally established musicians and community members who could support their shared ideas about the connection between labor and music and organize Chicago's emerging folk community.

Quickly, the combination of Broonzy, Stracke, and Terkel put in motion a folk music culture in Chicago that would rival that of the East Coast. Broonzy's songs covered a wide variety of social issues in a manner respected by musical and political collaborators such as People's Songs. Broonzy also

I Come for to Sing 111

knew dozens of local Chicago musicians who could lend their music and talents to the cause. Stracke and Terkel held strong connections with many mass-media outlets in Chicago that might provide opportunities for Broonzy to perform and record.

Broonzy appeared at Iowa State College's Memorial Union Hall in 1949 as a member of "I Come for to Sing."[53] While visiting Ames, Broonzy became close friends with the English Department faculty member Leonard Feinberg, who held a reception for the troupe at his home after the performance. Following the end of the tour, Broonzy returned home to Chicago only to be told by a physician that the combination of decades of heavy drinking, smoking, and sleepless nights traveling the country was catching up with him. With this in mind, Broonzy learned through his tour of college campuses that he could change his musical style to fit the new tastes of the blues audience and industry to continue on as a successful performer and artist. Taking a chance, Broonzy wrote to Feinberg to inquire about work on campus. In the letter, he offered his services as a laborer for the college's extensive agricultural research facilities, but the "farm" was so "sufficiently mechanized that additional laborers weren't needed." Feinberg suggested that if Broonzy was willing, there might be custodial work available. With his music career at a standstill and his health waning, he packed a suitcase and his guitar for Ames, Iowa, to take a job as a janitor for Iowa State College's Friley Hall. As a thank-you to Iowa State, Broonzy later wrote and recorded his 1951 track "The Moppin Blues" and posed for a publicity photo in Friley Hall in full janitorial regalia.[54]

Faculty and alumni alike remembered fondly Broonzy's respite in Ames. For a year, Broonzy lived alone in what was essentially a barracks—a hastily constructed Quonset hut community on campus named Pammel Court. Following World War II, Iowa State experienced a massive uptick in enrollment, choosing to solve its housing shortage with inexpensive, prefabricated housing. Having lived in far worse conditions in the Jim Crow South, Broonzy settled in easily. Quickly, he became friends with both faculty and students, including the Shakespearean scholar and classically trained pianist Albert Walker, Broonzy's neighbor on Pammel Court. On any given weekend night, residents in the community or wandering across campus might find the Feinbergs, the Walkers, Iowa State College faculty, and Broonzy jamming at the feet of Walker's upright piano, singing songs and trading licks from their deep repertoires of blues and jazz numbers.

One student remembered a "tame by Ames' standards" summer party in Pammel Court that featured Broonzy performing on his guitar in the company of several interracial couples in attendance. He asked Broonzy why he had moved to Ames, and Broonzy quickly replied that it was his desire to live in a "friendly place." Given the present company, the student interpreted Broonzy's response to mean that he enjoyed Ames's relaxed atmosphere and racially progressive worldview. When Broonzy was not at the center of Pammel Court's social scene, he found the time to offer guitar lessons to a young student named Louie Thompson, who learned from Broonzy about "style," singing, and song interpretation.[55] Broonzy's most celebrated night at Iowa State College came on Friday the thirteenth, in October 1950. It was homecoming weekend, and a makeshift stage had been constructed on the east side of the stadium for a rally to drum up support for a Saturday football victory over the University of Kansas. Residence life had organized two campus performances by the legendary Louis Armstrong and his band, with special guest Jack Teagarden on trombone. The band hit the stage for what was Armstrong's first concert at Iowa State. Halfway through the performance, Armstrong stopped the show to introduce the audience to their very own "Big Bill," who played a few songs with the group before exiting the stage to great acclaim and applause. Broonzy later remarked how good it was of his old friend "Louie" to continue to keep "tabs on the old musicians, and inviting them to perform with him whenever possible."[56]

As Broonzy had in Chicago, he quickly developed relationships that would last long after his departure from Iowa State College. Whenever the Walkers or other English Department faculty visited Chicago, Broonzy invited them to his flat, even sharing pressings of his latest recordings. Those who were in contact with him for that year would cherish their time with Broonzy. One student fondly remembered of Broonzy, "I never saw 'Big Bill' wield a broom, but I'm sure it was with a flair and a certain amount of gracefulness."[57] Life seemed easier for Broonzy as he transitioned from a blues icon to a folk hero at Iowa State. He planted a southern vegetable garden in the Feinbergs' backyard and even was continuing to write new blues songs.[58] To the faculty and students around him, he seemed content with his surroundings and happy to be in a place that appreciated him without having a separate agenda.[59]

This peace did not last long. While at Iowa State, Broonzy received a phone call inviting him to Europe. Nearly thirty years had passed since his last visit. As a black soldier during World War I, he had enjoyed Europe's more racially relaxed atmosphere, even though the army had exploited him for his labor. This time around, Europeans wanted something completely different: they wanted "Big Bill Broonzy" and his music. In 1951, Broonzy left Ames, Iowa, for England to, as he explained it, "awaken white people to an interest in blues."[60] By the beginning of 1951, Broonzy was nearly sixty years old. For half of his life, he had navigated American music culture and its industry with frequent success. Throughout his career, he fostered critical personal relationships with individuals who held power within a world that he was determined to master. Above all, Broonzy understood that his music was symbiotically linked to the changing expectations of and trends in the music industry and its audience, whether black, white, American, or European. He was often taken advantage of, and his journey was difficult, frequently forcing him to make great social and economic sacrifices. Yet, unlike so many of his peers, he survived many of the industry's drastic changes. Broonzy was a historical actor, and his malleable celebrity persona—from country musician to solo male blues artist to black pop pioneer to folk music hero—was not an accident.

In the face of often-insurmountable odds, Broonzy was wise enough to employ his skills—his charm, wit, good looks, and potent musical abilities—toward becoming one of the most important blues musicians of the twentieth century. Broonzy was raised as a country musician in Jim Crow Arkansas who played for segregated picnics within the confines of the South's rigidly segregated power structure. As a World War I veteran and southern migrant, Broonzy had recorded in Chicago in the late 1920s, only to produce recordings that sold poorly. Yet Broonzy continued to explore American vernacular music and its expectations for nearly thirty years, emerging from the latter stage of his career's evolution as celebrated as ever within white folk music culture. He had helped to pioneer the blues as a form of black popular music recorded for black audiences, only to see his blues transformed into a genre that explained white folklorists' understanding of a black vernacular music tradition. He could not have foreseen these changes in the music he loved so much, but he managed the resulting expectations nonetheless. By the beginning of the 1950s, Broonzy was poised to become one of the first blues artists to take American blues to Europe.

CHAPTER SIX

We Love the Blues, but Tell Us about Jazz

On May 13, 1952, Big Bill Broonzy and Alan Lomax sat in a Paris hotel room, recording a "two-hour interview of songs and talk on such subjects as pride, race, and black culture in America."[1] Eventually, these anecdotes found their way into one of Lomax's most important works and helped define Broonzy's legacy for a generation.[2] By the time of that Tuesday afternoon in 1952, Lomax had aided in the transformation of Broonzy's professional image and reputation as an exemplar of the folk. This recording session reveals a fascinating glimpse into how Broonzy was beginning to view his final career transformation—could he begin to teach and explain to Europeans the history of black music in the United States? On this, Broonzy reflected, "The people in France are good people. They're a good congregation to play to. The best people I've met in my life, . . . and I never was treated no better nowhere in the world I've been than I've been treated in France. The people of France are just like the Negro of America—they've been pushed around, . . . they've been done bad, all their lives, they've been in sorrow, they've been in the shape of the blues all their lives. And I think the people of France is just like my people."[3] To Broonzy, four decades of the horrors and destruction caused by the deadliest wars in human history had taken their toll on the French, so much, in fact, that they related to his blues in ways that other audiences—even some in the United States—simply could not. In reality, African American music had found a welcoming home in France and Europe long before that spring in 1952. But Broonzy was beginning to see himself as a critical link between European and American forms of music, perhaps even as a harbinger of a new era in the history and popularity of black music in a transnational setting. By transforming his image at critical professional moments and by finding creative ways to engage new audiences, Big Bill Broonzy sustained a long career among American and European audiences. Broonzy's ongoing project of re-creating himself— and the forces he faced to do so—highlights the cultural dynamics that both constrained and enabled twentieth-century black cultural architects as they lived their lives and shaped their celebrities within and beyond the United States.

For some music intellectuals, Broonzy's life and career were paradoxical. On the one hand, his life and music explained the history of the blues and black southern music in the United States, giving meaning to a distinctive American folk music tradition rooted in southern history and the black experience. At the same time, for Europeans, his work as the leader of five- and six-piece jazz-based blues bands fit notions they espoused about the blues as an antecedent to jazz. To Europeans, Broonzy was a figure in whom they could identify a seamless connection between the two genres. Yet the tensions housed within the "Big Bill" persona were profound. Was he the slick, urban performer from Chicago who could lead a five-piece jazz band through some of the sexually explicit hits he had recorded in the 1930s and 1940s? Or was he the humble, part-time janitor steeped in rural folk music who could explain the history of the blues, connect its messages to European audiences, and share aspects of the African American experience through his music and storytelling? Broonzy had navigated this dichotomy for decades in the United States, and he seemed at ease negotiating these networks, their expectations, and these professional personas throughout Europe. Ultimately, Broonzy became a touchstone for Americans' and Europeans' burgeoning interest in black music. Along the way, he became more than just "Big Bill" from Chicago: he became Big Bill Broonzy, international blues celebrity. In effect, Broonzy's career demonstrates that a musician's talent and skill alone do not make for a long and successful career. His path to success was often difficult and financially challenging as he traveled around the country and the world, frequently separated from his friends and family. And yet Broonzy understood that he could find and sustain celebrity by continually reinventing his career and recognizing the changing tastes of his audiences and how they understood black music. Quite successfully and without precedent, Broonzy transformed himself from a rural country musician to a black pop musician to a national and international icon for folk music enthusiasts and jazz aficionados. His career reveals a distinct path for black blues artists who carved out their celebrity among white audiences and found national and international acclaim.

As Europe rebuilt its physical and cultural infrastructure following the devastation of World War II, the dissemination of African American music and culture provided important building blocks for the continent's musical future. Since the early twentieth century, Europe had enjoyed the frequent visits of black entertainers as they toured Europe, satisfying the increasing interests of European jazz enthusiasts. As early as 1920, when the first jazz records were pressed for manufacture in the United Sates, black music spread to the Soviet Union, France, Sweden, and Great Britain. After World War II, the United States' presence in Europe increased dramatically, placing American GIs and the U.S. military-industrial complex (and its culture) in increasing proximity to Europeans. This "Americanization" of European culture became as important to Big Bill Broonzy's career and legacy as his days as the king of Chicago's blues culture were. Broonzy helped establish a path for wave after wave of American blues artists looking to follow in his footsteps.[4]

The blues made its first appearance in Europe well before Big Bill Broonzy's first tour in 1951, perhaps with Lonnie Johnson's blues-influenced jazz guitar work in a British touring music review in 1917. The classic blues singer Alberta Hunter performed in Europe from 1927 to 1929 and again from 1933 to 1934, touring France and Great Britain. It should be noted that the blues performers visiting Europe in the 1930s would have been heavily influenced by the vaudevillian and tent-circuit jazz-based blues styles of the classic female blues singers, styles that differed markedly from the blues carried over by Lead Belly, Josh White, and Bill Broonzy years later. The growth in popularity of the blues in Europe—and particularly in Britain—coincided with an emerging folk music revival beginning after World War II. Although not as complicated or contrived as the emerging folk revival in the United States, the British folk revival, indeed, shared connections to developments across the Atlantic. Dating back to the eighteenth century, British song hunters had eagerly sought out local traditional balladry, employing a combination of fieldwork, archival materials, and published collections to develop a canonical body of work that helped launch an interest in folk music in Britain and the United States by the 1910s.[5] One of these connections, Alan Lomax, played a seminal role in incubating the folk music boom in Britain.

By the late 1930s, the British Broadcasting Company (BBC) film critic Alistair Cooke injected a fascination with American folk tunes and hobo songs into cultural programming for BBC radio that was rare at the time, featuring popular culture on *New York City to the Golden Gate* and eventually a thirteen-part series "featuring a variety of southern field recordings," titled *I Hear America Singing*.[6] Cooke garnered attention from leading American folklorists of the period, including then assistant in charge of the Archive of American Folk Song at the Library of Congress, Alan Lomax. By 1944, Lomax was serving in the United States Army's Armed Forces Radio Service, editing "network radio shows . . . for overseas broadcasting," by providing "short musical selections" to replace commercial advertisements.[7] More importantly, Lomax continued his collaboration with the BBC, begun the year before in an effort to bring the United States and Great Britain closer together for the wartime effort, by offering biweekly folklore programs intended for air on the Columbia Broadcasting System (CBS) and the BBC. By the end of World War II, the American Forces Network and the Office of War Information had ensured that American music—blues, jazz, swing, country, crooner pop, and folk—became extremely popular in Britain. Ultimately, the BBC aired exclusively for British audiences several shows that were produced by Lomax and featured a bevy of American "folk" talent, including Paul Robeson, Josh White, Sonny Terry, Brownie McGhee, Burl Ives, Woody Guthrie, and Pete Seeger.[8]

That Lomax's name appeared in the June 1950 tract *Red Channels* as a communist sympathizer and subversive was probably no surprise to the seasoned folklorist. After all, the Office of War Information and the House Un-American Activities Committee had been investigating him since 1944, eventually influencing the Federal Bureau of Investigation to secretly trail him for sixteen years. By 1950, afraid that the dangers of the McCarthy-era purges might quickly ruin his already substantial career, Lomax grabbed his recently renewed passport and left the United States for England from 1950 to 1958. The folk music craze that emerged in Britain in the 1950s can be directly linked to Lomax's work there throughout the decade.

In London, Lomax immediately went to work establishing lasting relationships with the English Folk Dance and Song Society at Cecil Sharp House, the epicenter for folklore and folk song in England, and with the pioneering British revivalist Ewan MacColl.[9] MacColl, a BBC-affiliated British actor, singer, playwright, and producer of theater, recordings, and radio, had dabbled in the American folk scene in the 1930s and knew Lomax's career and reputation quite well. Consequently, his direct contact with Lomax in the 1950s marked the "moment when he [MacColl] understood the importance of folk song as a specific, free-standing art form."[10] MacColl reflected that upon his first meeting with Lomax, "folk music had been for most of us [British revivalists] a pleasant medium of relaxation, but after that night we all became confirmed addicts; in the jargon of the time we were 'committed.'"[11]

Lomax's connections with the growing British folk scene and the BBC, in turn, led to an immediate radio-programming job, offering a series of programs to British audiences for the BBC, including *Adventure in Folksong* and *The Art of the Negro*. With these radio shows, Lomax introduced Great Britain to his concept of the American folk music tradition—prison, work, and field songs, as well as "recordings of Jelly Roll Morton, Vera Hall, Big Bill Broonzy, . . . Robert Johnson, Sleepy John Estes, and Muddy Waters."[12] Within a few years, Lomax moved on to collecting Scottish, Irish, and English folk music, but his initial presence and popularity through his work with the BBC helped lay the groundwork for an explosive and prominent folk music revival in Britain that MacColl and others would carry forward. This revival welcomed with open arms an erstwhile blues singer turned folk hero named Big Bill Broonzy.

The folk music craze was not the only American popular music consumed and lauded by Europeans following World War II. American jazz had arrived in Europe following World War I, with the arrival of James Reese Europe, Will Marion Cook, and Sidney Bechet, and had by the 1950s established a loyal following, despite criticisms of the genre by many music critics and scholars.[13] Jazz was an important musical phenomenon that captivated a small but growing audience of Europeans eager for new sounds. The growth in the popularity of jazz, moreover, led Europeans to discover a new musical idiom that they believed was its precursor—the blues. The appearance of Alberta Hunter by the beginning of the 1930s suggests that the French appreciated black music. Other events added to the popularity of blues and jazz in France as well. Columbia Records had begun to distribute blues and jazz records throughout France, and radio shows and jazz publications began to recognize the importance of American blues.[14] In time, Big Bill Broonzy helped a generation of jazz enthusiasts understand that the blues traced a path that was analogous with but parallel to jazz. If American audiences understood black music, including the blues, in terms of race and segregation, then European artists began to understand the blues through their notions of its relationship to jazz.[15]

Broonzy's first tour of Europe, during the second half of 1951, relied on the hard work and dedication of two of his most devoted European fans: the French Jazz Hot Club president Hugues Panassié and Belgian jazz critic and radio host Yannick Bruynoghe. Since the 1930s, Panassié, a fascinatingly complex individual in his own right, had helped pioneer the field of jazz criticism and remained one of the leading academics on the subject for nearly four decades. By 1932, Panassié organized the Hot Club de France, dedicated to promoting traditional jazz, swing, and blues across France (and Europe), ultimately serving as the society's president from 1934 until his death in 1974. At age eighteen, he had contributed to French music magazines and remained a voracious writer and scholar of the subject, eventually authoring more than ten volumes on the subject. By 1935, he had established *Jazz Hot*, one of the first jazz periodicals in the world. By 1937, Panassié and his partner, Charles Delaunay, owned and operated the Parisian record label Swing, the first of its kind in its complete dedication to jazz.[16]

To many European jazz enthusiasts such as Panassié, the ascension of bebop had destroyed the primacy of the blues in jazz. As bebop created an intense movement that diverged from traditional jazz, Big Bill Broonzy and other bluesmen became lenses through which European jazz devotees could articulate their distaste for bebop. Bop's fast pace, heavy reliance on complex harmonies and improvisation, and antidance aesthetic moved far away from the slow, gutbucket blues that had peppered jazz since its formation. European jazz "traditionalists," then, introduced many black American bluesmen in Europe as examples of the interconnectedness of jazz and blues and, more important, evidence to why bebop had ruined jazz. This debate among Europeans—between those who supported bebop and those who hated it—sparked deep passion and an unparalleled understanding of American jazz that became critical for Broonzy as an international blues celebrity.[17]

Yannick Bruynoghe was, like Panassié, one of several Europeans who were convinced that the blues held an important connection to American jazz. Born in Leuven, Belgium, in 1924, Bruynoghe was transformed during a 1947 trip to New York's Harlem from the unassuming son of a university physician and professor into a fanatical devotee of black music. Trained as a lawyer, Bruynoghe joined the vibrant jazz-enthusiast scene blossoming across postwar Europe, even contributing to the Hot Club de France and operating a jazz radio show. Moreover, he had already participated in blues pilgrimages to the United States' famous blues cities, hoping to uncover the origins of both genres. In 1950, for example, Bruynoghe visited Chicago on his own personal "blues safari" and "rediscovered" Broonzy.[18] For nearly a year, Panassié and Bruynoghe devised a plan to bring Broonzy to Europe in hopes that he might experience success similar to those of the tours of Lead Belly and Josh White (in 1949 and 1950, respectively).

By the outbreak of World War II, the blues genre was gaining popularity in both France and Great Britain. But many jazz enthusiasts were limited in their familiarity with traditional blues—blues recorded during the 1910s and 1920s—as their collections tended to focus on the classic female singers and blues shouters associated with jazz and vaudeville and tent shows.[19] With the arrival of U.S. troops in Europe in 1942, the American war machine began manufacturing twelve-inch, 78 rpm "Victory" discs, or V-Discs, often featuring the black artists Josh White, Lil Green, and Big Bill Broonzy.[20] American

GIs who were stationed in Europe during World War II and the American Forces Network radio broadcast that arrived with them exposed many Europeans to the blues on V-Discs.[21] By 1942, many British jazz enthusiasts, including Paul Oliver, Derrick Stewart-Baxter, Ernest Borneman, and Max Jones, began a lifelong fascination with what Oliver described as "the strangest, most compelling" music they had ever heard.[22] European blues and jazz audiences, therefore, were familiar with the blues when the first wave of black performers arrived in the 1950s. To Europeans, though, pioneering urban artists such as Broonzy represented antecedents to the development of their true interest: American jazz. In time, Broonzy tried his best to understand and meet their expectations, often sharing his own recollections on the history of the blues, the meaning of folk music, and the origins of jazz.

Broonzy first arrived in Europe on July 18, 1951, in Brussels, Belgium, where he met Yannick Bruynoghe and began participating in one of the most important musical exchanges in twentieth-century American history: the dissemination of black blues and its culture across Europe. With great success, Broonzy handled the expectations of emerging European blues audiences in the same manner that he had navigated the city of Chicago and his thirty-year career. When Broonzy received the first call to go to Europe in 1951, his life and career had already changed dramatically. One year earlier, he had left his home and a failing marriage in Chicago, in ailing health and in need of respite from the city's constant and buzzing lifestyle.[23] When he left Chicago for Ames, Iowa, in the summer of 1950, he had already begun navigating the burgeoning white folk music scene by forgoing the five-piece jazz-based blues he had helped pioneer in Chicago to return to the solo acoustic blues of his earlier career that had become popular to white folk audiences. Although he still maintained close contact with Win Stracke and Studs Terkel back in Chicago, he seemed at ease in Ames when he received the call for his first tour of Europe. Following the "I Come for to Sing" tour, Broonzy's popularity had grown tremendously within the collegiate and intellectual circles that were beginning to recognize the blues as an important component of American folk music.[24] In Europe, however, Broonzy's appeal originated from a different current, and he began to reinvent his career on the basis of Europeans' understanding of American jazz.

Broonzy had twenty-five years' experience performing in many of the largest cities in the United States with his "Big Bill from black Chicago" celebrity. Yet, as he soon discovered, traveling and touring throughout Europe with its many languages, currencies, cultures, and nationalities could be challenging for a black Chicagoan with virtually no formal education and little precedent to follow. Broonzy's friend Josh White had toured Europe in 1950 and was touring in 1951 when Broonzy arrived. European blues audiences throughout the continent, moreover, were still a small but devoted group of record collectors, jazz writers, and music-industry professionals with limited experience managing the European tours of black bluesmen.

Nevertheless, as Broonzy approached his first European tour, he was well equipped with skills that could help him spark yet another successful phase in his already-prolific career. Throughout his career's earlier phases in the 1930s and '40s, Broonzy had relied on many intermediaries and promoters—Charlie Jackson, Lemon Jefferson, Ink Williams, Lester Melrose, Lil Green, Joe Glasser, Alan Lomax, Studs Terkel, and Win Stracke. From creating important introductions to networking performances and recording sessions to organizing travel arrangements, these individuals were as integral to Broonzy's musical success as were his musical abilities and affable personality. And the situation was no different abroad.

Right from the start, Broonzy began performing for small jazz audiences in France and was presented as an antecedent to American jazz. Although Bruynoghe had arranged Broonzy's trip overseas, Panassié organized his earliest successful performances. While Broonzy was working as a janitor at Iowa State College and tending to his garden on Pammel Court, he received a phone call not from Yannick Bruynoghe but from Hugues Panassié, who urged him to leave Ames for his first European tour. Panassié was quite familiar with Broonzy's music and the blues.[25] Quickly, Panassié convinced Bruynoghe, then a writer for *Jazz Hot*, through the blues forum and jazz publication to help support a small tour for Broonzy.

Like Bruynoghe, Panassié had seen Broonzy in the United States and had a familiarity with black bluesmen. In 1938, John Hammond had personally invited Panassié to New York's "From Spirituals to Swing" concert, where he was initially introduced to the blues-singing Arkansas sharecropper named "Big Bill." Panassié and the Hot Club, moreover, had helped bring Lead Belly to France in 1949, the first folk bluesman to tour Europe. Lead Belly's ailing health, however, had forced him back to the United States, where he died from complications caused by amyotrophic lateral sclerosis a few months later.[26] Panassié convinced Broonzy that despite this setback, an audience for blues was rapidly developing in Europe, especially in France and Great Britain.

Broonzy had experienced some success among white audiences back in the States as a folk-blues performer among both left-leaning intellectual and folk music circles. But Panassié knew that Broonzy was more than just a folk entertainer. He was familiar with Broonzy's recordings from the 1930s and

1940s and arranged for Broonzy's first performance to be accompanied by a small jazz band "in fear that he might not go down well on his own."[27] Panassié, of course, argued that Broonzy's first trip to Europe would help European jazz audiences "feel and understand where jazz comes from" and "where it still gets its substance and nourishment."[28] Whatever concerns Panassié may have held about Broonzy's arrival, he could not have anticipated the success and impact that the Chicago blues great would make throughout Europe.

On September 21 and 22, 1951, Broonzy spent two days recording in a Parisian studio for Vogue Records in what was to become a landmark studio session documenting his transition to the last phase of his career. Nearly twenty-five songs from these sessions were released, many of which he had recorded decades before. In this particular session, however, Broonzy recorded solo, self-accompanied on the guitar for the first time since the 1930s. Offering a rich mixture of slow blues, urban Chicago blues, and traditional songs, Broonzy's performances were masterful. He had come so far since the late 1920s. His playing could easily shift between slow, traditional spirituals to upbeat, swinging shuffles, while his smooth baritone echoed across the performances with powerful tone and timbre. His take on "Make My Getaway," for example, showcased Broonzy's skills with the slow-tempo, vocally driven blues popularized by more rural country blues styles. His guitar approach featured a much softer plucking attack, serving only as a buttress to his intense, field-holler vocal delivery. After so many years of playing Chicago blues with its formulaic, proto-R&B sound, with these recordings, Broonzy had finally mastered the country blues. In these sessions, the folk blues celebrity he had been crafting since 1946 had arrived, and he gave it to this French recording studio in a manner that made him an incredibly potent force for blues revivalists in Europe.[29]

Interestingly, in live settings, French jazz enthusiasts were attracted to Broonzy's black urban pop, heard in literally hundreds of urban blues recordings from the 1940s. That was the "Big Bill" Broonzy they had heard on record, and that was the Broonzy they were determined to introduce to Europe. During Broonzy's first tour of Europe, he was presented as a vanguard of the urbane, Chicago style he had helped pioneer. He embraced the role, even though he had more or less abandoned his urban blues image years before. Frequently appearing onstage with five- and six-piece jazz bands, Broonzy was even depicted in a photograph printed in *Melody Maker* magazine from his first tour wearing a brimmed fedora, dark suit with an open collar displaying gold neck jewelry, and adorned with two-toned brogues. Clearly, he was willing to play the part of Chicago's "Big Bill."³⁰ European interest in blues stemmed from a small but active group of enthusiasts who often disagreed with one another about the future of jazz. Soon these devotees began looking backward into the history of New Orleans jazz and found what they believed to be primitive protojazz within Broonzy's black pop style from the 1930s and 1940s.

Those in the audience who were familiar with Broonzy's transition from black pop star to white folk-blues darling seemed shocked by his first European performances. Ron Sweetman, a teenager in 1951 when he attended his first Big Bill Broonzy concert in Menton, France, remembered being surprised by the "sophisticated" nature of one of Broonzy's first French performances:

> Wandering through the streets of Menton, I was amazed to see a flyer announcing a concert at the Grand Casino in Menton by Big Bill Broonzy on Wednesday August 22nd. I had read about Big Bill in magazines and books, but none of his recordings had been issued in England, so I had only a vague idea of what to expect. . . . The instrumentation was not dissimilar to the groups Big Bill had been recording with in recent years in the United States, but because of my unfamiliarity with these recordings, I was rather surprised that his accompanists were so numerous and so sophisticated.³¹

Broonzy was willing to appear as a bridge between Europeans' interpretations of blues and jazz because he understood what his audience and his tour organizers expected. Broonzy presented the same black pop, protojazz persona in Germany. Beginning in 1941, German jazz enthusiasts, including Horst Lippmann and Olaf Hudtwalcker, had established the Hot Club of Frankfurt after its French predecessor, which offered a community of musicians and enthusiasts the chance to organize and share their passions until the war's end.³² Following the end of the war, the Hot Club of Frankfurt began working in concert with the Hot Club de France and the American-backed radio network AFN. This network of jazz enthusiasts, like their French counterparts, quickly began organizing and producing radio broadcasts and community performances featuring jazz and blues artists, including Broonzy.

Following Broonzy's performances in France, including an August 23 opening stint for the jazz legend Sidney Bechet at the Vieux Colombier Club, a jazz and dance club in Juan-les-Pins, Broonzy visited Dusseldorf and performed at least one concert at the Robert Schumann Saal with a seven-piece "Hot Dixieland" jazz band. On September 15, Broonzy performed with the Australian jazz pianist and composer Graeme Bell in Dusseldorf.³³ Offering solo folk-blues classics such as "John Henry," "In the Evening," "Trouble in Mind," and "Keep Your Hands Off Her" during part of the show, Broonzy then collaborated with Bell's jazz band for more traditional jazz arrangements such as "I Feel So Good," "Who's Sorry Now," "Mama Don't Allow," and "When the Saints Go Marching In." Emceed by Olaf Hudtwalcker, these shows offered German audiences a chance to witness the breadth of Broonzy's repertoire and live performance capabilities. At this and other concerts, Broonzy offered the black, Chicago, jazz-tinged blues style he had helped pioneer during 1930s and 1940s. While in Germany, Broonzy also met Gunter Boas of the jazz Hot Club of Frankfurt, with whom he would correspond throughout the 1950s. In this correspondence, Broonzy shared his woes of touring Europe, felt out Frankfurt for possible future touring dates, offered personal stories about his mother, connected Boas with other German blues enthusiasts, and coordinated his touring schedules.[34]

Big Bill Broonzy's performances in France and Germany suggest that while in Europe, he was continually willing to reinvent his image and style as a performer and artist. For the next several years, Broonzy toured Europe and then found a home in France, but he was not always completely as welcomed as some blues devotees had hoped. In 1952, Henry Kahn of *Melody Maker* seemed frustrated and disappointed at French reactions to Broonzy's January performances there. In January and February 1952, Broonzy once again toured as an opening act for Sidney Bechet as part of the Vieux Colombier Club, this time in Paris, at a club of the same name as its counterpart on the French Riviera where Broonzy had played in August of the previous year. On January 16, Broonzy began his act. Introduced as the antecedent to Bechet's jazz, Broonzy offered "some magnificent numbers: some slow blues and some good swinging blues, all in that inimitable style of his."[35] Yet many in the crowd clearly expressed apathy in response to Broonzy's set, talking throughout his performance and inevitably prompting one annoyed critic to proclaim that "the music was over the head of the long-haired existentialists who profess to know so much about jazz."[36]

Broonzy's trip to England created an even greater stir and helped establish the last public persona that he would share with the world for the rest of his career in both Europe and the United States. England had developed an almost cult-like following of blues music and culture that praised Broonzy's presence and performances in London and permanently transformed him into a folk-blues icon and the last of the "authentic" blues artists. In England, the blues were also discussed as the springboard for jazz "whose sole vestigial remains were the twelve-bar chorus, blue notes, and the output of the classic blues singers."[37] Classic female blues singers such as Bessie Smith and Ma Rainey and boogie-woogie pianists such as Fats Waller and Jelly Roll Morton were collectively categorized as jazz in most record outlets. The historian Roberta Schwartz has suggested that before World War II, blues records remained scarce in England, and those who did possess the occasional classics reflected the "isolated passion of a few interested souls."[38] Occasionally, however, young Britons stumbled across the recordings of blues from the likes of Sleepy John Estes, whose "atypical form" became the "subject of intense speculation."[39] Following World War II, the blues gained such significant popularity in England that jazz critics and record collectors began holding recitals for rare blues records throughout the war. These devotees, like their contemporaries in France, were equally engaged in a bitter campaign that pitted modern jazz aficionados, those who recognized bebop as a legitimate jazz form, against those who were dedicated to revitalizing more traditional modes of Dixieland and swing jazz. This disagreement between "modernists" and "revivalists" led members of the latter group to dig deep into the history of jazz and track its relationship to the blues. The post–World War II blues boom in England was born of this musicological tug-of-war, and Broonzy's first concerts provided important fodder for the revivalists' campaign and their growing understanding of the blues idiom.[40]

Some scholars have suggested that the increasingly "evangelical" nature of blues devotees in Britain—namely, Ernest Borneman, Albert McCarthy, Sinclair Traill, Paul Oliver, Derrick Stewart-Baxter, and Max Jones—helped fuel the blues' growth in Europe.[41] Yet beyond the sonic properties attracting British folk enthusiasts to the music itself, the blues and its culture appealed to them as a reflection of the black experience. Part of these revivalists' interests in the blues as a separate idiom from jazz stemmed from an intellectual current that echoed American folklorists' perceptions of traditional black blues. To the revivalists, then, the blues represented a window into a fascinatingly alien and disappearing past—one centered on the tumultuous history of the African American experience. The historian Neil Wynn suggests, "Blues and jazz both could trace their origins back to the music of black slaves and could . . . trace their roots back to Africa, if only indirectly. . . . Their songs reflected a bygone era for most white audiences, a pre-modern era with an oral tradition and references to mojos, black cat bones, and John the Conqueror; they also reflected a life of hardship and suffering. For some British converts to black music, there was a sense of identification with the socio-economic hardships of African Americans."[42] Broonzy understood the fundamental differences between jazz and blues and tried his best to accommodate European notions of blues as a music-evolutionary precursor to jazz. What Europeans believed to be the blues' antecedent to jazz, what they expected of him upon his first tour, Broonzy called the "dressed up" style.[43] He considered the urban style, with its jazz-like arrangements and delivery, as "dressed up blues," and for Broonzy, the "real blues" came from Mississippi.[44] Broonzy felt that blues and jazz were "separate" idioms, and to him, jazz "belonged to those Creole people . . . who came from New Orleans."[45] In order to explain the nature of "real" blues to British audiences, Broonzy continued to present himself as the stripped-down folk bluesman from Mississippi. His skills and experience had taught him throughout his career to give these "revivalists" what they were looking for.

Periodicals such as *Melody Maker* and the *Jazz Journal* featured specific articles anticipating Broonzy's arrival in Britain, containing often-hyperbolic descriptions of a legendary blues musician who was "the finest blues singer living."[46] British revivalists were committed to portraying Broonzy in a wholly different manner than the French and Germans. British revivalists introduced Broonzy as a vanguard of the early solo male blues performer now popular among folk communities in the United States—the very style he had shed decades before. Before he even set foot on British soil, Broonzy was portrayed as a "passionate lover of the blues" whose art "goes way back into the past."[47] His success stemmed from his ability to combine an "almost inexhaustible" repertoire with a "smooth delivery" and from his "conscious artistry," a trait "which had completely transformed him into an international success."[48] Unlike his performances in France and Germany, where he offered his "Big Bill" urban image, in Great Britain, Broonzy presented himself as the last of a great line of American bluesmen in the folk-blues tradition. After his first European tour, Broonzy eschewed his urbane "Big Bill" celebrity for good.

On September 22, 1951, Broonzy performed two concerts at Kingsway Hall in the Holborn district of central London. Sponsored by the Wilcox brothers, owners and promoters of the London Jazz Club, and by Max Jones from *Melody Maker*, the first performance featured Broonzy alone with his acoustic guitar serving up some traditional folk blues for an enthralled audience of collectors and fans who had become acquainted with Broonzy's music as his records and reputation spread across Europe.[49] This first British performance included hits such as "House Rent Stomp," "John Henry," "Careless Love," and a moving performance of "Black, Brown, and White," which introduced the audience to, as the British music journalist Derrick Stewart-Baxter observed, "a man who had experienced racial discrimination, but had come through the ordeal with a smile."[50]

The performance on September 22 offered a surprisingly different experience, with a rare guest appearance as a special treat that both confused the European jazz cognoscenti in attendance and bolstered the blues evangelists' understanding of blues. Alan Lomax, then living in Scotland, had driven to Kingsway Hall to pay a visit to his old friend and to emcee the second show. Lomax's work in collecting and presenting English, Irish, and Scottish folk music from 1951 to 1957 made his presence critical for Broonzy's and American folk music's acceptance in Great Britain and helped explain the blues' divergent path from jazz. One folklorist has suggested, "Taken overall, Lomax's presence in London certainly altered, mainly for the better, the development of the folk-song revival in England. Many of his BBC broadcasts were magnificent. . . . The revival would no doubt have occurred without him, but its pace would have been slower and its gestation more difficult."[51]

At the second performance, Lomax and Broonzy offered those who were in attendance, including the music critic Ernest Borneman, "a conversation between old friends . . . with songs from both and the wonderfully happy air of a family reunion."[52] Of course, Broonzy had known Alan Lomax for quite some time, and they had worked together to shape Broonzy's career since the *Blues in the Mississippi Night* sessions. In some respects, Lomax and Broonzy had forged their relationship around Lomax's wish that Broonzy embrace the blues-as-folk narrative and embody it in his music and persona. In order for Lomax to satisfy his curiosities and to further his research agenda at the time, he urged Broonzy to employ these analytics as a didactic tool for his new audiences, in hopes that they might learn more about the function of racism, the black experience, and Jim Crow segregation in the United States. Indeed, Broonzy seemed to trust Lomax, at least in part, as it was quite unusual at the time for a black man to share such intimate knowledge of African American life with a white man with Lomax's background in federal administration, folklore, and academia. The performance at Kingsway Hall and Broonzy's subsequent interviews with Lomax and other oral interviewers seem to reflect this trust. Although several critics found Lomax's probing and upstaging banter "unnecessary"—jazz critics in attendance were "let down" and frustrated by Lomax's self-promotion and what they perceived as the paternalistic tone he used with Broonzy—the two friends shared their knowledge of black folk music, often prodding each other with questions and responses that left the audience feeling "as if they had wandered more or less by accident into one of those fabulous jazz parties" that were so prevalent in jazz communities throughout the States.[53] Overall, those who were in attendance seemed impressed, with critics suggesting that, despite the shows' low attendance and their frustrations with Lomax, the performances offered British audiences "a rich and rewarding experience" featuring one of "the best and most memorable" concerts "of the last few years."[54]

Alan Lomax's presence at the concert and his stature as "one of the foremost authorities on folk music in the world" helped solidify Broonzy's reputation as an authority on blues in Great Britain.[55] Broonzy was a master of the blues "as they were sung and played before jazz music really started," and with a personal endorsement from Alan Lomax, Broonzy quickly became a "touchstone" to an obscure and vanishing musical style that was as deeply rooted in American folk music as it was in jazz.[56] Throughout subsequent European tours, then, Broonzy began discussing the blues, its history, and what it meant to audiences that he perceived might not understand the blues' origins and historical context. Broonzy left England for Chicago on Tuesday, September 25, after the two London concerts that were the best ever heard there by the *Melody Maker* columnist Ernest Borneman.[57]

When Broonzy returned again to England in 1952, his image and performances had changed to fit the image he was desperately attempting to create as one of the last old-time blues singers. Ron Sweetman attended another Broonzy concert the following year, and to his amazement, Broonzy had almost completely transformed. Sweetman recalled,

> On the afternoon of Sunday February 24th, 1952, Big Bill Broonzy appeared at the Cambridge Theatre in London. The program photo showed him in working clothes, a cigarette in his mouth, and promised "A Programme of Blues, Folk Songs and Ballads." For some numbers he was accompanied by the Crane River Jazz Band, described as "Britain's foremost revivalist band. . . ." While in France Bill was presented in a setting that mirrored his current urban-style activities in the United States, in England he was presented as the unsophisticated rural artist found on his earliest recordings. . . . After a brief intermission, Bill came on stage in a suit and tie (not overalls) with his guitar, a solitary figure on a vast and imposing stage, but his presence galvanized the audience, whom he held in the palm of his hand throughout the afternoon. . . . After the concert my friend Ron Glass and I somehow managed to infiltrate backstage, where Bill obligingly posed for some photos by Ron Glass, until one of the Wilcox brothers chased us out, claiming that he had a "copyright" on all photos of Big Bill.[58]

The tension between Broonzy's appearances at the two shows that Sweetman attended highlights Broonzy's adaptation to British folk, blues, and jazz audiences. Broonzy openly admitted to the jazz writer and musician Humphrey Littleton that much of the repertoire he was performing for his first European dates consisted of songs that his promoters suggested he learn or relearn in hopes of gaining favor with specific audiences.[59]

An examination of Broonzy's first European tour reveals how these performances set the patterns he would follow for the remainder of his European career. In effect, he relied on a network of producers, promoters, musicians, writers, old friends, and music industrialists to navigate nearly every facet of his first tour of Europe, including, crucially, how he would be presented. In France, he was presented as a vanguard and a figure representative of the antecedents of jazz, in the conception of jazz history espoused by French jazz enthusiasts. In subsequent tours, he would never again perform with five- and six-piece jazz bands of his former "dressed-up" style. Occasionally he enlisted the help of a blues pianist—when he performed within another musician at all—but he mainly performed night after night alone, with a glass of whiskey, a lit cigarette, and his acoustic guitar.

By identifying and engaging with European assumptions about African American music, Broonzy developed a new public celebrity rooted in the desires and misconceptions of European audiences. Along the journey, through the last decade of his prolific career, he established important relationships that facilitated his success in a foreign land. But his tours of Europe were not trouble-free; Broonzy frequently experienced many of the same difficulties he had faced in the United States—management mishandling his money, the effects of European racism, and uncertainty about his new audience. Nevertheless, as Europeans began to see the blues as distinct from jazz, Broonzy embraced the image of a rural folk-blues musician and never looked back.

CHAPTER SEVEN

Big Bill Broonzy
The Making of a Legend

In 1978, blues legend Muddy Waters first met Big Bill Broonzy's son Michael van Isveldt in Amsterdam while touring as an opening act for Eric Clapton. Michael, an Amsterdamer who at the time was twenty-two, was the son of an immensely talented city theater costume designer named Pim van Isveldt. He had never met his father but had long heard of his affiliation with and importance to Chicago blues. As Waters gripped Michael's hand, the striking similarity between Broonzy and his handsome young son was astounding. For nearly a minute, while fighting back tears, Waters clasped Michael's hand, perhaps transported back to State Street or to one of the clubs in Chicago's South Side where he and Broonzy had shared a song, a laugh, and a whiskey all those years before.[1] In so many ways, Michael van Isveldt is one of the most important parts of Broonzy's legacy in Europe and one of the last touchstones to Broonzy's important career there.

In 1951, Broonzy was still legally married to his third wife, Rose, but the marriage was for all intents and purposes over. As Broonzy's recording career in Chicago had begun to wane, so too had his ten-year marriage. When he left Chicago for Iowa, Rose had disappeared, and Broonzy had filed for divorce. Judge Joseph Sabath of the Superior Court of Cook County argued on Broonzy's behalf, arguing that Rose had "willfully deserted and absented herself from the Plaintiff without any reasonable cause for over the space of one year since June 16, 1948."[2] As Broonzy toured Europe in the 1950s, he looked for a fresh start to both his career and his love life.

Broonzy quickly found solace in France. In April 1953, he lived in Paris with a woman named Jacqueline, whom he was ready to marry. Broonzy had written Alan Lomax, then living in Scotland, to find two "white plain" shirts and "2 rings" for their upcoming wedding. Broonzy relied on Jacqueline to mediate financial transactions, suggesting that she would repay Lomax for the purchases upon delivery. The letter reveals an introspective Broonzy who seemed at ease sharing religious and philosophical quips with his friend and even joking that he was "still alive and still singing the blues . . . and making love to a beautiful woman."[3] The relationship eventually fell apart, as Broonzy sought the comforts of home whenever possible. Moreover, sometime

Broonzy holding his newborn son, Michael van Isveldt, 1957. Courtesy of the Michael van Isveldt Collection.

between 1953 and 1956 in Chicago, Broonzy met Rose Lawson, whom he married in July 1956.[4]

Broonzy's love interests were not limited to France and Chicago, however, as he formed perhaps his most intimate and important romantic relationship of the European phase of his career in Holland. Broonzy met Pim van Isveldt during November of his 1955 tour, at the Doelenzaal Auditorium in Amsterdam, a theater designed to promote the interests of the working classes. Van Isveldt came from a working-class family in Amsterdam and was a costume designer in the city's municipal theater. She was an enormous fan of Broonzy's music and knew of his emerging European celebrity. She had watched intently from the audience as Broonzy performed at the "Ons Huis" in Amsterdam two years earlier in 1953, admitting in a 2004 interview that she was "crazy about that man" from the very beginning. When Broonzy visited Amsterdam again in 1955, van Isveldt was introduced to Broonzy in his dressing room; she later admitted, "It was love at first sight for both of us."[5] For the next three years, Broonzy and van Isveldt maintained a somewhat tumultuous relationship through frequent visits and numerous correspondences, with van Isveldt traveling to Paris and Brussels whenever Broonzy performed there. Their relationship produced a son named Michael on December 4, 1956. From 1955 to 1957, Broonzy wrote Pim nearly every week in a series of more than fifty letters, through which he tried to make sense of their relationship.

Both onstage and in letters, Broonzy shared elements of his personality, essentially allowing van Isveldt, his fans, and his friends a chance to intimately share in the struggles he endured with romantic relationships, financial challenges of the music industry, and Europe's and the United States' racial undertones. One friend remembered that Broonzy was essentially "human": "good natured" and "temperamental" and equally "kind" yet "difficult."[6] In many ways, these descriptions serve as metaphors for Broonzy's experience as an international blues celebrity. His tours of Europe offered specific challenges that brought to the surface the complex nature of his character and the inherent difficulties he experienced forging his celebrity.

Even with the help of Broonzy's network, his tours of Europe from 1951 to 1957 were not always easy nor operated smoothly; Broonzy experienced financial and social difficulties that made his travels and performances in Europe challenging. But the importance of these individuals in shaping Broonzy's career in Europe cannot be overemphasized. In Belgium, France, the Netherlands, and the United Kingdom, Broonzy's network held personal and professional expectations of him that shaped how he as a man and as a performer might be understood. Most of Broonzy's professional contacts expected to share in his success in Europe, assuming that their support of his career transition would benefit their careers as well. As Broonzy toured Europe during these years, his network of intermediaries expanded to include many individuals beyond Europe's burgeoning blues and jazz culture. Broonzy often found good company among his admirers, and those who truly accepted his art form and personality and bolstered his celebrity status in Europe.

The Netherlands became a special place for Big Bill Broonzy; he once proclaimed, "You can't go to a better place than Holland." There he had "been treated the best," better than any other "place in the world."[7] Broonzy's first appearances in the Netherlands took place on November 7-8, 1952, when he and his friend the pianist Blind John Davis appeared in The Hague and in Scheveningen. Broonzy toured Holland in 1953 and again in 1955, appeared in concerts for the Haarlemse Jazz Club in Haarlem, for the Dutch public broadcasting network Algemene Vereniging Radio Omroep (AVRO) television and radio programs. He also performed for receptive live audiences in Rotterdam, Amsterdam, and The Hague. Organized by promoter Paul Acket, Broonzy even lodged at the home of the famous Dutch jazz critic Michiel de Ruyter, where he performed for the intimate crowd.[8]

After Broonzy's first visit to the Netherlands, he donated the proceeds from at least two concerts to victims of the Zeeland floods, one of the worst natural disasters in Dutch history.[9] Part of Broonzy's appreciation for the Dutch people and their culture stemmed from the noticeably relaxed racial environment of Holland and the flat, swampy land closely akin to the vistas of his proclaimed Mississippi Delta childhood. Broonzy's admiration of the Netherlands certainly had much to do with his romantic relationship with Pim van Isveldt.

Rather quickly, van Isveldt became an important cog in Broonzy's European network, with Broonzy often relying on her to place phone calls, write letters, market records, and promote his shows throughout Europe. Van Isveldt admitted that one of the only reasons she would date a man thirty years her senior stemmed "from the fact that Bill had something childlike and naïve about him."[10] The letters, now in the possession of her son Michael, seem to support this interpretation. Throughout this correspondence, Broonzy seems jealous, confused, patriarchal, lonely, mistrusting, and demanding. And yet he is equally kind, gracious, loving, and supportive. This mix of emotions suggests that sustaining his celebrity persona was not easy. He had also learned by that point that revealing his childlike deference, naiveté, and volatility could be useful for navigating important relationships and fostering tangible material gains.

For Broonzy, handling his reinvented career as an international blues celebrity involved more than just the development of personal relationships. He had to navigate professional relationships as well. He often felt "taken advantage of" and occasionally struggled with the demands and circumstances of being an American artist navigating new social and professional networks within several different countries. In 1952 and 1953, Broonzy toured France, Belgium, the United Kingdom, Spain, and the Netherlands with his friend and fellow Chicago bluesman Blind John Davis. Throughout his tours, however, he relied on the managerial services of Herbert Wilcox of the London Jazz Club. By the early winter of 1952, their relationship, at least in Broonzy's eyes, had begun to sour. On January 24, 1953, Broonzy sent a typed letter to Win Stracke in Chicago indicating that his 1952 tour of England had not unfolded as smoothly as he had hoped. The roots of his disagreements with Wilcox, as usual, were financial. Broonzy was upset that he had to pay for both his and Wilcox's travel expenses, including meals, train and cab fares, and lodging expenses.[11]

The tone of the letter was angry and resounds with disappointment. Wilcox had also managed Broonzy's British savings account and often suggested that Broonzy keep money available in Britain that Broonzy could access or use to transfer funds to Chicago, if necessary. In one instance, Wilcox cashed a check written to Broonzy without his signature. As financial transactions for performances began to accrue from concerts in Belgium, Holland, and London with Mahalia Jackson, the receipts did not seem to match the financial statements. Broonzy closed his letter with obvious disappointment:

> This is written by William Lee Broonzy known on records as Big Bill Broonzy and is known all over the world and played all over the world but never was treated by nobody like Mr. Wilcox treated me in my life. I don't think he has a heart in him at all. To say one thing today and change so soon in two weeks time he must have dollar signs for eyes. He has such a good wife and a lot of good friends that while I did not get a receipt for everything because I did trust him, but I trust him too much with my money.[12]

As he had told Alan Lomax years before about being a traveling musician in the United States, the road in Europe was also expensive, with a large percentage of his earnings covering "rent," "food to eat," and fees for his "clothes to be clean."[13]

After 1953, Broonzy soon relied particularly on Yannick Bruynoghe to manage his money, and in letter after letter, Broonzy seemed concerned about where his money was located and why Bruynoghe was taking so long to move it for him. The confusion arising from the financial aspects of Bruynoghe and Broonzy's professional association seemed a critical and constant issue between Broonzy and van Isveldt and often created rifts in their relationship. Though he relied on Bruynoghe to secure funds for van Isveldt and their son, Michael, he warned her not to completely trust Bruynoghe.

Money problems stemming from difficulties with international financial and labor agreements posed problems for Broonzy as well. Following his first European tour, as he traveled more regularly into other parts of the continent, simply acquiring a travel visa became a consistent challenge without legitimate documentation in the form of work contracts.[14] After his first few tours, and especially after 1955, Broonzy suggested that he was having a difficult time securing contracts to perform in Holland and Europe. By 1956, he was not even allowed to "carry his guitar" into Europe without contractual agreements that he could present to immigration. This fueled his continual frustration over sending money to van Isveldt when she needed it, especially following the birth of Michael.[15]

In Europe, Broonzy seemed to experience both new financial frustrations and familiar ones he had dealt with in Chicago with American intermediaries. In some ways, Broonzy seemed surprised that his intermediaries would treat him in such a manner; yet by this point in his career, he understood the unscrupulous practices of the music industry. Broonzy was not alone in the difficulties he experienced while navigating European networks. His fellow folk-blues artist Josh White was challenged by the same problems as he became an international celebrity. White's and Broonzy's careers both became deeply enmeshed within European jazz and folk music circles in the 1950s, with some people preferring White's more "sophisticated style" and other audiences preferring Broonzy's "earthy style."[16] Broonzy and White were not competitors on a personal level, but professionally they often toured many of the same European circuits.

Like Broonzy, White had toured Europe beginning in 1950 and found success almost immediately. Throughout the 1950s, White traveled almost incessantly, crisscrossing the Atlantic, North America, and western Europe. His first tour produced excited reactions from British, French, and Italian fans, but in a manner similar to Broonzy, touring in Europe presented White with troubles. In Italy, White experienced language-barrier problems that inhibited his travel plans, punctuality, and ability to judge his audiences' reactions. Like Broonzy, White soon grew frustrated with his financial difficulties in England, suggesting that he was intentionally being "ripped-off" by British concert promoters and his British booking agency.[17] In a letter to his wife, White clearly seemed aggravated: "The people that are paying me or should I say that are supposed to didn't live up to the contract. I am supposed to receive weekly $1,000 my 11th + 12th week salary in cash given to the Foster agency. Well this is what happened they gave Fosters a post-dated check which we know will bounce so if they don't get the cash by Monday I am taking them to court meaning this I won't be working for them after today."[18] From 1956 to 1957, White's situation became even more difficult, as American appearances were beginning to dry up and as he sank deeper in debt to British agencies because of "unrealized advanced payments."[19] On tour in England in 1957, White experienced a problem with a British bank where he had deposited the British equivalent of fifteen hundred guilders. His managers suggested he deposit the money for easy accessibility, as Wilcox had done for Broonzy. In an attempt to withdraw his deposit, White enlisted the help of mutual friends of Broonzy and van Isveldt's, Trixie and David Stevens; they helped White discover a suspicious paperwork mistake that was part of a ploy to prevent him from obtaining any of his money.[20]

The shared experience of similar financial and logistical troubles led Broonzy and White to develop a close friendship. Broonzy referred warmly to White as "the old cotton picker," and the two often shared drinks, song ideas, and general companionship with each other whenever possible in Europe.[21] Both were quickly becoming icons for Europeans' admiration of black music.

Much of Broonzy's frustration may have stemmed from his perspectives on race. While the open system of segregation that existed in the United States at the time did not exist in Europe, racism existed there nonetheless. In Great Britain and France, ideas of race slowly transformed in the immediate postwar era as a reaction to the defeat of racist fascism and the legacy of white supremacy. The sociologist Howard Winant writes, "The old racism had retained a commitment to biologism and notions of superiority/inferiority. The new racism broke with that viewpoint: it rejected (at least officially) concepts of 'natural' inequality and instead stressed 'cultural' differences."[22] In Germany, one of the global centers for fascist eugenics and biological determinism during the interwar years, the presence of American culture, the military industrial complex, and African American service members complicated the already complex racial picture of the early Cold War period.[23] Cultural differences within German notions of race immediately following World War II expose the lingering tension between biology and culture, based on sexual morality and fear of "sexual relations between races."[24] Before one European tour, while Broonzy was waiting for his next contract and payment for the last one, he expressed disdain and disappointment in a letter to van Isveldt filled with resentment over racial dynamics: "You know I'm an American Negro and over here I can't do nothing without a white man's helping me. I can't get my money I made over there. A white man has to get it for me about the money I made in England. Yannick did get it, but he was to send to the USA, but he hasn't done it yet. All the money he got over there went to his ticket."[25] Broonzy's race consciousness in Europe was not solely limited to financial interactions. He also felt challenged by his lack of formal education and his black southern dialect:

> In France they speak French, in Belgium they speak French and also in Switzerland they speak French. In Spain they speak a different language. And in Italy they speak a different language. Also in Germany they speaks a different language. And they don't understand the American Negro's language. Because the American Negro do not speak correct English. Some of the people could understand the American Negro, if

he spoke correct English. And the Mississippi Negro, which is where the blues came from—Mississippi, Arkansas, Georgia, Alabama and Texas—they do not speak correct, the blues singers, I'm not saying all Negroes. Because some of the Negroes do, from those states do speak correct English. But the Negro that really sings the blues, that's off of those farms and levee camps and extra gangs and things. Those people do not speak correct English and I am one of them.[26]

While Broonzy faced challenges in Europe, he also showed a part of his persona that was willing to push back against overt and systemic racism. Night after night, he performed his most racially combative songs to European audiences. One of these songs, "Black, Brown, and White," became a mainstay in Broonzy's repertoire. Broonzy suggested in an interview with Studs Terkel that he had written "Black, Brown, and White" in 1939 after his trainee in a Chicago foundry took his job as foreman because he was white and Broonzy was black. The lyrics give a poignant depiction of racism in American life:

> This little song that I'm singin' about
> People you know it's true
> If you're black and gotta work for a living
> This is what they will say to you
>
> They says if you was white, should be all right
> If you was brown, stick around
> But as you's black, m-mm brother, git back git back git back
>
> Me and a man was workin' side by side
> This is what it meant
> They was paying him a dollar an hour
> And they was paying me fifty cent
>
> They said if you was white, 't should be all right
> If you was brown, could stick around
> But as you black, m-mm boy, git back git back git back[27]

Broonzy once suggested that these lines reflected his life's experience and that he performed this and other socially conscious songs during his concerts as tools for explaining the black experience in the United States: "Black, Brown, and White" was "for a fact, written about my life. A lot of people don't like it because of the words 'get back.' Well a lot of people in this world haven't never had to get back but I wrote it because I had to get back."[28] "Black,

Brown, and White" became one of the most important antisegregationist songs in Broonzy's career and in American music. The social consciousness conveyed in "Black, Brown, and White" and similar songs became an integral part of this stage of his career as a black musical touchstone and international blues celebrity.

Beyond Broonzy's songs, his commentary on his time in Europe reveals him to be quite perceptive about racial encounters on the continent. He remembered that when he arrived in Germany, several "white girls" standing on the train platform "looked strange," and as he tried to shake one girl's hand, "she fainted" because he was black.[29] While in England, Broonzy was turned away from a hotel in Nottingham due to the management's explicit policy of not renting rooms to "Negroes."[30] During his second wave of sold-out Dutch appearances, organized by the Dutch jazz photographer Wouter van Gool, the Amsterdam Jazz Society, and Hans Rooduijn of the "Le Canard" Foundation, Broonzy visited Amsterdam in February 1953 and performed for a receptive crowd at the capital city's "Ons Huis," or Our House.[31] Following the performance, Broonzy was taken to a local public house in old Amsterdam, where his hosts asked him to sing a few more songs for the crowd gathered there. To their surprise, Broonzy refused, claiming that "he was afraid of being arrested for being black." Once his hosts explained with bewildered amusement that the Dutch did not carry such racial pretensions, Broonzy delightfully "played for an hour."[32]

Even Broonzy's relationship with van Isveldt was affected by racial tension. Right after they met, Broonzy seemed concerned that "living together would be hard."[33] After all, interracial marriage and dating were social taboos in the United States, and interracial marriage remained illegal in many states until 1967. Of course, interracial dating in western Europe was not widely accepted either. Broonzy discovered in February 1956, right after they had begun their courtship, that van Isveldt had lost her job as a costume designer for the community theater. Broonzy was convinced that she was fired because of their relationship, suggesting that she had lost her job because he was a "negro."[34] In the summer of 1956, Broonzy discovered that van Isveldt was pregnant with his "brown skinned baby," and he seemed ambivalent about "bringing another Broonzy in this world."[35] The letters that Broonzy wrote to van Isveldt from 1955 to 1958 are extremely important because they reveal more than just the challenges created by international romance: they reveal that inventing and reinventing his career as an international blues celebrity was extremely difficult. Several letters, for example, focus on a racially charged altercation in 1956 with the Dutch jazz critic and producer Michiel de Ruyter that provoked old feelings from a lifetime of being scammed in the recording studio.

De Ruyter and Broonzy had established a significant relationship through correspondence and frequent visits, sharing personal stories and openly enjoying each other's company. Although de Ruyter was an important jazz critic and promoter in the Netherlands, he and Broonzy were first and foremost friends. Broonzy had lodged at de Ruyter's home during his first Dutch appearances. De Ruyter was an enormous fan of Broonzy's music, and likewise, Broonzy admired de Ruyter as a leading European jazz promoter, writer, and producer.[36]

In February 1956, Broonzy was scheduled to record eight songs with de Ruyter in Bearn, Holland, for the Philips label, but the session quickly turned sour. Broonzy accused de Ruyter of purposefully intoxicating him in hopes of pushing the contracted eight-song session to a doubled number of sixteen. De Ruyter, or "Mr. Mike," as Broonzy called him, however, wrote that Broonzy had become too intoxicated to perform and record properly, and rather than confronting Broonzy directly, out of respect he had secretly informed Yannick Bruynoghe of the debacle. Broonzy, in turn, accused de Ruyter of breeching their trust and friendship, going as far as to suggest that the awkward situation stemmed from Broonzy's being a "Negro." Clearly offended, Broonzy threatened, "I did think you was my friend. You told me you would take care of everything and I trusted you. I know the peoples in Holland like to know you better and to know who you really are. And I'm going to tell them and every newspaper and magazine I know to print this story."[37] In several letters to van Isveldt, Broonzy seemed openly upset over the incident, justifying to her that "Mike" was truly not his friend, that he was not drinking, and that Bruynoghe laughed at the entire situation.[38] For several months following the recording incident, Broonzy seemed uncomfortable and concerned about how his career might be affected, as he clearly did not want to jeopardize his professional opportunities. This anecdote, then, suggests that balancing his personal and professional relationships within his new life was much more difficult than he expected and that the issue of race was clearly on Broonzy's mind as he navigated this new persona.

Despite the social and financial struggles Broonzy experienced while touring in Europe, his tours were highly successful. They had reinvented his recording career and quickly ignited an array of new performing and recording opportunities back in the United States. George Adins, a friend of Bruynoghe's, blues revivalist, and frequent writer for *du Hot Club du France*, revealed in a 1957 letter to van Isveldt that his family had been greatly affected by Broonzy's presence in Belgium. Adins explained that, through Broonzy, he had gained an "intense and deep admiration for the Negro population," suggesting that "they are the most loving and joyful people ever created." To Adins, Big Bill Broonzy was "the best and most kindhearted" man he had ever met, and some of the happiest moments he had ever experienced were having Broonzy in his home.[39]

Although Broonzy enjoyed the European phase of his career, the financial and social challenges he faced in foreign countries on tour served to strengthen his love of Chicago even further. Despite consistently promising van Isveldt from 1955 until his death that he was leaving the United States to move to Europe, Broonzy always returned to his home in Chicago's South Side.[40] When he returned to the United States, however, his career began to take a different turn. The Chicago blues community where Broonzy was once king now worshiped at the altar of Muddy Waters, Little Walter, Howlin' Wolf, Sonny Boy Williamson II (Rice Miller), and Willie Dixon. Their electrified "down-home" styles had superseded the slick urban blues of Broonzy's past and the rural country folk-blues of his present persona.

But just as the preferences of black audiences and the white-operated recording industry had changed, American academic, intellectual, and left-wing political circles had placed in motion an enormous revival of interest in American folk music, of which blues were viewed as an integral part.[41] Broonzy employed his newfound international celebrity to refuel his career, becoming highly active in the development of the American folk music movement.[42] The revival's organizers and promoters recognized Broonzy's potential. This was fitting, as many of its leaders had helped forge the solo folk-blues persona that Broonzy had perfected among European audiences, dating back to his first stint with "I Come for to Sing" in the late 1940s.

For this group of folk enthusiasts, Broonzy could embody juxtaposed identities simultaneously: the early blues pioneer in the United States and one of the most prolific recording artists in urban blues history and now an international celebrity who had toured the world sharing the blues and his recollections of the black experience. Upon his return to the United States, his career gained significant momentum. From 1951 to 1957, Broonzy appeared in Studs Terkel's "I Come for to Sing" traveling program along with Win Stracke, Larry Lane, and Chet Roble; Broonzy served as the show's folk-blues component. Moreover, gigs in the form of residencies at new folk clubs such as the Blue Note, the Gate of Horn, and the Blue Angel began to emerge with help from Terkel and Stracke, along with increasing recording opportunities for smaller independent labels such as Chess, Verve, and Folkways.⁴³ At the same time, however, Broonzy was also involved in Chicago concerts explaining the history of jazz that were eerily similar to his first European performances. Similarly, in a manner reminiscent of his European celebrity, he was frequently featured in the *New York Times* and other national newspapers as a linchpin for understanding jazz's development in the United States.⁴⁴

Occasionally, new opportunities involved more than just music. In Chicago, Broonzy had helped establish a local tavern dubbed Big Bill and Moore's Lounge on the city's South Side.⁴⁵ Broonzy also helped Win Stracke and the local folk musician Frank Hamilton open Chicago's Old Town School of Folk Music, on December 1, 1957, providing the school its very first folk music lesson with a demonstration of his masterful guitar work.⁴⁶ Although Broonzy's reinvented career had provided new musical opportunities in Chicago, he still had to work to supplement his income. Nearly every summer from 1953 until his death, Broonzy worked as a cook for a folk camp in Hastings, Michigan, called Circle Pines. Throughout the 1940s and 1950s, the Circle Pines Center thrived as a progressive, family-centered folk camp where a racially integrated mix of children and adults from the Midwest participated in a cooperative culture through a specific emphasis on education.⁴⁷ Former campers recalled Broonzy's lackluster cooking skills but incredible musicianship during his residency there, including a remarkable performance with Pete Seeger in 1956 on the lawn of the camp's farm house.⁴⁸ Vera King, a longtime board member, has suggested that Broonzy's presence at the camp was memorable for campers and families. She recalled, "[Broonzy] would sing all night with the kids and couldn't get up in the morning. The kitchen manager was furious with him. . . . Apparently he was an alcoholic at the time, but he never drank while he was here, and he never sang any of his off-color songs to the kids."⁴⁹

Broonzy's celebrity in Chicago and in Europe, however, was quite different. In Europe, he was accustomed to performing for packed crowds to great acclaim and praise, in elaborate music halls in the continent's greatest cities. Many major European music publications hailed Broonzy as an incredibly gifted musician. Broonzy loomed large in the imaginations of the burgeoning group of black-music devotees and was crucial to their understandings of the music. His fans opened their homes, lauded him with gifts and their affections, and captured their respect in photographs. He developed a network of friends and colleagues whom he could usually depend on and who seemed to care for his well-being as much as his music. But for many of his closest European admirers and fans, he also fed a fascination with black primitivism and exotica that defined the shifting terrain of race in post–World War II Europe. Hugues Panassié, for example, continually wrote of Broonzy's purity and his primitive, simplistic style in an attempt to link New Orleans traditional jazz to it blues roots. Repeatedly, he pointed to "fantasies of black exceptionalism and Noble Savagery" in his writings on African American music, suggesting that African Americans exuded innate cultural differences that made them inherently musical.[50] This idea, of course, completely ignored the countless hours Broonzy had spent studying songs, crafting new melodies, practicing his instrument, and learning about and navigating the American recording industry. Other jazz critics similarly deemed Broonzy a "simple and sensible artist" with a "pure and poignant voice," appearing in France as one of "the last authentic blues singers."[51]

Broonzy's less glamorous, U.S. employment situation—playing small folk clubs and college campuses and his work as a cook for Circle Pines—is indicative of the plight of many black musicians in a country where African Americans were considered second-class citizens. Broonzy's celebrity in Europe had granted him unprecedented access to many European spaces of privilege and citizens' homes, but in the United States, Broonzy was still just a black musician from Chicago's South Side. While he was an important element of Chicago's vibrant folk music community and a well-respected celebrity in black Chicago, his status was diminished when compared to the electrified blues currently popularized by the Chess sound.

By 1957, Big Bill Broonzy's career, considered in its totality, could sustain success and acclaim and provide sufficient opportunity for recording and performance both at home and abroad. He was increasingly recognized as one of the most important national and international blues artists, and his professional associations in Europe, Chicago, and the greater Midwest's folk music revival had kept him constantly on the move. Yet the sad irony of all of this reinvigorated success and hard work was the fact that this larger-than-life elder statesman of the blues was slowly dying. His doctor had warned him in the late 1940s that twenty years of traveling and living the itinerant musician's lifestyle was dangerous for his aging body and health. Part of his decision to leave Chicago for Ames, Iowa, in 1950 and his frequent summer stints at the Circle Pines Center's summer camp were based on this suggestion. By 1956, however, Broonzy was becoming increasingly sick.

In letter after letter to van Isveldt, beginning in 1956, Broonzy complained of "feeling ill," ultimately revealing through his correspondence with her a two-year battle with cancer.[52] Initially, his doctors had suggested that he was eating the wrong foods and that the continuous changes in his diet as he traveled might be the root cause of his problems.[53] He also seemed emotionally spent; at age sixty, he had crafted a new image that had reinvigorated his career, but his career was now in the hands of many intermediaries whom he did not completely trust. He was constantly traveling all over Europe and back to the United States. He had fathered a child with his Dutch girlfriend without really being able to be around. His drinking was beginning to affect his ability to work. By June 1956, he clearly seemed frazzled, explaining to van Isveldt that his "nerves" might be bad.[54] From 1956 and into 1957, Broonzy's condition grew increasingly worse throughout his last tour of Europe, after which he was diagnosed with cancer in July 1957.[55] Despite his ailing health, Broonzy still found time to appear at Circle Pines as a camp cook and performer with Pete Seeger and recorded *The Big Bill Broonzy Story* for Verve Records.

These July 12-14, 1957, recordings in Chicago were Broonzy's last. During one of the stormiest midsummer weekends in the city's history, he recorded over ten hours of his favorite songs at Universal Studios in Chicago, with the legendary promoter and producer Bill Randle.[56] This session led to the 1960 release of a five-album, Grammy Award-nominated box set on the Verve label, titled *The Big Bill Broonzy Story*. The nearly seventy tracks offered a tour de force of Broonzy's long career, presenting the flexibility of his wide-ranging repertoire as he tore through blues songs, spirituals, and traditional ballads. In an attempt to highlight the final stage of Broonzy's career, Randle had Broonzy perform all the material solo, with only his famous 1946 Martin 000-28 acoustic guitar as accompaniment. The hi-fi sound of the recording mix yielded one of the most sonically clear recordings in Broonzy's long career. Despite his ailing health, his voice is powerful, and his guitar playing marks him as a true master of the blues tradition on the instrument. Randle recalled, "the choice of the material was largely Bill's; he dominated the sessions and strongly resisted direct requests for favorite blues, work songs, and background materials."[57] In between takes on classics such as "Key to the Highway" "Joe Turner Blues," "See See Rider," "It Hurts Me too," and "Trouble in Mind," Randle nudged Broonzy to elucidate his musical past, in terms of his understanding of his own influences, style, repertoire, and general philosophy about black music. Further, Broonzy recorded, for the very last time, the song he had made famous nearly twenty years earlier, "Just a Dream." At nearly four minutes, this is the longest and perhaps best-recorded version of the song. It remains one of the only versions of the classic without any piano or drums accompaniment, capturing Broonzy one last time, alone with his most beloved guitar. His masterful vocal delivery leads the performance. Many performances and years had passed since Broonzy first recorded "Just a Dream" in 1939, and his 1957 vocals, full of melismas and timbral variations, reflect a seasoned and world-traveled artist who simply did not exist twenty years earlier. His guitar work similarly conveyed the mastery of a veteran recording and performing artist, with its single-note runs, quarter- and half-step bent notes, hammer-on and pull-off effects, and intermittent chord strumming serving as both melodic and rhythmic accompaniment. It is impossible to know if he thought this session for Verve Records would be his last, but the sheer power and emotion of this recording has led listeners to suspect that indeed he may have.[58]

The following September, still in Chicago, Broonzy wrote van Isveldt to explain that he had been in the hospital for two weeks after having an operation for cancer that removed a lung.[59] Ever the optimist, Broonzy tried to convince van Isveldt that he would soon be returning to London, but he would never tour Europe again. The cancer metastasized from his throat to his lungs. A second operation on his throat in the fall of 1957 severed his vocal chords, silencing his powerful singing voice forever. Although another operation was planned in the early winter of 1958, in hopes of repairing his severed vocal chords, Big Bill Broonzy never performed again.[60]

As Broonzy's hospital bills accumulated, his meager savings dwindled. The reputation he had built throughout his long and distinguished career brought together dozens of friends and colleagues eager to help him and his family through these difficult times. In Chicago, dozens of black musicians, folk music enthusiasts, blues aficionados, and jazz cognoscenti organized a benefit concert to help with Broonzy's mounting medical debt. The sold-out show raised approximately $2,000 for Broonzy's cause. Broonzy stood onstage with tears streaming down his face to thunderous applause after the two-and-a-half-hour performance, thanking his friends and colleagues in a whisper for "making the evening so memorable."[61]

Across the Atlantic, two benefit concerts held in London in March featured European jazz and blues revivalists as well as musicians from across the continent.[62] The first, held at the London Coliseum and sponsored by *Melody Maker*, featured Alan Lomax as the master of ceremonies and included over fifty "top stars of British jazz," ultimately raising £500 for the cause. The second concert, promoted by the National Jazz Federation, featured a midnight performance at the Dominion Theatre that included performances from the Lonnie Donegan Skiffle Group, the Chris Barber Band with Ottilie Patterson, and the Ken Coyler Band. It also raised approximately £500 for Broonzy.[63]

A comparison of the American and European benefit concerts reveals that, to the very end, Broonzy's audiences and his respective identities in the United States and Europe were different. In the United States, the benefit was held at the Pilgrim Gospel Baptist Church in the heart of Chicago's South Side and included performances from a who's who of local and national blues, folk, and gospel giants. Broonzy's friend the Chicago media personality Studs Terkel emceed the evening's proceedings, and many of his closest friends—including Tampa Red, Mahalia Jackson, J. B. Lenoir, Pete Seeger, and Memphis Slim—were in attendance.[64] The concert reflects Broonzy's status in the United States as a black musician: "Big Bill" from black Chicago.

In England, Broonzy was recognized as a musician whose importance went further than the "Big Bill" figure of Chicago. The British concerts were held in two of the country's largest theaters in the heart of London and offered audiences a chance to hear some of the United Kingdom's brightest jazz and skiffle celebrities.[65] Alan Lomax provided emcee services for the events. Most of the performers were white, and *Melody Maker* and the National Jazz Federation sponsored the events. Broonzy was treated as an international celebrity at these events in London, whereas in the United States, the scope of his influence seemed limited to Chicago's blues and folk communities.

Broonzy did not attend the London concerts on the advice of his physicians, though he admitted, "there's nothing I want to do more."[66] Broonzy's last letter to van Isveldt, written in March 1958, reveals just how dire his health had become. Broonzy complained of crippling headaches and failing vision, which were greatly affecting his ability to write. He expressed excitement that his friends in Europe and Chicago were trying to raise funds for his operations and expenses but seemed overwhelmed by the mounting debt created by his vast medical bills. He seemed convinced that he would sing again and that his health would improve.[67] By July, Broonzy had succumbed to the reality of his prognosis, apologizing to his British friends David and Trixie Stevens: "Please don't think hard of me for not writing you all. I can't see, I am almost blind, and my mind is not so good. I am so nervous. I am writing to let you know that I haven't forgotten you. I am yet thankful for all you did for me."[68] One month later, on Friday, August 15, 1958, Big Bill Broonzy died of cancer in an ambulance on his way to Billings Hospital from his home at 4716 South Parkway, Chicago.[69] The proud singer affectionately known all over the world as "Big Bill," who had developed an image and personality around his larger-than-life blues persona and six-foot-three, two-hundred-pound frame, had wasted away to a mere eighty pounds.[70] News of his death spread rapidly across the United States and Europe as folk and blues media outlets, his social and professional networks, and major newspapers and magazines shared the sad news.[71] After memorial services attended by Broonzy's friends Studs Terkel, Win Stracke, Brother John Sellers, J. B. Lenoir, Muddy Waters, Tampa Red, Little Walter, Lil Armstrong, Mahalia Jackson, and Chet Roble, Broonzy was laid to rest in Chicago's Lincoln Cemetery on August 19.[72]

Broonzy's long career is an extremely fruitful case study for understanding black cultural construction in the United States in the first half of the twentieth century. When Broonzy first landed on European shores to perform in 1951, he had seen his two-decade career transformed from the hit-making machine "Big Bill," "from black Chicago," into "Big Bill," "folk-blues hero." As his music lost favor among black audiences, he navigated folk music's growing influence in the United States in a manner that helped connect his music to a new audience across the Atlantic with budding interests in black vernacular music. To a new audience of blues revivalists and jazz enthusiasts, he became the edifying link between blues and jazz history. Along the way, he became a celebrity as a black musician who explained African American music and traditions to white audiences in Europe. The magnitude of his achievement becomes more apparent when we recognize that Broonzy invented and reinvented himself as a man and as a musician in a country that maintained a system of legal racial segregation and discrimination. For almost thirty years, Big Bill Broonzy engaged the music business and the expectations it held of black musicians in a manner that led him to unprecedented success as both a national folk icon and an international blues and jazz performer. As Broonzy toured Europe and found new fame in the United States, he encountered new audiences that held more expansive expectations about what his life and career represented. These new fans expected an opportunity to intimately celebrate the wise and affable blues musician as a romantic, if not exotic, touchstone to the African American past. Similarly, they anticipated that his didactic storytelling and unmatched musicianship would shed further light on the creators of this music tradition that they loved, creators about whom they knew very little. Broonzy knew what they wanted, and night after night onstage and in recording studios, he was willing to give it to them to maintain his identity and advance his career, even if it killed him in the process.

CHAPTER EIGHT

Escaping the Folk

The "Authentic" Career of a Black Pop Star

The legendary blues and rock guitarist Eric Clapton first saw the Chicago blues pioneer William "Big Bill" Broonzy on British television in 1955: Broonzy was sitting alone in a dimly lit nightclub with an acoustic guitar. By Clapton's account, he would never be the same. The image presented by the broadcast was a far cry from the dressed-to-the-nines Chicago bluesman and rhythm-and-blues songster Broonzy had been in the 1930s and 1940s. Clapton's discovery of Broonzy left him with the belief that Broonzy was "the main man." Immediately, Clapton recognized Broonzy's immense guitar talent as he toured Europe in the 1950s and was fascinated that the Chicago bluesman was "so readily available during" the period.[1] In a sense, Broonzy's music helped Clapton find his own aesthetic on his journey as a musician and fan of the blues. Clapton was drawn to the raw folk-blues style that Broonzy exhibited throughout the 1950s:

> I saw a clip of him [Broonzy] on TV, playing in a nightclub, lit by the light from a single light bulb, swinging in its shade from the ceiling, creating an eerie lighting effect. The tune he was playing was called "Hey, Hey," and it knocked me out. It's a complicated guitar piece, full of blue notes, which are what you get by splitting a major and minor note. You usually start with the minor and then bend the note up toward the major, so it's somewhere between the two. . . . When I first heard Big Bill . . . I became convinced that all rock 'n' roll—and pop music too, for that matter—had sprung from this root.[2]

Broonzy's stunning virtuosity and the unforgettable image he presented in that dark, Belgian nightclub motivated Clapton to discover the roots of the music that he loved, and Clapton used what he had learned about Broonzy's music as he meshed the blues into the British rock music pioneered in the 1960s. What Clapton could not have known at the time, however, was that Broonzy had presented multiple professional identities throughout his long career: first as a rural, southern, migrant musician in the 1920s; then as a black pop entertainer in the 1930s and early 1940s; and, finally, as an exemplar of "the folk," embodying the ideals of folk, blues, and jazz revivalists in the late 1940s and 1950s.

In 1992, Clapton released one of the highest grossing albums of his lengthy and prestigious career, *Eric Clapton Unplugged*. Recorded live in Great Britain for an MTV audience, Clapton played a fourteen-song set covering old blues standards and new arrangements of his own work to a receptive audience. Featured in this performance was a tribute to one of his guitar heroes: a searing rendition of Big Bill Broonzy's virtuosic "Hey, Hey." Self-accompanied with an acoustic guitar, Clapton performed the song in a precise note-for-note reconstruction of how he had first heard Broonzy perform it thirty-seven years earlier. In effect, Clapton introduced a new audience to Broonzy, but only to one of Broonzy's several phases. The popularity of the album ensured that Broonzy's memory would live on in the musical world of solo acoustic folk blues. Clapton's influence on the public memory of Broonzy was enormous, as Clapton is now recognized as perhaps the greatest living blues guitarists. The *Unplugged* album won six Grammy Awards, including Album of the Year, and proved that Broonzy's musical legacy was still relevant thirty years after his death, even if it represented only one aspect of his multifaceted life in music.

Eric Clapton's career-long devotion to Broonzy exemplifies a kind of posthumous chapter in the narrative of Broonzy's life and legacy, as well as an important element of the history of the blues' growth in a transnational context. In public memory, Big Bill Broonzy's four-phased, thirty-year career has been defined by its last stage.[3] Before the late 1940s, most music criticism written about Broonzy focused on his extensive music career in Chicago as a veteran blues musician, his role as a "From Spirituals to Swing" alumnus, and his frequent performances in New York.[4] By the 1950s, as Broonzy transitioned from black pop to white folk, his public image changed as well.

Focusing on the last decade of Broonzy's career, chroniclers have tended to minimize his successes as a black pop music entertainer. When British guitarists such as Clapton, Jeff Beck, and Keith Richards first heard Broonzy's blues in the 1950s, they were quickly convinced that he was one of the greatest of all country blues singers and guitarists. And yet the Broonzy they "discovered" in the 1950s barely resembled the sophisticated urban blues pioneer of the 1930s. Those who have remembered Broonzy's importance to black audiences—such as Muddy Waters and the blues historian Mike Rowe—have been silenced by the consistent focus on the last decade of his career, when he became the embodiment of white American and European

Broonzy performing in his country-blues-as-folk style, ca. mid-1950s. This is the Broonzy that Eric Clapton was introduced to. Courtesy of the Frank Driggs Collection at Jazz at Lincoln Center.

interest in the folk, protojazz, and primitive blues. Key elements of Broonzy's historical legacy reflect as much about these culture brokers' worldviews as they do about the artistic significance of Broonzy's music.

First, by positioning Broonzy within the realm of the Mississippi Delta blues tradition, folklorists such as Alan Lomax tended to focus on his experience as a victim of southern racism in the Jim Crow South. Through

Broonzy, these culture brokers discovered the blues' intricate connections to race and the black experience in the United States. Central to their interpretation of Broonzy was a tendency to focus on his "otherness"—his large physique, his southern roots, his race consciousness, his ability to survive in Chicago—in a manner that overshadowed Broonzy's own agency as an architect of black culture and that undervalued his importance to black audiences. These elements became key components for explaining Broonzy's importance to the white folklore community that Broonzy navigated near the end of his career, and to a certain extent, his memory has remained part of the folk-revival legacy ever since. As discussed in chapters 5 and 6, one of Broonzy's most important professional relationships in the United States was with the folklorist Alan Lomax. For almost two decades, these two giants of American music culture kept close tabs on each other, often communicating and corresponding on both personal and professional matters. Lomax was not alone in his interest in and close association with Broonzy.

While Alan Lomax became acquainted with Broonzy following a "From Spirituals to Swing" concert in 1939, by the mid-1940s, Broonzy and Lomax were corresponding through a series of letters in which Broonzy laid out for Lomax his story and influence within Chicago's blues community. Through their correspondence, Lomax recognized Broonzy's value as a veteran of Chicago's music world and as someone with deep connections to the Arkansas and Mississippi River bottoms in which Lomax had conducted fieldwork throughout the period.

The 1947 recording *Blues in the Mississippi Night*, produced by Lomax and featuring Broonzy, Peter "Memphis Slim" Chatman, and John Lee "Sonny Boy" Williamson, offers oral interviews and music intended to explain the blues from three of Chicago's most celebrated bluesmen.[5] But Lomax had more in mind than simple descriptions of the blues' origins and meanings. In reality, Lomax applied his philosophy of folk music collecting, his political beliefs, and his conception of American history to *Blues in the Mississippi Night*, and these three Chicago bluesmen were, for a brief moment, his muses. What Lomax had intended to discover the night of the recording was not an investigation into the ethnomusicology of the blues but, rather, an investigation into one of his true passions—the interplay of race and music in the development of culture. To Lomax, "Here at last, black working-class men had talked frankly, sagaciously, and with open resentment about the inequities of the Southern system of racial segregation and exploitation. An exposé of that system was on record. Also, a new order of eloquence in documentation had emerged out of a situation where members of a tradition could present their own case to each other. They had themselves stated why and how the blues had arisen in their homeland in the Mississippi Delta."[6] More than just a recording of three commercially successful Chicago blues veterans reminiscing on life and music in the South, *Blues in the Mississippi Night* captures what Lomax hoped would be "a real breakthrough" into "a dark period of history that had previously been hidden."[7] Lomax, of course, was familiar with Broonzy's overtly antisegregationist songs and race consciousness, and he knew that with a "midnight bottle of bourbon," he could push Broonzy into a "Socratic Role" that would pull "his young friends into deeper and deeper levels of the drama."[8] Lomax intended this conversation to bring the "Mississippi night" to New York by capturing unprecedented revelations about racism in the United States.

Filled with frightening anecdotes about the struggles and hardships of southern blacks of the period, *Blues in the Mississippi Night* claims to capture on record the perspectives of blacks themselves about life in the United States. Through their discussions and performances of protoblues, levee-camp and field hollers, prison songs, and gang-labor shouts, the three bluesmen discussed southern racism's intrinsic connection to poverty, exploitive agriculture, gang labor, prison culture, and mob violence experienced by blacks throughout the Jim Crow South. With humor, storytelling, and song, these blues giants offered a glimpse into the sordid world that had driven all three of them—not to mention hundreds of thousands of others—out of the South along the paths of the Great Migrations and into Chicago.

Of course, Lomax knew that these interviews would be highly provocative given the racial mores of the period. The sense of danger that this recording created essentially bolstered Lomax's reputation as a folklorist willing to push the edge of race relations in the United States and gave the project unprecedented appeal to Lomax's audience of folklorists. These recordings posed a threat to all three of the African Americans who participated; they believed their respective southern families might be in danger from such revelatory interviews. Broonzy and his band, at first, were extremely reluctant to answer Lomax's questions, and Lomax had to ply the men with liquor to get them to participate more fully. Not until 1959, moreover, did any record company agree to release the recordings commercially. Even then, Broonzy and Williamson—both deceased—and Chatman were given pseudonyms in hopes of protecting their southern family members from any backlash the album might create.[9]

What is most striking about the recordings is what Lomax failed to transmit. All three of these men were incredibly important architects in the construction of Chicago's blues community, yet Lomax showed no interest in discussing their new lives in Bronzeville. Broonzy had left the South because of Jim Crow—the very subject of Lomax's investigation—and had created one of the most important careers in Chicago blues. Rather than portray Broonzy, Chatman, and Williamson as active agents in the creation of Chicago's vibrant blues culture, Lomax chose instead to introduce these men as victims of the South's system of apartheid, whose personal lives existed outside the law. Lomax knew that the sophisticated urban sounds and personas these men produced at the time did not mesh with his romanticized ideas about the Deep South and folk music. Therefore, he constructed the conversation and its presentation so as to make each of the narrators seem as if he had just left the plantation fields of Arkansas, Tennessee, and Mississippi.

> I wasn't sure exactly where I was and I didn't much care. The man who owned the little country tonk [honky tonk] was named Hamp, they told me. This was Hamp's place, somewhere out in the Arkansas backland across the river from Memphis. It was a one-room shanty store that doubled as a bar room at night, a place where the people who made the cotton in this fat land came to dance and gamble and commit a bit of friendly mayhem. . . . It had been a refuge for the three blues musicians and myself—"where nobody *gonna* bother us," they said. "No laws or nothin."[10]

There is little doubt that Lomax was quite familiar with the type of place described in the preceding excerpt. But this recorded conversation would have never happened in the Deep South, where these men came of age. What is more, in great detail, these three men openly revealed specific ways in which African Americans resisted the open racism of the region, yet by the end of their conversation and only "for an instant," they "understood each other." To Lomax, capturing these gripping and powerful testimonies had eroded "the absurdity, the perversity, and the madness" that held sway over the Jim Crow South, "a beautiful and fecund land, rich in food and genius and good living and song, yet turned into a sort of purgatory by fear." This sort of purgatory, whether in the Arkansas Delta, on the bustling streets of Chicago, or in the booming nightclubs of New York, had not disappeared in the United States of 1947, and "the brutalizing lies of race" never lost their "fallacious dignity" for these three African Americans. Broonzy, Williamson, and Chatman were born in an openly segregated society that reminded them daily and in humiliating fashion of their subordinate position in U.S.

society. Only Chatman lived long enough to witness the limited fruits of the civil rights movement, as Broonzy and Williamson spent their entire lives within the nation's system of segregation.[11]

Lomax and Broonzy continued to correspond until Broonzy's death in 1958. They also spent a significant amount of time together in Europe in the 1950s, when Broonzy became one of the first blues artists to tour Europe. The two remained close friends through the 1950s, as Broonzy's career transitioned into its final blues-as-folk phase. In 1993, thirty-five years after Broonzy's death, Alan Lomax finally published his fifty-years-in-the-making magnum opus, *The Land Where the Blues Began*. Included within the book's five hundred pages on Mississippi Delta folk culture is a revelatory chapter titled "Big Bill of the Blues." Relying on years of interviews and correspondence, Lomax carves out a history of Big Bill Broonzy that has added to Broonzy's historical memory.

With *The Land Where the Blues Began*, Lomax attempts to firmly situate Broonzy within the Mississippi Delta blues tradition, and ultimately within the folk music tradition, through the association of folklore with the Mississippi Delta blues culture. The first half of the chapter "Big Bill of the Blues" retraces Broonzy's southern past through careful discussions of his family, his early music tutelage, his discovery of the opposite sex, his short career as a country musician, his brief stint as a country preacher, and his conscription into the AEF during World War I. This material is peppered with discussions of the inequality and poverty from which Broonzy had escaped in an attempt to cement his role within the "cult of authenticity" and its reliance on musicians' "otherness."[12]

For Lomax, Broonzy's authenticity as a "true folk composer" derived from three elements. First, Broonzy had survived "all the humiliation and injustice" suffered by African Americans in the United States with an "unbroken . . . spirit" and "undistorted" "vision of life," and more than any other bluesman of the period, he had "struck back against Jim Crow" with his music.[13] For Lomax, then, Broonzy's appeal was deeply rooted in American racism and stemmed from the respectability and dignity that his life experience and personality commanded from all who knew him. Lomax portrays Broonzy as a victim of racism and the unscrupulous practices of Chicago's recording industry, which had "cheated black country bumpkins" at nearly every turn.[14] Second, Broonzy had fled the South to settle in an often violent and rapacious city filled with blues musicians who had "lived by violence and died by violence."[15] As a southern rube turned South Side blues celebrity, Broonzy had also survived the "ghetto jungles of Chicago and Harlem . . . basically untouched, still merrily-hearted, strong, and dignified."[16] Essentially, Broonzy was a passive agent who was "lucky to be alive," lucky to have survived in an exotic world filled with the "otherness" of less fortunate African Americans who "came to Chicago without education or skills to help them."[17] Never mind that Broonzy had worked extremely hard for nearly two decades, traveling the country honing his craft and developing one of the most important blues careers of the twentieth century. In Lomax's portrayal, such a victim could not possibly be an active agent in the development of black vernacular and popular music for black audiences that respected his talents and role in the community. Finally, what made Broonzy authentic in Lomax's blues romanticism was his large, imposing physique. Throughout his chapter on Broonzy, Lomax propounds the idea that Broonzy's "otherness" was manifested through his physical presence (six foot three, 215 pounds). For Lomax, this "otherness," along with Broonzy's undying luck, were at the crux of his survival abilities, suggesting that both Broonzy's intimidating frame and his charming ways were much more responsible for his success as a Chicago migrant and bluesmen than were his musical skill, intelligence, and crafty determination. It also suggests that Lomax, at five foot eleven, may have been intimidated by Broonzy's large build and most likely fascinated by his dark skin and handsomeness. Lomax's descriptions of Broonzy's physicality and charm, moreover, highlight Lomax's interest in an exoticized notion of the violence, sexuality, and physicality of black Chicagoans, while at the same time corroborating Lomax's stereotyped definition of the kind of person who could create authentic blues.

The Big Bill Broonzy who emerges from the pages of Lomax's work does not reflect the "Big Bill" persona that Broonzy had crafted for two decades in black Chicago. Though Lomax does offer accounts of Broonzy's most active years as a recording artist, he portrays Broonzy as someone who was continually at odds with his success, economic conditions, the music industry, studio musicians, and race relations in the United States. Ultimately, Lomax's depiction of Broonzy obscures his role as a cultural actor shaping sounds and tastes for black and white audiences with diligence, determination, and intelligence.

Lomax has been the most influential stakeholder in Broonzy's public memory, but beginning in the 1950s, jazz writers also began to mold Broonzy's image. For jazz scholars and enthusiasts, Broonzy was a source of excitement because he represented a figure who challenged one of their earliest misconceptions about the blues—that it was a kind of evolutionary precursor to jazz. As jazz writers and critics in Europe and the United States began systematically and intellectually chronicling the history of jazz in the 1930s and '40s, they quickly discovered that blues was not, in fact, a precursor to jazz but, rather, was a parallel genre with a history of its own. Broonzy's career and recordings helped them to this realization.

As New Orleans jazz of the 1920s evolved into the big band and swing jazz of the 1930s and 1940s, Europeans and white Americans took a much greater interest in black music. A crowd of young, middle-class whites in the 1940s had fallen in love with the up-tempo, swinging style of the big band jazz that American jazz musicians such as Count Basie were performing in dance halls and performance theaters in the United States and across Europe. Yet some jazz fans found this new jazz to be a commercially oriented and diluted version of the older and purer jazz hailing from New Orleans. This rift became evident as jazz scholars and enthusiasts of the period began writing about the fundamental differences between the two sounds, with some arguing for a return to the more traditional New Orleans style (which incidentally had been recorded primarily in Chicago during the 1920s). These "traditionalists" argued, moreover, that real fans of jazz—unlike swing and big band devotees—should know the history of jazz and its antecedents. Most of these scholars looked toward the blues as a precursor to New Orleans jazz, because of the many harmonic and rhythmic similarities between the two. As these traditionalists studied the history of New Orleans jazz, however, they discovered that the blues was a different genre with a separate history. Part of Broonzy's public memory is tied up in jazz writers' understandings of this distinction.

Broonzy was first covered in a jazz publication in the 1940s, when his career was beginning to change from its black-pop phase to his role as a representative of white folk culture. In 1946, Broonzy appeared in the Art Hodes-edited jazz magazine the *Jazz Record*, under a featured article titled "Baby I Done Got Wise." Written by Broonzy (the article does not mention any contributors but surely included a ghost writer), the article features a three-and-a-half page biography of the famed Chicago blues great. The article begins with a brief description of Broonzy's childhood and introduction to music in Arkansas; the majority of the text focuses on Broonzy's important role in shaping Chicago's blues community. The piece offers detailed accounts of Broonzy's experiences navigating black Chicago's incredibly vibrant music scene, describing many of Broonzy's professional relationships as well as the recording companies he had worked for, the venues where he performed, and his experiences in New York as a "From Spirituals to Swing" artist. Moreover, the article offers anecdotal glimpses of Broonzy's experience in black Chicago, especially the often violent and unscrupulous world of Chicago's underground blues culture.

Essentially, "Baby I Done Got Wise" reflects how jazz enthusiasts viewed the development of Chicago's music scene and its deep connection to New Orleans jazz. As jazz enthusiasts began studying and interpreting Broonzy's career, the idea that the black music of Chicago derived in some way from New Orleans remained at the core of their investigations. Like Lomax, Hodes was interested in the violent and exotic world that had produced so many of these urban musicians, even going as far as to print Broonzy's anecdote about a rent party that turned into a riotous affair featuring brandished knifes, broken furniture, and stolen whiskey.[18]

Across the Atlantic Ocean, jazz writers were also discovering the importance of the blues' parallel path to jazz, and Broonzy became an invaluable voice in their accounts. As Broonzy toured Europe in the 1950s, he befriended many European jazz critics and blues revivalists interested in his story. At every turn, Broonzy tried his best to explain the parallel paths between jazz and blues. By doing so, he met someone who became another close friend, the Belgian jazz critic Yannick Bruynoghe. Bruynoghe help Broonzy write his 1955 autobiography, *Big Bill Blues*. For several years before 1955, Broonzy corresponded with Bruynoghe in a series of letters, sharing anecdotes, remembrances, and mementos from the past sixty-two years of his life, which the Belgian jazz writer then incorporated into a fascinating, if limited, portrait of a blues legend.

Organized into three chapters, *Big Bill Blues* is a short book documenting Broonzy's multifaceted life in all its splendor and hardship: his life in the South, his experience as a World War I veteran, his participation in the Great Migration, his participation within black Chicago and its music culture, his love of women and vice, his interpretations of race in the United States, his involvement in taking blues to Europe, his musical repertoire and influences. But such a broad stroke is undoubtedly filled with holes that have greatly affected Broonzy's historical legacy and the public's memory of him.

Taken as a whole, *Big Bill Blues* employs similar analytical devices as those used by folklorists such as Lomax. There are far more discussions and revelatory anecdotes about rural, southern life in the first two-thirds of the book than about black urban life in Chicago. Similar to the work of folklorists, Bruynoghe and Broonzy employ many devices demonstrating Broonzy's legitimacy and authenticity as a Mississippi bluesman.[19] One reviewer finished the book wholly believing that Broonzy "was a country blues singer" whose "memories are charged with the everyday intimacy that belongs to country life."[20] Indeed, discussions of Jim Crow, white southerners, agriculture, southern culture, and southern labor run throughout chapters 1 and 2. The majority of the text attempts to firmly place Broonzy in the Mississippi Delta tradition by focusing on his early life and the creative impetus behind his prolific songwriting. Both folklorists and jazz enthusiasts of the 1950s, then, were committed to discovering the next great authentic Mississippi Delta bluesman. Both Broonzy and Bruynoghe seemed aware of that desire.

The book opens with Broonzy explaining the importance of his story and the need for a printed work on his life. Broonzy argues, "The reason I'm writing this book is because I think that everybody would like to know the real truth about Negroes singing and playing in Mississippi. I'm one of the oldest still alive and I want everybody to know that we Mississippi musicians care just as much about our way of singing and playing as anyone else."[21] Right away, the reader is presented with a revelation that becomes ironic when juxtaposed with the actual facts of Broonzy's life. First, Broonzy was born in Pine Bluff, Arkansas, in 1893 but moved outside of Little Rock at age eight, first to Langdale and then to Scott's Crossing, a small agricultural community located twenty miles outside the state's capital.[22] The fact that Broonzy describes himself as one of the last of a great line of Mississippi bluesmen is a direct reference to white folklorists' growing "cult of authenticity" and plays to jazz enthusiasts' fascination with a romanticized version of black music history. More than any other subgenre of the blues, the vaunted Mississippi Delta style, associated with Delta luminaries such as Charley Patton, Son House, and the legendary Robert Johnson, became fetishized and sought after by folklorists, collectors, and enthusiasts because of its inherent "authentic" quality.[23] The Mississippi Delta lineage, moreover, could be traced forward in time to the extremely popular and prevalent style of Chicago blues greats such as Muddy Waters and Howlin' Wolf.

The first chapter of *Big Bill Blues* carries readers from Broonzy's life in the segregated U.S. South through war-torn Europe to his participation in the Great Migration, revealing the complexity of his experiences. More than just a pioneer of Chicago blues and a black celebrity musician, Broonzy is portrayed with imagery centered on his southern roots and hardscrabble life: the son of a former slave and a free black, a country musician for possessive and controlling white land owners, a country preacher and family man, a veteran of World War I, a southern migrant, a borderline alcoholic, a recording-industry pioneer, and an urban laborer. In the same manner as Alan Lomax, jazz scholars of the 1950s saw their political and social viewpoints reflected in Broonzy's experience. Their histories, while considering the aspects of Broonzy's life related to race, focused more squarely on the music of the South and Broonzy's connection to its rich past. Both Bruynoghe and Broonzy understood their target audience and realized that firmly centering Broonzy's legacy in this way would solidify his importance to the history of Mississippi blues and black vernacular music traditions. From the very beginning, the authors of *Big Bill Blues* constructed the book to cement the "truth" about blues from Mississippi. Central to this approach was an examination of the Jim Crow South and the complex machinations of black southerners' daily lives. With the stroke of a pen, the veteran Chicago blues entertainer and recording artist whose southern musical heritage stemmed from Arkansas became a Mississippi Delta bluesman.

Big Bill Blues is the first in-depth biographical study of any bluesman and an incredibly important text in establishing Broonzy's public memory. Bruynoghe's approach to organizing the autobiography around themes of the U.S. South reflect larger trends in history and social science scholarship on the United States that was rewriting the history of African Americans and their culture.[24] As new audiences of jazz enthusiasts in Europe began engaging with African American culture, Bruynoghe knew that investigating the nuances of life in the Jim Crow South—especially by adding dangerous and provocative elements of black music's past and Mississippi roots—would make Broonzy's story all the more compelling.

Big Bill Blues offers more than just evidence of jazz and blues critics' widespread interest in the Mississippi Delta blues tradition. The book also emphasizes its subject's political ideology. Throughout Broonzy's long career, he had composed some of the most openly antiracist music of the twentieth century. The songs that Bruynoghe chose to discuss suggest that he understood the white blues and jazz enthusiasts who would be interested in reading Broonzy's autobiography; therefore, the book's song selection offers examinations of Broonzy's then-current phase as a vanguard of the blues-as-folk tradition. Roberta Schwartz has argued that "Broonzy's reception as a representative of the early, primitive blues required some selective memory on the part of critics, collectors and cognoscenti," suggesting that this new audience chose to ignore Broonzy's career as a jazz-tinged blues crooner.[25] That was the Broonzy that Bruynoghe's target audience wanted and expected, and he was willing to give it to them even if it masked important facets of Broonzy's long career. For instance, the second chapter, "My Songs," analyzes more than fifteen songs, including "Big Bill Blues," "When Do I Get to Be Called a Man," "WPA Rag," "Looking Up at Down," "Black, Brown,

Escaping the Folk 159

and White." Here Bruynoghe's interest in Broonzy's political music is readily apparent, as he seemed to have selected the majority of Broonzy's most political songs. "When Do I Get to Be Called a Man" and "Black, Brown, and White," for example, were highly evocative for their direct commentary and criticism of racism in the United States. What is so striking is the limited glimpse of Broonzy's vast and broad repertoire offered in the second chapter. By the 1950s, he had written and recorded hundreds of songs. Moreover, the chapter offers no discussion of the urban blues and Tin Pan Alley songs of the interwar period, with their often obscenely sexual and openly misogynistic lyrics, such as 1937's "Horny Frog" or 1938's "Flat Foot Susie and Her Flat Yes Yes," which Broonzy had recorded by the dozens for some of the country's most successful record labels.[26]

Big Bill Blues, like *The Land Where the Blues Began*, also suggests that Broonzy's otherness—his apparent affability and outgoing deference to Jim Crow life and his large physical size—had safely guided this bluesman through difficult environments and situations. Bruynoghe implied that Broonzy's physical presence defined him and guided his survival, suggesting, moreover, that he was as imposing physically as he was emotionally and intellectually. In Bruynoghe's *Big Bill Blues*, Broonzy's personality and physical presence served as the means by which he commanded respect and formed lucrative relationships within Chicago's blues community. Of course, Broonzy was in fact large and was addressed affectionately among his peers in Chicago and across the country as "Big Bill." But such a strong emphasis on his physical presence masks his intellectual prowess as a brilliant and successful architect of twentieth-century American culture.

Despite the autobiography's strong focus on Broonzy's southern roots and Mississippi Delta lineage, the third chapter demonstrates that Bruynoghe's was equally interested in investigating an "unknown Chicagoan world" and the dozens of relationships Broonzy had made within Chicago's blues culture.[27] Chapter 3 reveals the scores of friendships Broonzy had fostered throughout his long career as an active participant in the Windy City's blues community. With its focus on the relationships Broonzy established as a pioneer of urban, Chicago blues, the final chapter of *Big Bill Blues* contradicts the overall theme of the autobiography by demonstrating that Chicago had really sustained Broonzy's successes.

In a haphazard and nonchronological manner in the chapter, Broonzy and Bruynoghe provide rich details of the black blues world that jazz enthusiasts and blues revivalists in the United States and Europe so desperately wanted to understand. To Bruynoghe, a jazz writer and critic, the blues was a key component to a complete understanding of jazz, and if Broonzy could share general information about the blues (and hokum and boogie-woogie) world and recording culture in Chicago, then perhaps Bruynoghe could gain a better understanding of American jazz. The chapter only briefly discusses the blues clubs, dance halls, rent parties, recording studios, and social gatherings that made Broonzy and Chicago synonymous with blues culture.

Rather than describe the structure of Chicago's blues culture, Bruynoghe offers interesting vignettes of Broonzy's relationships with Chicago blues celebrities such as Tampa Red, Memphis Slim, Sonny Boy Williamson, Memphis Minnie Douglas, Lillian Green, Lonnie Johnson, Maceo Merriweather, Sleepy John Estes, and many others. Ultimately, the chapter presents whimsical and limited glimpses into the day-to-day workings of performance, recording, rehearsal, and musicians' lifestyles. In rich sentimental detail, Broonzy described to Bruynoghe the physical and emotional characteristics of each of his closest friends, suggesting that they had remained alive in his mind long after their deaths. This focus on characters further ensured that readers could relate to Broonzy's experience. What emerges from these reminiscences are Broonzy's personal reactions to the evolving Chicago blues community, the death of his friends, the long hours he spent traveling around the country, and the high value he placed on friendship. Collectively, Bruynoghe presents Broonzy's blues world in Chicago as one of passion, danger, creativity, humor, camaraderie, and exuberance, fused with a highly exotic, folksy, and generally romanticized depiction of the world of Chicago blues.

Unlike folklorists' often socially and politically driven investigations, Bruynoghe was interested in Broonzy's community and his importance to black Chicago's music culture. Chapter 3 of *Big Bill Blues* served as a tribute to Broonzy's importance to black blues and black audiences. But the manner in which Bruynoghe wrote about black Chicago revealed his keen interest in the "otherness" associated with the more exotic elements of black Chicago's rough and tawdry blues culture.

Only one chapter in *Big Bill Blues* reveals an exotic blues world full of black blues for black audiences with rent parties, theater and club performances, recording studios, and talent competitions in a city where African Americans were free to consume alcohol at Negro League baseball games and to fish in Lake Michigan.[28] To be sure, Chicago was home to racism and de facto segregation. And Broonzy may have been a "country bluesman," born in Mississippi and raised in farm communities around Little Rock, but in

1955, he had lived in Chicago for thirty years. Trying to label Broonzy as a Mississippi Delta bluesman is as specious as labeling Robert Johnson as a Chicago bluesman because he performed and recorded "Sweet Home Chicago."

The final pages of the autobiography's epilogue suggest that Broonzy held his own ideas about the public's memory of him, and he wanted the book to be the key for unlocking his importance to future generations. Broonzy writes, "As for me, I would love to pick up a book and read a story about Big Bill Broonzy. I wouldn't care if it's just a story about how I live or how drunk I was the last time that they saw Big Bill. . . . But when you write about me, please don't say I'm a jazz musician. Don't say I'm a musician or a guitar player—just write that Big Bill was a well-known blues singer and player and has recorded 260 blues songs from 1925 up till 1952."[29] As much as Broonzy may have wanted to steer his own public memory in a particular direction in the early 1950s, individuals who held their own understandings of his importance were quickly crafting his legacy, and he knew it.

The epilogue of *Big Bill Blues* documents Broonzy's frustration with how enthusiasts and folklorists of black vernacular music had portrayed Broonzy's legacy. Bruynoghe's choice to include Broonzy's lament seems to contradict his own work and intellectual agenda as a jazz critic. The language is clear and direct. Broonzy does not want to be remembered as a "jazz musician," as European enthusiasts understood him. Nor does he want to be remembered as a "musician or a guitar player" in the way that white American folklorists had intended. Rather, Broonzy wishes to be remembered as a "blues singer and player," who, above all, was creatively and commercially successful for nearly thirty years. He wants to be remembered as a good friend who had helped pioneer Chicago blues and was "liked by all the blues singers."[30] Throughout the epilogue, fascinatingly titled "Envoi," Broonzy chooses his words carefully. In effect, Bruynoghe was addressing several key elements that were shaping Broonzy's career and memory at that moment. Through their close correspondence, Broonzy convinced Bruynoghe that the details of his life beyond music were just as interesting and important to history as his career in music was.

First published in 1955 in London by Casell, the autobiography received republication rights in Brussels and Paris and again in London in 1957, as part of the Jazz Book Club series.[31] *Big Bill Blues* was marketed as a jazz-related European publication for almost a decade. Essentially, Broonzy's autobiography represented a study of what Europeans understood as an element of the larger jazz spectrum.

Bruynoghe visited Chicago in 1957 shortly after the book's publication, once Broonzy was left voiceless after undergoing the risky operation intended to remove the cancer in his throat. When Bruynoghe arrived, he found Broonzy as cheerful and warm as ever, despite his bad health. Bruynoghe recalled, "My first call in town was of course to Big Bill. I could not recognize the voice at the other end of the wire. It was Bill, after the operation that mutilated his vocal chords. A few hours later I was at his flat, located on South Parkway, just opposite the Regal Theatre. Fortunately, Bill is physically unchanged; just as wonderful and young looking as ever, and in excellent spirits. A short while later, some other guests joined the party: Little Brother Montgomery, Memphis Slim, his wife and four kids, and Tampa Red."[32] With Big Bill Broonzy as his tour guide, Bruynoghe was able to venture into "rather rough" Chicago neighborhoods and step behind the velvet ropes of blues clubs such as Silvio's, Ricky's Show Lounge, The 708, the Green Door, and Smithy's.[33] Through Bruynoghe's correspondence with Broonzy, the Belgian jazz writer had been introduced to a world that seemed unimaginable: a place where all of his blues and jazz heroes mingled openly in the city. Bruynoghe was mesmerized as he shook hands and watched the performances of Broonzy's friends such as Little Walter, Howlin' Wolf, and Muddy Waters and marveled at the seemingly exotic world of which these blues masters were a part.[34]

Blues writing began to come into its own as a genre of music criticism because jazz writers started to move away from the historical narrative that linked blues to jazz in favor of positioning the blues as a separate genre altogether. This transition marked a significant shift in how the blues was beginning to be understood and marketed. A new generation of blues revivalists began to challenge the idea that the blues was a backwater derivation of traditional jazz. The successful studies of former jazz traditionalists turned blues "revivalists," such as Samuel Charters's *The Country Blues* and Paul Oliver's *Blues Fell This Morning*, seemed to suggest that the moment was right for Bruynoghe to update the autobiography for an American edition of *Big Bill Blues* that firmly planted Broonzy within the "country" blues tradition. Oak Publications in New York printed the American edition of *Big Bill Blues* in 1964, six years after Broonzy's death.[35] The American edition indicates that Bruynoghe felt the need to address critical issues arising from the first jazz-based edition. Blues revivalists were beginning to approach the blues in a wholly different manner than Bruynoghe had attempted with Broonzy. Indeed, the blues' increasingly literary audience and growing intellectual community had high standards for investigations of the blues. Jazz critics, scholars, and readers had convinced the autobiography's coauthor that Big Bill Broonzy may have not told Bruynoghe the complete truth in their series of correspondence. To this, Bruynoghe quips, "More than being the truth about the blues, [*Big Bill Blues*] is the truth about a man whose psychology it perfectly reflects. This man having been one of the great blues representatives of this time, it is also his truth about the period and all that made his life and his blues."[36] In response to these questions, Bruynoghe corroborated new evidence and added footnotes in the American edition, especially concerning the dates of Broonzy's recordings, the age of his friends, and Broonzy's birth date. Rather than portraying Broonzy as a smart and savvy self-promoter, Bruynoghe's additions construe Broonzy as something of an unreliable narrator with selective memory, willing to embellish his history for a new audience.

More importantly, the 1964 edition offers a new fourteen-page foreword meant to stand as a brief and objective biography documenting Broonzy's fascinating life and career, in the hope of providing a similar analytical framework offered by other published blues studies. Bruynoghe commissioned the jazz critic, Folkways record producer, and *New York Times* critic Charles Edward Smith to map out Broonzy's long career in the foreword. Smith cements Broonzy's historical memory with an analysis rooted in black history, ethnomusicology, and the history of the blues. To be sure, Smith situates Broonzy firmly within the realm of the then-popular "country blues" by tracing his rural roots to the blues in Chicago.[37] Yet most of Smith's documented sources rely on the same published works of jazz critics and folklorists who interviewed Broonzy throughout the 1940s and 1950s. These resources, moreover, should be contextualized within Broonzy's experience and audience of that specific phase of his career.[38] For example, many of Smith's conclusions falsely dismiss Broonzy's early commercial success among black audiences and the race-record industry in Chicago.

Essentially, Smith's introduction to the American edition negates the earlier periods of Broonzy's career, even stating that Broonzy "was hardly known outside the ground floor operation of the 'Rhythm and Blues,'" which had defined Broonzy's "Big Bill" black-pop image.[39] Smith also argues that only in 1939, when Broonzy appeared at Carnegie Hall's "From Spirituals to Swing" concert, did "blues and jazz enthusiasts" recognize Broonzy's "unforgettable" talent as one of the "great country blues singers."[40] Only upon Broonzy's discovery by whites, that is, did his career and music become recognizably important. This element of "discovery" figures prominently in folklorists', blues revivalists', and jazz enthusiasts' approach to studying black vernacular music. Moreover, it serves as key evidence for the perpetuation of what one scholar has called the "cult of authenticity."[41]

As previous chapters in this book discuss, by 1939, Broonzy could be described as a seasoned performer within black Chicago's rent-party, blues-club, and black-theater circuits. He was not, as Smith suggests, an unknown entity. But as jazz scholars pushed the boundaries for new audiences of black blues, Broonzy's music remained popular to a certain degree, even if it resembled the blues-as-folk element of the folk music revival and even if it omitted earlier stages of his long career. The evidence Smith does provide of Broonzy's success and popularity among black audiences in the 1950s occurred long after the height of Broonzy's popularity in black Chicago.[42]

Smith and Bruynoghe were only beginning to understand that the blues represented a parallel musical genre with a history of its own. The country blues featured on the highly coveted recordings of the late 1920s and early 1930s was only one phase of blues history. Smith's and Bruynoghe's studies represent mainstream white culture's discovery of a black vernacular tradition rather than an understanding of these discoveries on their own terms. In reality, the blues was originally constructed, performed, and marketed as black music for black audiences, and as with all audiences, the aesthetic tastes of African Americans continually evolved.

The literature of this period shows that European jazz enthusiasts and emerging blues revivalists were equally attracted to Broonzy's otherness, especially as his career progressed from the 1940s to the 1950s. Article after article in European jazz and blues magazines in the 1950s retell the same stories and anecdotes covered in the autobiography and from Lomax's work. Through Broonzy, folklorists and jazz scholars and the respective communities they served discovered that race, the U.S. South, and the African American experience were inextricably linked to the blues, its culture, and black history. This linkage added a new element to Broonzy's "otherness."

By the time that folklorists and jazz enthusiasts discovered Broonzy in the 1950s, Broonzy was well aware of this paradigm that linked the blues, American racism, and African American history, and he discussed these elements almost as easily as he performed his music. Ultimately, a large part of Broonzy's historical memory is tied to revelations concerning the connection between black vernacular music and race in the United States. European jazz journalists and critics helped craft this legacy as they interviewed Broonzy throughout the decade.[43] Posthumous biographical articles and anecdotes from these magazines followed throughout the 1960s. The blues that Broonzy loved so much had become an integral part of explaining the history of folk music in the South and of jazz then popularized in Chicago and New York. Through these media, Broonzy's public memory was constructed in a way that firmly planted him in the last stage of his career.

As blues scholarship began to solidify as a field in its own right, the composite picture of Broonzy created by music critics gained nuance and detail. One of the first authors to address the dialectic between the last stage of Broonzy's career as a folk artist and his popularity as an urban black bluesman among black audiences was the Folkways Records field researcher, jazz writer, and burgeoning blues historian Samuel Barclay Charters.[44] Charters explains, "There were two Big Bills. There was the Big Bill who described himself as 'a well-known blues singer and player and has recorded 260 blues songs up till 1952,' and there was the Big Bill who could stand up at a concert stage and sing work songs he'd learned from phonograph records and back country blues he'd picked up from books on country music, and fascinate the audience just talking about himself. They were both the same man, but one was a singer entertaining a Negro audience and the other was a man entertaining a white audience."[45] Charters's groundbreaking study of what he describes as "country blues" attempts to trace the emergence of rural black music in the southern United States as it evolved from a "rich confusion of music from the fields" into a popularly recorded "fabric of Negro life itself."[46] First published in 1959, Charters's work examines the lives of several vanguards of the country blues tradition, including Blind Lemon Jefferson, Leroy Carr, Lonnie Johnson, Robert Johnson, and one chapter on the popular Chicago bluesman "Big Bill Broomsley."[47]

Charters situates Broonzy's history within the evolution of the blues as an artist emerging out of the reorganization of the record industry following the catastrophic collapse during the Great Depression. Charters introduces Broonzy as a key element of a newly developing style in Chicago and describes him as "one of the most prolific blues artists the record business had ever seen."[48] Rather than trying to cement Broonzy within the Mississippi Delta lineage, as folklorists and jazz researchers attempted, Charters understood that Broonzy belonged in a completely different category. In the course of about four pages, *The Country Blues* traces Broonzy's transformation between 1927 and 1947 from a "blues shouter in the grand tradition" (i.e., a solo male blues artist) to a "strutting" and "ingratiating" blues crooner, prolific songwriter, and leader of "four- and five-piece jazz and swing bands" (i.e., "Big Bill," urban blues pioneer).[49] To be sure, Charters recognized that Broonzy represented a newer and smarter urban blues musician, filled with "bitterness and cynicism" brought on by life in the city.[50]

The Country Blues argues that Broonzy was an important component of urban blues culture in Chicago whose success stemmed from his engagement with a newly emerging blues world and changing audiences. Charters seemed disturbed by the bifurcated nature of Broonzy's legacy. Indeed, Broonzy's autobiography clearly resonated within white folk and European jazz culture in its selective memory of Broonzy's commercial success in the 1930s and 1940s. Charters's book was the first systematic study of the blues and its history as a whole, and it sparked an enormous wave of research in a then-nascent field. Despite his groundbreaking approach to Broonzy's public memory, Charters shares culpability with other culture brokers and stewards of Broonzy's public memory by pigeonholing Broonzy, and other artists for that matter, into a generalized category known as "country blues," which cannot encompass his entire career. Even if Charters recognized the complexity of Broonzy's four-phased musical journey, his positioning of Broonzy within this blues subgenre ultimately added to other culture brokers' ignorance of the more commercial phase of Broonzy's career and its importance to black audiences.

Beginning in the late 1970s, scholars of the blues began to consider the blues' importance to the larger narrative of American history and changed their conception of blues history from a static focus on the blues' early period to a discussion of its diachronic evolution as a genre. The first full treatment of Broonzy as an important representative of Chicago blues for black audiences was published in 1973. The veteran British blues scholar and *Blues Unlimited* editor Mike Rowe offered blues enthusiasts a full-fledged treatment of Chicago's rich blues culture in his book *Chicago Blues*. In a little more than two hundred pages, employing methodology rooted in social history, Rowe documented the history of Chicago blues from its fledgling stage in the late 1920s through the 1960s, when blues' popularity began to decline among black audiences. Central to Rowe's understanding of Chicago blues is his assertion that "the nature of the blues is always the result of the mood of the black masses" and, more specifically, a "commercial interpretation of that feeling."[51] *Chicago Blues* appropriately places Broonzy at the center of Chicago blues from the 1920s until his death in 1958. Rather than offering "great man"-style analysis of Chicago's blues greats, Rowe's narrative focuses on the city and its blues scene. Although Rowe contextualizes black migrants' southern roots on a macro level, *Chicago Blues* focuses on Broonzy's contributions to the creation of Chicago's distinctive urban blues culture in a wholly different manner. Rowe's investigation of Broonzy's time in the city's rent parties, recording companies, blues clubs, dance halls, and performance theaters negated the "otherness"—the racism, danger, poverty, sexuality, physicality—that pervades the work of folklorists and jazz writers. In Rowe's hands, Broonzy becomes, for the first time, an important architect and leader of Chicago's blues community.

Rowe adds a new component to Broonzy's public memory—his role in successfully providing a pathway to other black musicians through mentorship and example. Throughout the text, Rowe indicates that Broonzy's "ingratiating exuberance" propelled him to become one of the most important vanguards for up-and-coming bluesmen of the period, including Little Walter, Jimmy Rogers, J. B. Lenoir, and Muddy Waters.[52] For instance, Rowe shares an anecdote involving the Arkansas migrant and blues musician Floyd Jones, who had been protected by Broonzy's intimate knowledge of the community. Jones had recently arrived in Chicago in 1945 and had become a regular performer on Maxwell Street. By 1945, Broonzy was an esteemed veteran of the community and frequently visited the Maxwell Street scene where he had once paid his dues. Floyd Jones had recently written and recorded a song about a labor strike at the Union Stockyards and the difficulties of city life. Broonzy witnessed Jones's impressive street performance of the new hit and instantly recognized the song's potential. Further, Broonzy understood quite well that Maxwell Street and Chicago's blues culture could be ruthless, and he suggested to the young bluesman, "you better play with me or somebody's going to take it."[53] Rowe uses this story to reveal Broonzy's importance to Chicago's blues community and younger musicians and his significance among African Americans eager to follow in his footsteps.

Perhaps more than any music writer, generations of younger musicians affected by Broonzy's music have affected his public memory. Jeff Beck and Eric Clapton, for example, have both credited Broonzy as an enormous influence on their introductions to the blues, therefore depicting him as an integral part of the pantheon of black blues artists with connections to British rock. More than the investigations of folklore, jazz, and blues researchers, this element of Broonzy's history is perhaps the most important component of his popular memory.

When Muddy Waters first arrived in Europe in October 1958, he was amazed to find how popular Broonzy had become among English audiences and how far removed they were from the changing form of Chicago blues of the period. British audiences expected to hear an acoustic guitar and Broonzy's smooth voice singing songs about plowing fields and damaging plantation floods as he shared anecdotes of his rural past. The folklorists, jazz traditionalists, and blues revivalists in Britain had only introduced their English audiences to Broonzy's older, solo male blues style then established within the folk music culture in the United States.[54] Muddy Waters and his band, however, were far removed from folk music. With a white Fender electric guitar and Otis Spann's billowing piano rhythms, Waters's first performances must have perplexed British audiences. The electrified, percussive, and wailing Delta guitar sound was light years from Broonzy's folk blues. Waters candidly admitted that British audiences mistakenly thought he "was a Big Bill Broonzy."[55] To British audiences, Broonzy had become an icon of black American blues. He represented the last of a great line of blues singers, and his music defined the blues and its history.

Muddy Waters equally paid respects to his mentor by fulfilling Chess Records' desire to fill the folk music void caused by Broonzy's death. In fact, he offered his first full-length LP as a posthumous tribute to his mentor, covering ten of Broonzy's most popular songs in Broonzy's folk-blues signature style.[56] Waters chose many of the songs Broonzy recorded between 1939 and 1950, including "When I Get to Drinking," "Hey, Hey," and the song Broonzy had offered the "From Spirituals to Swing" crowd, "Just a Dream."[57] Essentially, the song selections covered the blues-as-folk style as Broonzy's career transitioned into its last phase. Yet the Waters tribute reflected Waters's Chicago sounds as much as it did the blues-as-folk music of Broonzy. The formulaic "country" piano sound was featured, but so too was the wailing harmonica and up-tempo percussive beats of Waters's signature sound.

Nevertheless, no single blues musician has had more influence over Big Bill Broonzy's public memory than Muddy Waters. In a sense, their careers are enmeshed, and Muddy Waters in large part owes his success to Big Bill Broonzy. Broonzy mentored Waters as the young migrant began navigating Chicago's blues culture. He guided Waters through the difficulties of the city's blues world when Muddy arrived in the early 1940s and brokered important introductions in the same manner that Charlie Jackson, Blind Lemon Jefferson, and Blind Blake had done for Broonzy years before. More important, Broonzy provided Waters a template to follow as the younger musician pursued his career. Waters's biographer Robert Gordon has argued, "For decades Big Bill's character resonated with Muddy. 'You done made hits, you got a big name, the little fellow ain't nothing,' Muddy said in the 1970s about the star attitude. 'But Big Bill, he didn't care where you were from. He didn't look over you cause he been on records a long time. "Do your thing, stay with it, man. If you stay with it, you going to make it." That's what Big Bill told me. Mostly I try to be like him.'"[58] A famous photograph from the 1940s reveals a smiling Broonzy leaning on the shoulder of a young and nervously excited Muddy Waters.[59] Broonzy had helped Waters with gigs in Chicago, and as Broonzy's career waned, Muddy reciprocated, lending opening slots to Broonzy as often as he could. Even as Broonzy navigated new European audiences, he spoke highly of Waters, telling blues revivalists in Great Britain that Waters was an authentic representative of the Mississippi Delta tradition.[60] When Waters arrived England in 1958, Broonzy had already paved the way and helped to establish his celebrity there.[61]

Despite Muddy and Broonzy's relationship, white European musicians discovering the blues would hold even more influence over Broonzy than Broonzy's own protégé. They ensured that Broonzy's public memory would emphasize the last phase of his career at the expense of the other phases. A new generation of white English musicians had heard Broonzy on BBC radio and had even seen him on British television. Eventually, they would push rock music to a worldwide audience, but one of their first blues discoveries was the acoustic folk blues of Big Bill Broonzy. Broonzy's musicianship, especially his guitar playing, seemed to captivate a young, white British audience. Jeff Beck, the eccentric lead guitarist of the British rock groups the Yardbirds and the Jeff Beck Group, understood Broonzy's importance to the history of the blues and its connection to rock music. Beck recalled,

> My interest in blues began when the Chicago blues albums began to reach England. I grabbed them. Muddy Waters, Buddy Guy. . . . I think they're just great. There's a special way the guitars sound: sort of tinny and rough. The Chicago sound—it's like nothing else. I was listening to Big Bill Broonzy trying to accompany himself, and I loved that thumping crudeness and the stomping foot. It's the kind of guitar playing that sounded crude until you tried to play it—you know what I mean? Then I went backwards—I went back to the Deep South, the blues, Cajun music.[62]

Beck's description of Broonzy's style as crude and the emphasis placed on the stomping foot connote a sense of primitiveness that had been associated with the version of Big Bill Broonzy that John Hammond had featured in the "From Spirituals to Swing" concerts. Beck, in fact, was describing Broonzy's then-current image as the folk-blues performer represented in England during the latter phase of his career. Throughout the period, Broonzy was marketed across the United Kingdom as the last of the great Mississippi bluesmen.

In 1955, for example, Broonzy appeared on the British public television show *Downbeat* as a self-accompanied blues performer singing to an audience in a dimly lit nightclub.[63]

Beck's reflections, moreover, suggest another component of Broonzy's public memory that moves beyond his image as a popular recording artist, folk hero, or protojazz performer. Beck and many others were drawn to Broonzy because of his unparalleled skill as a guitarist. Nearly all of the culture brokers discussing Broonzy's life and career have tended to focus on his personal history, his race consciousness, the connections he held within the blues world, and his storytelling and stage presence. In the interpretation and reception of young British rock musicians, Broonzy figured as one of the best and most influential guitarists of the twentieth century and a critical link to the development of rock music.

Since Big Bill Broonzy's death in 1958, folklorists, jazz enthusiasts, blues scholars, and a younger generation of musicians influenced by him have defined Broonzy's legacy in a manner that reveals fascinating elements of twentieth-century culture. The intersections of race consciousness, music, and the mass consumer marketplace, as well as the creation of African American musical celebrity within specific communities in the rural South, the urbanized North, and across the Atlantic in western Europe, are part of the revelatory framework for understanding Broonzy's impact on American, European, and transnational history and culture. In addition, his life and career serve as a guiding hand in an understanding of the mechanisms through which black music is interpreted and remembered. His memory, moreover, informs notions of the history of race in the United States, the blues' relationship to jazz music, its appeal to white audiences, and the adoption of the blues by a new generation of young, white, European musicians who devoted themselves to it.

The stewards of Broonzy's public memory have consistently undervalued Broonzy's importance as a pioneer of specific developments in African American culture that were geared toward African Americans themselves. Many of these culture brokers have tended to focus on Broonzy's otherness and his importance to their own (white) perspective on African American culture in a manner that has misrepresented his importance to black audiences. Both scholars and musicians have overlooked the urban blues stage of Broonzy's career, when his performances and recordings reached black audiences across the country. Those who *have* remembered Broonzy's importance to black audiences—such as Muddy Waters and Mike Rowe—have been silenced by the consistent focus on the last decade of his career, when he became the embodiment of white American and European interest in the folk, protojazz, and primitive blues. Big Bill Broonzy's life history reflects the mutability of African American identity during the twentieth century by providing an example of how African Americans created identities based on leisure culture rather than labor. Minimizing this important aspect of Broonzy's public memory has neglected his important contributions to American culture and history.

A consideration of Broonzy's posthumous reception by various kinds of cultural actors allows historians of the blues and of the African American experience a new vantage point to see the ways in which music, memory, celebrity, and legacy are crafted over time. Nearly sixty years after his death, scholars, researchers, music critics, blues fans, and many others are continuing to construct around Big Bill Broonzy a lasting body of work that should be explored and at times contested. His successful navigation of white American and European scholars' romantic interest in the blues as "down home" has contributed to our failure to understand Broonzy as a profoundly resourceful, urbane, and intelligent artist. Broonzy began recording in the mid-1920s, and for the next twenty years, he became an extremely important black musician who recorded and performed hit after hit for black blues audiences. As one who was both deeply immersed and musically engaged with a specifically black audience—in many ways providing African Americans with a soundtrack as they made themselves over as modern—Broonzy's ability to explain black culture to white American and European audiences became so much a part of his legacy that his days as a black entertainer for black audiences were overshadowed. At his death, he had achieved new fame and had carefully crafted a celebrity around the anticipations of his new audience.

Epilogue
This Is Your Father's Guitar

Michael van Isveldt sat in Chicago's Old Town School of Folk Music at 4544 North Lincoln Avenue in May 2013 awash in a sea of mixed emotions. As Big Bill Broonzy's Dutch son, he had arrived in Chicago for his first trip to the United States. In a room full of five or six teachers at one of Chicago's longest running schools of music, Michael was handed a glass of water and asked to sit at a nearby table. At the time, BBC Four had begun production of a documentary on Broonzy's impact in Great Britain as he toured there throughout the 1950s.[1] The BBC desperately wanted to capture Michael's responses on film as he revisited his father's past and legacy in the Windy City and brought him to America to do so. The BBC's intent seemed pure enough to Michael, and one can only imagine the tremendous weight he carried as he came so physically close to a man he never knew.

Enjoying the polite conversations circling around the room concerning the weather back home in Amsterdam, Michael caught, out of the corner of his eye, two young men carrying what appeared to be an instrument case. At first glance, he paid little attention to the young men. After all, he remembered, "it was a music school, . . . and people were coming in and out of there all the time with flutes and horns" and various other instruments. Within a minute, however, he noticed that the students had placed the case on a table merely six feet from his chair. With curiosity, Michael observed that one of the young men had slipped on a pair of white gloves and began opening the case. Cradling the enclosed guitar in his gloved hands like a Stradivarius, the student walked toward Michael and handed it to him while a voice at the table announced, "Michael, take it. That's your father's guitar." Astounded, Michael replied without missing a beat, "But I don't have any gloves on!" Once the laughter subsided, Michael held closely the guitar made so famous by decades of fanfare and respect in what had become the legacy of Big Bill Broonzy. While holding the instrument and examining its contours, Michael, for the first time in his life, "had an emotional moment" with his father.[2]

In many ways, Michael van Isveldt, the six-foot-six Amsterdamer of black and Dutch ancestry, has become the steward of Big Bill Broonzy's legacy and celebrity. Tall, handsome, modest, and exceptionally bright—and bearing

Michael van Isveldt holding his father's famous Martin 00-28, 2013. Courtesy of the Michael van Isveldt Collection. Photo by Bob Riesman.

a definite resemblance to his father—he has made a name for himself as one of Amsterdam's leading minds in Dutch theater. But for sixty years, he has wrestled with the reality that his father was a black American he never knew in a country not wholly comfortable with either blackness or fatherless children. For decades, both he and his mother, Pim, resented Broonzy's contradictory assertions and unfulfilled promises that had made their lives uniquely complicated. After all, Broonzy had, in letter after letter from the late 1950s, promised to leave his then current wife, Rose, marry Pim, and raise Michael as his son (whom Broonzy wanted to name William Lee Conley or perhaps Little Bill), all the while supporting a wife and family in Chicago.[3] For decades, Michael harbored deep disappointment in the man who "was the love of his mother's life" but ultimately the cause of a lifetime of heartache. Michael was raised knowing that his father was a famous American bluesman while the rest of his countrymen and women either had no idea or refused to believe it even if told.[4]

Growing up without Broonzy in Amsterdam was particularly difficult for Michael because his skin is black. In the Amsterdam of Michael's adolescence, the black Surinamese and Antilleans teased Michael, essentially re-

Broonzy holding Michael van Isveldt while showing Michael how to fret his father's guitar, 1957. Courtesy of the Michael van Isveldt Collection.

jecting him for being a "bounty," or "black on the outside and white on the inside." On more than one occasion, Michael faced Dutch discrimination against both his blackness and his whiteness, even though he was raised in what he believed to be a completely white environment, "with a white attitude, a white culture," and a "white background."[5] As a younger man, whenever someone would probe him on his own sense of black consciousness, Michael would simply reply, "Fuck off."[6] Much of what he learned of African American culture in Europe and beyond came from the television or from his love of popular music. In some ways, Michael was always seen as someone exotic, someone who never quite belonged in black or white Amsterdam, despite his desperate attempts to foreground his whiteness. Quite simply, for so long he resented his father because the latter was never there to teach him how to be black or how to handle a lifetime of frequently embarrassing and challenging moments caused by his race. For years, because of this, Michael "hated the guy."[7]

In 2005, everything began to change. Michael had always remained close to his mother, deeply admiring her for providing him with a wonderful childhood, despite all of the challenges they faced. As long as they remained close, he would always respect her encouraging wish that Michael leave the

Michael van Isveldt, the author, and Bettina Weller at van Isveldt and Weller's home in Amsterdam, the Netherlands, 2016. Author's private photograph. Photo by Andrew Wiest.

memory of his father behind and "live a life without" Big Bill Broonzy.[8] During her lifetime, she could control how and when their connection to Broonzy could be handled and associated. In 2003, for example, Pim had begun giving interviews with Dutch and American academics interested Broonzy's European travails, but Michael remained uninterested in their inquiries. Pim passed away in 2006, leaving Michael alone to carry his mother's and father's memory and legacy into the future.

After Pim's death, Michael became more curious about the growing interest in Holland and the United States in his father's music and career. Soon, Michael began answering emails and phone calls from researchers and reporters, even giving an interview in early 2006 for an award-winning piece in Amsterdam's newspaper *Het Parool*, which essentially introduced Michael to Amsterdam and the Netherlands as Broonzy's European son.[9] Slowly, years of pent-up anger and frustration began to transform into a growing desire to learn more of the father and legacy he often glimpsed in the mirror each day—a change, Michael said, "that was mainly inside of me."[10] From 2006 to 2008, word began to circulate that Michael had inherited from his mother a virtually untouched archive of letters, photographs, and other ephemera documenting the short but passionate relationship between Pim and Big Bill as they toured Europe together in the late 1950s. By the summer of 2009, Michael began receiving unsolicited emails from a young American graduate student working on a dissertation investigating Broonzy's past and his European career. Of course, when it came to his parents and the then-growing fascination with their story, "he never trusted anyone" and felt a strong desire "to protect his mother."[11] Nevertheless, he agreed, in the summer of 2010, to share an extraordinarily intimate part of his life with a complete stranger from North Carolina, ultimately helping the student earn his doctorate and achieve unexpected career successes. The result of that trip and the strong relationships formed through that encounter have deeply shaped this book.

Sixty years old now, Michael has come to terms with his relationship with Broonzy and has learned "that his father was something special" and "very important" to a great many people across the globe. Even further, through his contact with biographers, historians, journalists, and ethnomusicologists, Michael now feels he is "closer to his father than his mother ever was" and admits that his mother would be disappointed by this fact.[12] In a sense, Pim had shielded Michael from the pain and frustration she had carried all those years. And yet years of intellectual inquiry and discovery directed toward Michael from those who were interested in his father's past and legacy have catalyzed a cathartic process for Michael, enabling him to accept his father's absence and shortcomings in a manner that has helped him to truly understand both his father's and his own place in the world in a way his mother never could. Michael has discovered that he and his father are, in fact, very much alike in some ways—tall, handsome, artistically gifted, modest, highly intelligent, and unfailingly kind. Since taking ownership of Broonzy's legacy around 2005, Michael has traveled to Chicago and New York to revisit elements of his father's life in America and even shared his story with the BBC. Michael's own family—his wife, Bettina; daughter, Veerle; and son, Leonard—have watched Michael embrace his American past and become proud of their father and grandfather. On trips to Chicago and New York, they, too, have witnessed Michael move past his estranged connection to Broonzy and closer to the formation of an emotional bond that had haunted Michael for decades in the past.[13] This has been Michael's path as he has taken ownership over his father's legacy and celebrity. As for Michael's understanding of Broonzy's perpetual reinventions of his public self, he does not think "anyone will ever know the truth" of who Broonzy really was. To Michael, "nobody can know what was in [his] father's mind."[14] Like a recurring dream and the unresolved conflicts from which they grow, Broonzy's legacy moves in and out of Michael's life one dream at a time.

In some ways, I think, Broonzy himself was "just a dream." In effect, he has become for me a tool for unlocking complex historical and sociological transformations in the twentieth century—the fluid and globalized construction of race, the juxtaposing tendencies of transnational cultural aesthetics, the uneasy realities that being a black celebrity entails, the shifting terrain of historical musical memory, the evolution of African American art. This book opened with the following quote, and the epilogue seems the most fitting place to revisit its fascinating relationship to Broonzy:

> And oh, how I wondered about the artist himself, that irreproachable magician! . . . Was he a worldling smothered in success? Was he coldly calculating, knowing how to tickle people in exactly that delicate, sensitive spot between their tear glands and their purses, which makes tears and dollars fall like rain, if one but understands the magic?
> Or was he a humble servant of the art, too modest to permit himself a judgment of his own, willingly and helpfully playing his role, making no protest against fate?[15]

Like Broonzy's son Michael, I, too, puzzle over the meaning of Broonzy's life, music, and legacy. Does an examination of his life and career reveal him to have been an important participant in the New Negro Renaissance, a beacon showing the power of black culture to combat racism and prejudice, or an architect of transatlantic culture? Is he now a vehicle through which academics and music enthusiasts define and redefine musical style and genre?

Big Bill Broonzy's lifelong efforts to remake himself highlight the importance of black innovators who employed flexible mixtures of accommodation and resistance to advance and engage modernity in the face of a country wrestling with the world's shifting relationship to blackness and music. With every passing decade following World War II, with help from artists such as Broonzy, black music figured more prominently in offering both a voice for those who were terrorized by global racism and "a critique of the system by which those groups are oppressed."[16] Essentially, this study seeks to situate twentieth-century black blues musicians in the fundamental continuation of black "intellectual and historical traditions" that place African American artists and activists—including Broonzy—as part of a vital community of global black citizens.[17] At the very moment when struggles for decolonization and human rights blanketed the world and defined much of the second half of the twentieth century, music became a powerful vessel for a reenvisioning of the African diaspora and its long past. From their beginnings, African American and black studies programs employed this idea as a powerful device for finding meaning in black aesthetics and the function of black culture across the diaspora.[18] In effect, Broonzy, like Paul Robeson before him and James Baldwin after, helped articulate the African American experience across racial and ethnic lines in the United States and around the world and, in doing so, should be seen as a black global citizen offering substance to the world's evolving understanding of blackness. Without a doubt, Big Bill Broonzy will continue to be a figure through whom biographers, scholars, and nonacademics alike work through that experience—the evolution of African Americans' place across the globe—in the twentieth-century United States and the larger world.

Notes

Introduction

1. Hammond, *From Spirituals to Swing*.
2. Dugan and Hammond, "Early Black-Music Concert."
3. Hammond, *From Spirituals to Swing*; Dugan and Hammond, "Early Black-Music Concert," 198.
4. Hammond, *From Spirituals to Swing*; Dugan and Hammond, "Early Black-Music Concert," 198.
5. John Hammond, "Liner Notes," *From Spirituals to Swing: Box Set*. Vanguard Records compact disc B00000JT6C; *Roy, Reds, Whites, and Blues*, 1.
6. Josephson and Trilling-Josephson, *Café Society*.
7. Hammond, *From Spirituals to Swing*.
8. Broonzy, *Big Bill Blues*, 117.
9. Smith, "Big Bill and the Country Blues," 13.
10. Kaye, *Pussycat of Prizefighting*, 14.
11. Kelley, "Notes on Deconstructing the Folk,'" 1405.
12. Brundage, "Working in the 'Kingdom of Culture,'" 20.
13. My mention of race consciousness refers to Du Bois's notion of "double consciousness," which Du Bois described as a "sense of always looking at one's self through the eyes of others, of measuring one's soul by the tape of a world that looks on in amused contempt and pity." See Du Bois, *Souls of Black Folk*, 2–3. Throughout the book, I also refer to or hint at a black consciousness—within the larger realm of black culture—that was malleable and fluid. This black consciousness ensured that black music always stood as much more than just a form of entertainment. This is one of the key arguments in Lawrence Levine's *Black Culture, Black Consciousness*, and it is an argument that broke solid ground in the field. Robin D. G. Kelley expounded on this and challenged parts of it as well. See Levine, *Black Culture, Black Consciousness*; Kelley, *Race Rebels*.
14. Sternheimer, *Celebrity Culture*, 2.
15. Gamson, *Claims to Fame*, 4–5.
16. Gamson, *Claims to Fame*; Marshall, *Celebrity and Power*; Sternheimer, *Celebrity Culture and the American Dream*; Cashmore, *Beyond Black*.
17. Sternheimer, *Celebrity Culture*, 2.
18. Filene, *Romancing the Folk*; Wald, *Josh White*; Hamilton, "The Blues, the Folk, and African American History"; Gussow, *Seems like Murder Here*; Wald, *Escaping the Delta*; Schroeder, *Robert Johnson*; Wynn, *Cross the Water Blues*; Evans, *Ramblin' on My Mind*; Miller, *Segregating Sound*.
19. Fitzhugh Brundage's excellent edited volume on the complex role played by African Americans in the creation of American popular culture and mass consumerism

soundly argues that black musicians were more than just entertainers in the early Jim Crow era. They were, in fact, active cultural and political architects who struggled to secure their own image and consciousness in a nation embracing elements of modernity. See Brundage, *Beyond Blackface*.

20. For a brief survey of this literature, see Locke, *New Negro*; Huggins, *Harlem Renaissance*; Lewis, *When Harlem Was in Vogue*; Wintz, *Black Culture and the Harlem Renaissance*; Lewis, *W. E. B. Du Bois: Biography of a Race*; Lewis, *W. E. B. Du Bois: The Fight for Equality*.

21. Cullen, "Fool's Paradise," 213.

22. Lipsitz, *Time Passages*.

23. For an in-depth investigation into the history and historiography (a field dominated by social scientists and literary theorists) of celebrity culture, see First, "Mechanics of Renown," 12-42. For investigations of black celebrity and the analytical use of the changing transnational landscape of how that might be understood see, Kelley, *Africa Speaks*; Runstedtler, *Jack Johnson*; Ransby, *Eslanda*; Cook, "Finding Otria."

24. House, *Blue Smoke*.

25. Grossman, *Land of Hope*; Cohen, *Making a New Deal*; Hunter, *To 'Joy My Freedom*; Sugrue, *Origins of the Urban Crisis*; Kyriakoudes, *Social Origins of the Urban South*; J. Gregory, *Southern Diaspora*; Green, *Selling the Race*; Heap, *Slumming*.

26. Baldwin, *Chicago's New Negroes*; Hine and McCluskey, *Black Chicago Renaissance*; Runstedtler, *Jack Johnson*; Baldwin and Makalani, *Escape from New York*.

27. Baldwin, "Introduction," 20-21.

28. Baldwin, *Chicago's New Negroes*, 8.

29. The minstrel show and vaudeville performer, pianist, and composer Perry Bradford understood that the blues represented a cultural construct far more sophisticated and modern than many New Negro intelligentsia who labeled the music as trash liked to lend credit. See Bradford, *Born with the Blues*, 97.

30. Baldwin, *Chicago's New Negroes*, 19.

31. Baldwin, "Introduction," 20.

32. The term "public memory" is taken from Benjamin Filene, who defines the term as "the vague and often conflicting assumptions about the past that Americans [and Europeans] carry with them and draw on, usually unconsciously in their daily actions and reactions." Public memory is also "formed by a recursive process" that "involves revisiting and revaluating the culture of the past in light of the present." Filene, *Romancing the Folk*, 5, 8.

33. "List of Records on Machines in Clarksdale Amusement Places," in Gordon and Neverov, *Lost Delta Found*, 311.

34. Broonzy, *Big Bill Blues*, 151.

35. Broonzy's song lyrics are important for deciphering his history, but scholars are now suggesting that music historians need to move beyond a reliance on song lyrics in their research. Hale, panel comments on "New Perspectives on Race and Music in the American South."

36. Kelley, *Race Rebels*, 47.

37. Kelley, *Race Rebels*, 47.

38. Broonzy, *Big Bill Broonzy Interviewed by Studs Terkel*.

Chapter One

1. Broonzy, interview by Bill Randle, recorded July 12-14, 1957, on Broonzy, *The Bill Broonzy Story*, Verve MGV 3000-5, 1960.
2. Broonzy, "Baby I Done Got Wise," 9; Lomax, *Land Where the Blues Began*, 426.
3. Broonzy, interview by Randle.
4. Lomax, *Land Where the Blues Began*, 426.
5. Lomax, *Land Where the Blues Began*, 428.
6. Broonzy, interview by Randle.
7. Big Bill Broonzy convinced the world that he was born in Scott, Mississippi, in 1893 and moved to Arkansas in 1900. Broonzy's biographer Bob Riesman spent a decade trying to retrace his story and has concluded that the bluesman may in fact have been born in 1903 in and around Pine Bluff, Arkansas. The only definitive document discovered as proof is a family ledger listing the name Lee Bradley in 1903. While not an official legal document, the ledger brings into question many elements of Broonzy's past. Nevertheless, Alan Lomax, the folklorist and longtime friend of Broonzy's, met Broonzy's sister Laney sometime in the 1950s, and she "produced certificates" documenting June 26, 1898, as Broonzy's actual birthday. The 1910 U.S. Census lists a Lee Bradley from Jefferson County, Arkansas, born in 1904, aged six. Broonzy's death certificate from 1958 in Cook County, Chicago, lists a birth date of 1893. Most of this back-and-forth with the details of his actual birth date has been used to prove or disprove Broonzy's self-proclaimed service in the American Expeditionary Force in World War I. I suggest that it is impossible to know the exact date of his birth, but I firmly believe the veracity of his declaration of military service. Throughout the mid-1940s, Alan Lomax conducted several oral histories with Big Bill and a final one in 1952. Lomax transcribed a portion of these interviews for use in the construction of *The Land Where the Blues Was Born*. Several of these undated oral history transcripts are located in folder 09.04.10 of the Alan Lomax Collection, American Folklife Center, Library of Congress; 1910 U.S. Census; Harold and Stone, "Big Bill Broonzy"; Riesman, *I Feel So Good*, 1-5; File 2405936, Illinois Office of Cook County Clerk.
8. Broonzy, interview by Randle.
9. Broonzy, *Big Bill Blues*, 55.
10. Broonzy, interview by Randle.
11. Broonzy, interview by Randle.
12. Malone and Stricklin, *Southern Music /American Music*, 1, 5-7.
13. Lomax, *Land Where the Blues Began*, 429; Broonzy, *Big Bill Blues*, 35.
14. Broonzy, *Big Bill Blues*, 35.
15. Broonzy, *Big Bill Blues*, 34.
16. Broonzy told Yannick Bruynoghe and Alan Lomax that in the South, he was not allowed to play with black musicians after local whites had discovered his music abilities. He used this anecdote to explain elements of southern racism in his autobiography and in his interviews. Broonzy, *Big Bill Blues*, 35-36; Interview transcript, folder 09.04.10, Lomax Collection.
17. Interview transcript, folder 09.04.10, Lomax Collection.

18. Miller, *Segregating Sound*, 57.
19. Miller, *Segregating Sound*, 58.
20. Broonzy, interview by Alan Lomax, March 2, 1947, Blues in the Mississippi Night Recordings, Lomax Audio Archive.
21. Interview transcript, folder 09.04.10, Lomax Collection.
22. Interview transcript, folder 09.04.10, Lomax Collection.
23. Broonzy recalled playing for segregated audiences in the South, with whites on one side of the stage and blacks on the other. See Broonzy, *Big Bill Blues*, 35-36; interview transcript, folder 09.04.10, Lomax Collection.
24. Interview transcript, folder 09.04.10, Lomax Collection.
25. Grace Hale's "blues model of individualism" makes the assertion that early blues artists—particularly black women—replaced notions of economic self-determination, or "I exist because I work for myself," with a new cultural self-determination that evoked a sense of "I exist because I express myself." See Hale, "Hear Me Talking to You," 248.
26. Radano, "On Ownership and Value," 367.
27. Szwed, *Alan Lomax*, 191-92.
28. Broonzy, *Big Bill Blues*, 61. Broonzy told Bill Randle a fascinating story about the juxtaposition between the blues and gambling and his mother, who would not allow either in her home. See Broonzy, interview by Randle.
29. Interview transcript, folder 09.04.10, Lomax Collection.
30. Burnim, "Spirituals," 54-68.
31. Du Bois, *Souls of Black Folk*, 251.
32. Levine, *Black Culture, Black Consciousness*, 167.
33. Levine, *Black Culture, Black Consciousness*, 170.
34. Litwack, *Trouble in Mind*, xvi.
35. Bechet, *Treat It Gently*, 212-13.
36. Wald, *Escaping the Delta*, xiii.
37. Wald, *Escaping the Delta*.
38. Handy, *Father of the Blues*, 72-74.
39. Miller, *Segregating Sound*, 13-15.
40. Knight, "He Paved the Way for T.O.B.A.," 153-81.
41. "Tolliver's Comedy Co.," *Chicago Defender*, May 29, 1915, 6.
42. Wald, *Escaping the Delta*, 19.
43. Wald, *Escaping the Delta*, 18-19.
44. Bradford, *Born with the Blues*, 117.
45. Bradford, *Born with the Blues*.
46. Interview transcript, folder 09.04.10, Lomax Collection.
47. Broonzy's military records were destroyed in the 1973 fire that gutted the National Archives' military service records of U.S Army veterans from World War I to the 1960s. See also Williams, *Torchbearers of Democracy*.
48. Williams, *Torchbearers of Democracy*; interview transcript, folder 09.04.10, Lomax Collection; Broonzy, *Big Bill Blues*.
49. Interview transcript, folder 09.04.10, Lomax Collection.
50. Williams, *Torchbearers of Democracy*, 110-13.
51. Interview transcript, folder 09.04.10, Lomax Collection.

52. Interview transcript, folder 09.04.10, Lomax Collection.
53. Interview transcript, folder 09.04.10, Lomax Collection.
54. Broonzy, interview by Lomax.
55. Broonzy, interview by Lomax.
56. Broonzy, interview by Lomax.
57. Interview transcript, folder 09.04.10, Lomax Collection.
58. Interview transcript, folder 09.04.10, Lomax Collection.
59. Williams, *Torchbearers of Democracy*, 110-13.
60. Du Bois, "Essay toward a History of Black Men in the Great War."
61. The veil in Du Bois's *Souls of Black Folk* visually symbolizes a three-pronged phenomenon defining African American life at the turn of the twentieth century. This metaphor perhaps still holds true today. First, and most important for this argument, is the idea that African Americans, according to Du Bois's observations, seemed incapable of viewing themselves as individuals and as a people beyond what white America had defined and constructed for them. Second, the veil cloaks African Americans in darkness, ultimately symbolizing the physiological differences between both races. Finally, the metaphor also represents white Americans' inability to accept Africans Americans for what they are—a central thread in the fabric of the nation. Broonzy's intellectual transition from adolescence to early adulthood, his lifting of the veil, reflects parts of this metaphor. See Du Bois, *Souls of Black Folk*, 1-12.
62. Du Bois, *Souls of Black Folk*, 2-3; "Paris: Big Bill Broonzy Interview," May 13, 1952, Lomax Audio Archive.
63. Williams, *Torchbearers of Democracy*, 225.
64. Interview transcript, folder 09.04.10, Lomax Collection.
65. Quotation from "Racial Clashes," *Savannah Tribune*, July 26, 1919. See also, "The Old and the New," *Washington Bee*, January 11, 1919; Dr. R. R. Moton's Mission Abroad," *Cleveland Gazette*, February 8, 1919; "Decatur County Welcomes Soldiers," *Savannah Tribune*, April 26, 1919; "Kansas City, MO., Mayor Backs Up for Dynamiters," *Topeka Plain Dealer*, May 9, 1919; "American Negroes Unite against Evil of Lynching," *Kansas City Advocate*, July 11, 1919; "Rev. S. E. J. Watson Speaks before White Minsters Union," *Topeka Plain Dealer*, December 19, 1919.
66. Interview transcript, folder 09.04.10, Lomax Collection.
67. Williams, *Torchbearers of Democracy*, 263-64.
68. Williams, *Torchbearers of Democracy*, 263.
69. Interview transcript, folder 09.04.10, Lomax Collection.
70. Interview transcript, folder 09.04.10, Lomax Collection.
71. Interview transcript, folder 09.04.10, Lomax Collection.
72. Broonzy, interview by Lomax.
73. Blackmon, *Slavery by Another Name*.
74. "Negro Drowns While Working on Revetment," *Pine Bluff Commercial*, April 4, 1919; "Fail to Find Body of Negro," *Pine Bluff Daily Graphic*, April 15, 1919; "Body of Negro Who Drowned Thursday Recovered Today," *Pine Bluff Commercial*, April 15, 1919; "Recover Body of Jim Bradley," *Pine Bluff Daily Graphic*, April 16, 1919. See Riesman, *I Feel So Good*, 272.
75. Interview transcript, folder 09.04.10, Lomax Collection.

76. King, *Blues All Around Me*, 93-95.
77. Interview transcript, folder 09.04.10, Lomax Collection.
78. Interview transcript, folder 09.04.10, Lomax Collection.
79. The Illinois Central Railroad operated its service from New Orleans to Chicago on the *Panama Limited* from 1911 to 1971, and the train has been memorialized in blues culture by numerous songs referring to its legendary run. See Downey, *Images of Rail*, 35-56.
80. 1930 U.S. Census, Cooke County, Chicago; Box 194, collection 06/02/03, Pullman Company Archives; Big Bill wrote Alan Lomax many times to share parts of his life story with the folklorist. The Lomax Collection contains hand written letters by Broonzy from 1946, 1948, and 1953. See correspondence, folder 23.06.44, Lomax Collection. Broonzy's death certificate is dated August 17, 1958, and lists 4706 South Parkway as his address. See Broonzy Death Certificate, File 24059362, Illinois Office of Cook County Clerk.

Chapter Two

1. Broonzy, *Big Bill Blues*, 88-90.
2. Alan Lomax affectionately described Broonzy as a veritable lowlife when he first arrived in Chicago in 1920. See Lomax, *Land Where the Blues Began*, 442.
3. Baldwin, "Introduction," 2.
4. Baldwin, "Introduction," 4.
5. Locke, "New Negro," 7. For works supporting this interpretation, see Huggins, *Harlem Renaissance*; Lewis, *When Harlem Was in Vogue*; Baker, *Modernism and the Harlem Renaissance*; Hutchinson, *Harlem in Black and White*.
6. Baldwin, "Chicago's New Negroes," 123; Baldwin expands this idea in his groundbreaking study *Chicago's New Negroes*.
7. Locke, "New Negro," 3-16.
8. Baldwin, *Chicago's New Negroes*, 13.
9. 1930 U.S. Census.
10. Grossman, *Land of Hope*, 133; interview transcript, folder 09.04.10, Lomax Collection.
11. L. Cohen, *Making a New Deal*, 38.
12. L. Cohen, *Making a New Deal*, 11-52.
13. J. Gregory, *Southern Diaspora*, 14.
14. Chicago Commission on Race Relations (CCRR), *Negro in Chicago*, 106; Drake and Cayton, *Black Metropolis*, 8; Gregory, *Southern Diaspora*, 14.
15. Hunter, *To 'Joy My Freedom*, 21-43; Kyriakoudes, *Social Origins of the Urban South*, 74-95.
16. Grossman, *Land of Hope*, 74.
17. J. Gregory, *Southern Diaspora*; Grossman, *Land of Hope*, 133.
18. Grossman, *Land of Hope*, 47.
19. Spear, *Black Chicago*, 11-12.
20. Langston Hughes, "Chicago Blues," *Kansas City Plaindealer*, October 15, 1943.
21. CCRR, *Negro in Chicago*; City of Chicago, *City Planning in Race Relations*; Drake and Cayton, *Black Metropolis*.

22. CCRR, *Negro in Chicago*, 108.
23. L. Cohen, *Making a New Deal*, 34.
24. Interview transcript, folder 23.02.02, Lomax Collection.
25. Interview transcript, folder 23.02.02, Lomax Collection.
26. Terkel, de Graaf, and Stein, "Guerilla Journalist as Oral Historian," 100.
27. Interview transcript, folder 23.02.02, Lomax Collection; Lomax, *Land Where the Blues Began*, 442.
28. Gaines, *Uplifting the Race*, 3.
29. Grossman, *Land of Hope*, 127.
30. Baldwin, *Chicago's New Negroes*, 28-29.
31. Baldwin, *Chicago's New Negroes*, 29.
32. Grossman, *Land of Hope*, 129-30.
33. Baldwin, *Chicago's New Negroes*, 29.
34. *Chicago Defender*, March 24, June 2, July 14, 28, August 4, 11, October 20, November 17, 1917; February 2, March 23, April 6, May 25, July 13, September 14, 1918; June 7, 1919.
35. Baldwin, *Chicago's New Negroes*, 16.
36. Baldwin, *Chicago's New Negroes*, 28. "Old Settler" was a common term used by both black and white Chicagoans prior to World War I. See Drake and Cayton, *Black Metropolis*, 66-76. The term is also used frequently in Tuttle, *Race Riot*; and Grossman, *Land of Hope*. Although Drake and Cayton used the term "New Settler," it has been further developed in Baldwin, *Chicago's New Negroes*.
37. Baldwin, *Chicago's New Negroes*, 19.
38. Grossman, *Land of Hope*, 145.
39. Broonzy, *Big Bill Blues*, 19.
40. Broonzy, *Big Bill Blues*.
41. Broonzy, *Big Bill Blues*.
42. Broonzy, *Big Bill Blues*, 83-90, 140-44; Gold, "Big Bill Broonzy," 38.
43. Hill, "Color Differences."
44. Broonzy, *Big Bill Blues*, 144.
45. Broonzy, *Big Bill Blues*, 143.
46. Grossman, *Land of Hope*, 146.
47. Interview transcript, folder 09.04.10, Lomax Collection.
48. Correspondence, folder 09.04.10, Lomax Collection.
49. Early historiography on black Chicago, for example, defined the city as having a "Negro Problem" as a result of the Great Migration. See CCRR, *Negro in Chicago*; City of Chicago, *City Planning in Race Relations*; Drake and Cayton, *Black Metropolis*; Spear, *Black Chicago*; Tuttle, *Race Riot*. Recent scholarship has moved away from the "ghettoization" model in favor of unmasking Black Chicago's and other cities' engagement with modernity and powerful contributions to American life. Whereas earlier studies tended to view the worlds of vice and leisure as degradation, these more recent works argue that the world of policy, sports, music, drinking, dancing, and illicit sex became places where African Americans contested entrenched social norms and reinvented themselves as a result of these tensions. Grossman, *Land of Hope*; Hunter, *To 'Joy My Freedom*; J. Gregory, *Southern Diaspora*; Green, *Selling the Race*; Baldwin, *Chicago's New Negroes*.

50. Baldwin's research focuses on the outward appearance of "New Settlers" by discussing Madam C. J. Walker's beauty empire and contemporary heavyweight champion Jack Johnson's open displays of race pride. See Baldwin, *Chicago's New Negroes*, 54-90, 195-204; Broonzy, *Big Bill Blues*, 153-55.

51. Broonzy, *Big Bill Blues*, 122.

52. Chicago Blues Museum, *Soul of Bronzeville*.

53. Broonzy, *Big Bill Blues*, 44-45.

54. For descriptions of friends Broonzy lost to alcohol see Broonzy, *Big Bill Blues*, 45, 140-44, 120-23; Interview transcript, folder 09.04.10, Lomax Collection; Lomax, *Land Where the Blues Began*, 444.

55. Cobb, *Most Southern Place on Earth*, 158-59.

56. Interview transcript, folder 09.04.10, Lomax Collection.

57. Hamilton, "Sexuality, Authenticity, and the Making of the Blues," 148-50.

58. Hamilton, "Sexuality, Authenticity, and the Making of the Blues," 148-50.

59. Interview transcript, folder 09.04.10, Lomax Collection.

60. Interview transcript, folder 09.04.10, Lomax Collection.

61. Interview transcript, folder 09.04.10, Lomax Collection.

62. Interview transcript, folder 09.04.10, Lomax Collection.

63. Employee record file for "Rosie" Broonzy, box 194, collection 06/02/03, Pullman Company Archives.

64. Correspondence, folder 09.04.10, Lomax Collection.

65. Broonzy, *Big Bill Blues*, 138.

66. Broonzy, *Big Bill Blues*, 138-40.

67. Interview transcript, folder 09.04.10, Lomax Collection.

68. 1930 U.S. Census, Cook County, Chicago.

69. Broonzy, "Baby I Done Got Wise," 11; Broonzy, "Truth about the Blues," 19.

70. Interview transcript, folder 09.04.10, Lomax Collection; 1930 U.S. Census, Cook County, Chicago. Broonzy's marriage certificate to Rose Lawson is dated July 11, 1956; see Marriage certificate, Historical Cook County, Illinois Office of Cook County Clerk, Vital Records.

71. Interview transcript, folder 09.04.10, Lomax Collection.

72. Big Bill Broonzy's Dutch son, Michael van Isveldt, is in possession of a large box he inherited after the passing of his mother in 2005. Contained in the box is correspondence between Big Bill and Pim van Isveldt throughout the 1950s as well as other correspondence among Pim, Big Bill, and the European network that aided Broonzy's tours of Europe. In addition, there are multiple pieces of ephemera and a few legal documents including divorce papers from Big Bill's marriage to his third wife, Rose, Box 1, van Isveldt Collection; Interview transcript, folder 09.04.10, Lomax Collection.

Chapter Three

1. Broonzy, "Baby I Done Got Wise," 9.
2. Broonzy, "Baby I Done Got Wise," 9.
3. Correspondence and interview transcript, folder 09.04.10, Lomax Collection.
4. Wald, *Escaping the Delta*, 15.

5. Hale, "Here Me Talking to You," 239-40; Levine, *Black Culture, Black Consciousness*, 237.

6. Miller, *Segregating Sound*.

7. Absher, *Black Musician in the White City*.

8. Kenney, *Recorded Music in American Life*, 44-49.

9. Minton, *78 Blues*, 3-25.

10. Kenney, *Recorded Music in American Life*, 3-22; Ayers, *Promise of the New South*, 70, 81, 373-74.

11. *Chicago Defender*, May 31, 1924, August 17, 1925, January 8, 1927, February 18, 1928.

12. Kenney, *Chicago Jazz*, 5-7; Green, *Selling the Race*, 52-53.

13. Demlinger and Steiner, *Destination Chicago Jazz*, 13-33.

14. Bluestone, "Chicago's Mecca Flat Blues," 391-93.

15. Bluestone, "Chicago's Mecca Flat Blues," 384.

16. Gioia, *History of Jazz*, 71.

17. Kenney, *Chicago Jazz*, 4.

18. Albertson, *Bessie*, 1-35.

19. Lomax, *Land Where the Blues Began*, 401.

20. Whiteis, "Blues Reality of Maxwell Street," 22-25.

21. Whiteis, "Blues Reality of Maxwell Street," 22.

22. Whiteis, "Blues Reality of Maxwell Street," 22-25.

23. Rowe, *Chicago Blues*, 47-49.

24. Heap, *Slumming*, 76.

25. Byrd, "Harlem Rent Parties."

26. Byrd, "Harlem Rent Parties."

27. Byrd, "Harlem Rent Parties."

28. Byrd, "Harlem Rent Parties."

29. Bontemps and Hughes, *Book of Negro Folklore*, 596-600.

30. Interview transcript, folder 09.04.10, Lomax Collection.

31. Barlow, *Looking Up at Down*, 65-66.

32. Interview transcript, folder 09.04.10, Lomax Collection.

33. Reid, "Mrs. Bailey Pays the Rent," 146.

34. Broonzy, *Big Bill Blues*, 70.

35. Chicago Blues Museum, *Soul of Bronzeville*.

36. Broonzy, *Big Bill Blues*, 68-69.

37. Baldwin, *Chicago's New Negroes*, 165.

38. Baldwin, *Chicago's New Negroes*, 165.

39. William Howland Kenney maintains that New York and Chicago became the centers of American recording from the late nineteenth century through the Great Depression and were primarily responsible for establishing and sustaining the American recording industry. Quote from Kenney, *Recorded Music in American Life*, 121; See also Kenney, 23-64, 65-134. For further statistics, see Gronow, "Record Industry," 59.

40. For the unethical practices of the early recording industry see Oliver, *Songsters and Saints*; Barlow, *Looking Up at Down*. For Chicago's music ties to the criminal underworld, see Morris, *Wait until Dark*.

41. Nearly all of Chicago's recording companies, except for Paramount, were owned by East Coast businesses, which were based almost exclusively in New York.

42. Mayo Williams's life reflects many of the elements addressed throughout this book, suggesting that Chicago's New Negroes experienced the New Negro Renaissance in ways specific to the Windy City.

43. Calt, "Anatomy of a 'Race' Label," 12-13; Cunningham, "J. Mayo 'Ink' Williams."

44. Calt, "Anatomy of a 'Race' Label," 13.

45. Calt, "Anatomy of a 'Race' Label," 13.

46. Calt, "Anatomy of a 'Race' Label," 14.

47. Barlow, *Looking Up at Down*, 131.

48. Barlow, *Looking Up at Down*, 132.

49. "Well Sir! Here He Is at Last! Papa Charlie Jackson," *Chicago Defender*, August 23, 1924, 6.

50. A contemporary of Broonzy, Tommy Johnson preformed widely throughout Mississippi until his death in the 1950s. Born in 1896, Johnson stood as one of the earliest proponents of an identifiable Mississippi Delta sound, studying under Charley Patton, among others, and recording a number of songs for Paramount and Victor between 1928 and 1930. Unique in his vocal approach, Johnson often sang in a high vocal register and falsetto quite different from other Delta musicians. At the same time, he offered an inflection, tone, and timbre in his vocals that others would try to emulate across generations. See Mississippi Blues Trail, "Tommy Johnson."

51. Baldwin, *Chicago's New Negroes*, 174.

52. Baldwin, *Chicago's New Negroes*, 172-73.

53. Broonzy, "Baby, I Done Got Wise," 9.

54. Uzzel, *Blind Lemon Jefferson*.

55. Interview transcript, folder 09.04.10, Lomax Collection.

56. The blues pianist Little Brother Montgomery recalled drinking, playing, and partying at Blake's Chicago apartment with Big Bill Broonzy. Quote from Barlow, *Looking Up at Down*, 86; see also, 85-87.

57. In the South, of course, performances in barrelhouses and juke joints, at picnics and parties, and even on back porches were critical for fostering young blues talent. Race-record companies, after all, seemed eager to popularize the bawdier, southern down-home style. Aspiring southern bluesmen, such as the young Broonzy in Arkansas with See-See Rider or the young Robert Johnson in Mississippi with Son House, expected to hone their skills by emulating popular artists from their communities whom they saw at local functions. These informal social gatherings defined when and where young musicians were introduced to the blues and how their styles as blues musicians would be perceived. These venues for cultural exchange, then, followed African Americans into urban areas as tens of thousands of blacks fled the South during the Great Migrations.

58. Interview transcript, folder 09.04.10, Lomax Collection.

59. Interview transcript, folder 09.04.10, Lomax Collection.

60. Interview transcript, folder 09.04.10, Lomax Collection.

61. Broonzy, *Big Bill Blues*, 47.

62. *Chicago Defender*, August 25, 1928, September 29, 1928.

63. Broonzy, *Big Bill Blues*, 47.
64. Interview transcript, folder 09.04.10, Lomax Collection.
65. Dixon, Godrich, and Rye, *Blues and Gospel Records*, 59.
66. Van der Tuuk, *Rise and Fall of Paramount Records*; interview transcript, folder 09.04.10, Lomax Collection.
67. Green, *Selling the Race*, 54.
68. Calt, "Anatomy of a 'Race' Label," 19.
69. Calt, "Anatomy of a 'Race' Label," 13, 19.
70. Calt, "Anatomy of a 'Race' Label," 13, 19.
71. Interview transcript, folder 09.04.10, Lomax Collection.

Chapter Four

1. Broonzy, *Big Bill Blues*, 48.
2. Broonzy, "Baby I Done Got Wise," 9.
3. Melrose, "My Life in Recording," 60.
4. Wald, *Escaping the Delta*, 40-41.
5. Drake and Cayton, *Black Metropolis*, 84; see also L. Cohen, *Making a New Deal*, 242-43.
6. Drake and Cayton, *Black Metropolis*, 83-86.
7. "Plantation Cabaret Dark Again," *Chicago Defender*, March 28, 1928.
8. Drake and Cayton, *Black Metropolis*, 508-9, 517.
9. Kenney, *Recorded Music in American Life*, 163.
10. Kenney, *Recorded Music in American Life*, 158-63.
11. Wald, *Escaping the Delta*, 36.
12. O'Neal and van Singel, *Voice of the Blues*, 18-30.
13. Interview transcript, folder 09.04.10, Lomax Collection.
14. 1940 U.S. Census.
15. Barlow, *Looking Up at Down*, 304-5.
16. The 1940 U.S. Census, Cooke County, Chicago, lists Dorsey living with his mother, sister, and two nieces at least since 1935 at 6525 South Vernon Avenue on the city's South Side.
17. "'Tight Like That' Sales Over $500,000," *Chicago Defender*, November 23, 1929, 7.
18. Barlow, *Looking Up at Down*, 301. For other explanations of hokum blues, see Wald, *Escaping the Delta*, 28, 37-38; Muir, *Long Lost Blues*, 102.
19. House, *Blue Smoke*, 188-91.
20. O'Neal and van Singel, *Voice of the Blues*, 1.
21. O'Neal and van Singel, *Voice of the Blues*, 29.
22. Correspondence, folder 09.04.10, Lomax Collection.
23. Charters, *Country Blues*, 171.
24. Melrose, "My Life in Recording," 59.
25. Melrose, "My Life in Recording," 59-61.
26. Melrose, "My Life in Recording," 59-61.
27. Dixon, Godrich, and Rye, *Blues and Gospel Records*, 59.
28. Barlow, *Looking Up at Down*, 133.

29. Quote from Green, *Selling the Race*, 52; Rowe, *Chicago Blues*.
30. Broonzy, *Big Bill Blues*, 107-48.
31. Dixon, Godrich, and Rye, *Blues and Gospel Records*, 61-63.
32. Charters, *Country Blues*, 182-93.
33. Filene, *Romancing the Folk*, 79-81.
34. American Federation of Musicians, Chicago Chapter Files. Broonzy's Local 208 card is stamped up to January 4, 1958, indicating his active membership. The card also lists Broonzy's Social Security number; see Big Bill Broonzy file, Chicago History Museum.
35. Halker, "History of the Local 208," 212-13.
36. "Musician's Plight."
37. Rowe, *Chicago Blues*, 41.
38. In 1946, Broonzy and Lomax began corresponding through a series of letters that detail all the artists whom Broonzy had performed with, the record companies he had recorded for, the number of songs he had either written and recorded as Big Bill or other pseudonyms or provided songwriting credits or instrumental accompaniment for throughout his twenty-year career. At the time, Lomax was gathering information and oral histories with Broonzy for what eventually became the chapter "Big Bill of the Blues" in Lomax's 1970 book *The Land Where the Blues Began*. See Interview transcript, folder 09.04.10, Lomax Collection; as well as Lomax, *Land Where the Blues Began*, 423-58.
39. Correspondence, folder 09.04.10, Lomax Collection.
40. Rowe, *Chicago Blues*, 40-45.
41. "Music: Spirituals to Swing."
42. One of the first discussions of this contradiction appeared in Charters, *Country Blues*, 177. Recently, the blues historian Elijah Wald has revisited the same theme in *Escaping the Delta*, 227; Liner Notes from John Hammond, *From Spirituals to Swing: Box Set*. Vanguard CD B00000JT6C, 1999, compact disc.
43. Bill Chase, "All Ears," *New York Amsterdam News*, December 30, 1938, 13.
44. Broonzy performed and recorded this version of "Just a Dream" in front of a live and captive audience at "From Spirituals to Swing," December 23, 1938.
45. Broonzy's only known offspring, Michael van Isveldt, born December 4, 1956, looks strikingly similar to his father and lives with his family in Amsterdam, where he was born and raised by Broonzy's lover Pim van Isveldt. Both Pim's and Michael's relationships to Broonzy are explored in chapters 7 and 8 and in the epilogue.
46. Broonzy, *Big Bill Blues*, 142.
47. Filene, *Romancing the Folk*, 113-14.
48. Bogdanov, Woodstra, and Erlewine, *All Music Guide to the Blues*, 69.
49. Broonzy, *Big Bill Broonzy: Complete Recorded Works, Vol. 12 (1945-1947)*.
50. "Apollo Introduces New Swing Outfit," *New York Amsterdam News*, June 2, 1945.
51. Interview transcript, folder 09.04.10, Lomax Collection.
52. In the epilogue of Broonzy's autobiography, Broonzy suggested that he did not expect to be remembered as a jazz musician or a guitar player and singer in the folk realm. He expected to be remembered as a bluesman. See Broonzy, *Big Bill Blues*, 151-52. He also discussed this problem with Alan Lomax in the 1940s as his career

was beginning to decline. See Lomax, *Land Where the Blues Began*, 455. In a 1956 interview with Studs Terkel, Broonzy discusses the problem of viewing the blues as a part of jazz history. See Broonzy, *Big Bill Broonzy Interviewed by Studs Terkel*.

53. Lomax, *Land Where the Blues Began*, 454-55.
54. Lomax, *Land Where the Blues Began*, 454.
55. Lomax, *Land Where the Blues Began*, 455.
56. Lomax, *Land Where the Blues Began*, 455.
57. "Display Ad 126," *New York Amsterdam News*, June 22, 1946, 26.
58. "Human Welfare Festival Attracts Capacity Crowd," *Chicago Defender*, March 15, 1947, 8.
59. Lomax, *Land Where the Blues Began*, 456.
60. "Petrillo Defends Ban on Recordings," *New York Times*, July 31, 1942; "All Recording Stops Today," *DownBeat*, August 1, 1942.
61. L. Cohen, *Making a New Deal*, 325-30.
62. Green, *Selling the Race*, 56.
63. Melrose, "My Life in Recording," 56.
64. DeVeaux, "Bebop and the Recording Industry."
65. Green, *Selling the Race*, 72.
66. Leadbitter and Slaven, *Blues Records*, 28; House, *Blue Smoke*, 178-79.
67. Rowe, *Chicago Blues*, 51-69.
68. Rowe, *Chicago Blues*, 61.
69. In the summer of 1941 and again in the summer of 1942, with the help and guidance of the Fisk University ethnomusicologist John W. Work III, Alan Lomax visited Stovall Farms, Mississippi, to record McKinley Morganfield, a local farmer and musician. He captured Morganfield on record for the Library of Congress Archive of American Folk-Song. These recordings reflect Muddy's early Delta blues style that was linked to Delta traditions established by Charley Patton, Son House, Robert Johnson, and Nehemiah "Skip" James. See Muddy Waters, "Country Blues."
70. Barlow, *Looking Up at Down*, 330.
71. The historian Tony Russell describes the jukebox collection of five jukeboxes in Coahoma County, Mississippi, surveyed by Fisk University's Lewis Jones in September 1941. Two of the machines listed songs by Chicago's own "Big Bill." See Russell, "Clarksdale Piccolo Blues," 30.
72. Russell, "Clarksdale Piccolo Blues."
73. O'Neal and van Singel, *Voice of the Blues*, 172.
74. Gordon and Neverov, *Lost Delta Found*, 311.
75. Intermission spots were small sets in between the full gig of a featured performer, which in this case was Muddy Waters. See Broonzy, *Big Bill Blues*, 13; Lomax, *Land Where the Blues Began*, 456; Gordon, *Can't Be Satisfied*, 110.
76. Green, *Selling the Race*, 53.
77. Rowe, *Chicago Breakdown*, 41.
78. O'Neal and van Singel, *Voice of the Blues*, 26.
79. O'Neal and van Singel, *Voice of the Blues*, 244.
80. O'Neal and van Singel, *Voice of the Blues*, 172.
81. Fry, "We Are the Blues," 7-8.

82. Gordon, *Can't Be Satisfied*, 3-68.
83. O'Neal and van Singel, *Voice of the Blues*, 172.
84. O'Neal and van Singel, *Voice of the Blues*, 172.
85. O'Neal and van Singel, *Voice of the Blues*, 173.
86. Filene, *Romancing the Folk*, 91-92.
87. Leadbitter and Slaven, *Blues Records*, 28.

Chapter Five

1. A Moore's Lounge business card with dates and a hand written note is contained in Michael van Isveldt's personal collection. See, Box 1, van Isveldt Collection.
2. Box 1, Vice President for Student Affairs. Contained in this collection are letters from alumni, alumnae, faculty and their families addressing the year the Big Bill lived on campus. Also, there are newspaper clippings and articles from the *Iowa State Daily*.
3. R. Cohen, *Rainbow Quest*, 115.
4. R. Cohen, *Rainbow Quest*, 151.
5. Email correspondence between historian Jorgen Rasmussen and Broonzy's former neighbors in Ames, Jauvanta and Albert Walker. The email, dated April 8, 2003, explains Broonzy's friendships with several members of Iowa State's faculty. Box 1, Vice President for Student Affairs.
6. Some music scholars employing methodologies rooted in sociology and American studies who are now examining the folk music revival have suggested that twentieth-century folk music—one piece of a much larger process—represents a complex cultural phenomenon in the form of a social movement, which reexamined core American societal values and unintentionally redefined them in the twentieth century. As the New Left, civil rights, and antiwar movements gained enormous momentum in the 1950s and '60s and embraced American vernacular music as a vehicle for political and social solidarity, the folk music boom provided an arch for bridging the Old Left with a new generation in search of similar but older democratic pluralism in the form of multiculturalism. It should be noted that this growing multiculturalism embedded within the folk music revival from the late 1930s to the 1950s exposes the racially contrived nature of the folk revival as social movement idea. See Mullen, *Man Who Adores the Negro*; Roy, *Reds, Whites, and Blues*, 1-27; Donaldson, "I Hear America Singing," 1-20
7. Donaldson, "I Hear America Singing," 2.
8. Benjamin Filene and Ronald Cohen smartly describe the political and problematic agendas in early folksong collecting represented by the Lomaxes and Lunsford, but prevalent among many folklorists of the era. To many, folk music stemmed from an authentic period of cultural formation and must be documented as such. This "cult of authenticity" marred much of early folk music collecting and had an enormous impact on Big Bill Broonzy place in the folk music revival. See R. Cohen, *Rainbow Quest*, 8-19; Filene, *Romancing the Folk*, 32-75, 9-46.
9. R. Cohen, *Rainbow Quest*, 8-38.
10. R. Cohen, *Rainbow Quest*, 8-38.

11. Filene, *Romancing the Folk*, 20-27; R. Cohen, *Rainbow Quest*, 8-19; Mullen, *Man Who Adores the Negro*, 1-20.

12. Mullen, *Man Who Adores the Negro*, 11, 12-13.

13. Filene, *Romancing the Folk*, 50.

14. Filene, *Romancing the Folk*, 52-55.

15. Filene, *Romancing the Folk*, 55.

16. Filene, *Romancing the Folk*.

17. John Lomax, quoted in Filene, *Romancing the Folk*, 59.

18. Broonzy, "Truth about the Blues," 19; Dance, "Perennial Blues," 53.

19. Wolfe and Lornell, *Life and Legend of Leadbelly*, 101-3.

20. Dixon, Godrich, and Rye, *Blues and Gospel Records*, 59-65.

21. Hammond, *On Record*, 202.

22. Miller, *Segregating Sound*, 221.

23. Filene, *Romancing the Folk*, 71-72.

24. The University of Chicago's archives contain a folder with clippings from newspapers, *Melody Maker* articles, articles on Broonzy in *Jazz Journal* from 1951-1953, and several undocumented periodicals. Box 83, folder 12, Steiner Papers.

25. Josephson and Trilling-Josephson, *Café Society*, 14-15.

26. Lomax, *Land Where the Blues Began*, 13.

27. Correspondence, folder 09.04.10, Lomax Collection.

28. Correspondence, folder 09.04.10, Lomax Collection.

29. Josephson and Josephson, *Café Society*, 58-59.

30. Szwed, *Alan Lomax*, 134-35.

31. Lomax, *Land Where the Blues Began*, 459.

32. R. Cohen, *Rainbow Quest*, 28-41.

33. "Paris: Big Bill Broonzy Interview," May 13, 1952, Lomax Audio Archive.

34. Broonzy, *Big Bill Blues*, 30.

35. R. Cohen, *Rainbow Quest*, 38.

36. R. Cohen, *Rainbow Quest*, 51.

37. Lomax, *Land Where the Blues Began*, 459.

38. Lomax, *Land Where the Blues Began*, 459.

39. "Blues in the Mississippi Night Interviews," March 2, 1947, Lomax Audio Archive.

40. "Blues in the Mississippi Night Interviews," March 2, 1947, Lomax Audio Archive.

41. Levine, *Black Culture, Black Consciousness*, 408.

42. "Blues in the Mississippi Night Interviews."

43. "Blues in the Mississippi Night Interviews."

44. "Blues in the Mississippi Night Interviews."

45. Riesman, *I Feel So Good*, 129.

46. Portelli, *Death of Luigi Trastulli*, 26.

47. R. Cohen, *Rainbow Quest*, 38.

48. Born in 1914 in Greeneville, South Carolina, Josh White became an ambassador of the folk music scene in the United States throughout the 1930s and 1940s, ultimately transforming his career into that of a cabaret and film star. Like Broonzy, he toured Europe in the 1950s but fell into obscurity in the United States because of his association with socialists during the McCarthy era. See Wald, *Josh White*.

49. R. Cohen, *Rainbow Quest*, 48-49, 55.

50. R. Cohen, *Rainbow Quest*, 55.

51. Newspaper clipping containing a picture of Big' Bill's pallbearers carrying his casket. Folder 12, Box 83, Steiner Papers.

52. William Grimes, "Studs Terkel, Listener to America, Dies at 96," *New York Times*, October 31, 2008; Studs Terkel, "Studs Recalls How One Man's Dream Became a Reality," *Chicago Tribune*, November 25, 2007; Grayson, *Biography of a Hunch*.

53. Email correspondence between Javunta Walker and Jorgen Rasmussen from April 10, 2003. See Box 1, Vice President for Student Affairs.

54. Class of 1951 Civil Engineering graduate Louis Legg documented his memories of Broonzy in a letter dated February 24, 2000. See Box 1, Vice President for Student Affairs.

55. Journalism student Louie Thompson studied guitar with Big Bill in Ames. See "Guitarist Thompson Taught by 'Big Bill' Broonzy," *Iowa State Daily*, October 2, 1958 in Box 1, Vice President for Student Affairs.

56. Letter from Legg, Box 1, Vice President for Student Affairs.

57. Letter from Legg, Box 1, Vice President for Student Affairs.

58. In 1951, Broonzy recorded a blues titled "The Moppin Blues," which he wrote while living in Ames. A former student corroborated this story in a letter to the university reflecting on Broonzy's time at the college. See Leadbitter and Slaven, *Blues Records*, 28; Letter from Legg, Box 1, Vice President for Student Affairs.

59. Gregg Gammack, "Big Bill," *Ethos* February-March 1964, Box 1, Vice President for Student Affairs.

60. Gammack, "Big Bill," Box 1, Vice President for Student Affairs.

Chapter Six

1. Harold and Stone, "Big Bill Broonzy."

2. This interview later became part of Alan Lomax's larger study of Broonzy that appeared in "Big Bill of the Blues," in *Land Where the Blues Began*, 423-58.

3. Broonzy, interview by Alan Lomax, May 13, 1952, T1007, Lomax Audio Archive.

4. Schwartz, *How Britain Got the Blues*, 1-45; Wynn, "Why I Sing the Blues."

5. Cohen and Donaldson, *Roots of the Revival*, 17-18.

6. Cohen and Donaldson, *Roots of the Revival*, 18.

7. Szwed, *Alan Lomax*, 210.

8. Szwed, *Alan Lomax*, 203-16; Cohen and Donaldson, *Roots of the Revival*, 5-24, 39-45.

9. Ewan MacColl's fascinating story is told quite well in his *Journeyman*.

10. Laing, "MacColl and the English Folk Revival," 156.

11. Quoted in Szwed, *Man Who Recorded the World*, 259.

12. Cohen and Donaldson, *Roots of the Revival*, 42-43.

13. Gioia, *History of Jazz*, 159.

14. Springer, "Blues in France," 236.

15. Wynn, *Cross the Water Blues*.

16. Perchard, "Tradition, Modernity, and the Supernatural Swing," 25-26.
17. Hot Club de France president Hugues Panassié explained this argument in 1949 for the growing post-World War II European jazz community in Paris and beyond. See Panassié, "Big Bill Broonzy."
18. Springer, "Blues in France," 243; Sacre, "Yannick Bruynoghe."
19. Springer, "Blues in France," 246-47.
20. Springer, "Blues in France," 236.
21. Springer, "Blues in France," 239.
22. Oliver, "Blue-Eyed Blues," 230-31.
23. Broonzy's divorce papers documenting the end of his marriage to his third wife, Rose, are located in the van Isveldt Collection. Broonzy used this document to convince Pim van Isveldt that he, indeed, had divorced his wife Rose (née Allen). But his claims were, in fact, disingenuous because he was in a relationship at the time with Rose Lawson, who became his fourth wife.
24. Will Davidson, "It's Jazz Week in the City's Cafes and Concert Halls," *Chicago Daily Tribune*, October 19, 1947; Claudia Cassidy, "On the Aisle: Gossip about West Coast Music, Singers of Folk Songs, Money Makers, and Some Other Things," *Chicago Daily Tribune*, November 6, 1947.
25. A clipping from Greg Gammack, "Big Bill," *Ethos* (February/March 1964): 6 in Box 1, Vice President for Student Affairs; Mezz Mezzrow, "Big Bill," 4; Folder 12, Box 83, Steiner Papers.
26. Springer, "Blues in France," 241.
27. Springer, "Blues in France," 242.
28. Panassié, "Big Bill Doesn't Sell His Music," 9.
29. Broonzy, *Complete Vogue Recordings*.
30. Hugues Panassie, "Big Bell doesn't sell his music—he gives it away," *Melody Maker*, September 15, 1951.
31. Sweetman, "Big Bill Broonzy in France and England."
32. P. Jones, "Horst Lipmann," 4; Bohländer, "Evolution of Jazz Culture in Frankfurt," 173.
33. Sweetman, "Big Bill Broonzy in France and England"; Broonzy, *Big Bill Broonzy in Concert with Graeme Bell*.
34. Two letters from Broonzy to Gunter Boas are in the Gunter Boas Collection at the Lippmann+Rau Musikarchiv in Eisenach, Germany. One is dated March 3, 1954. The other is undated but may well be from 1953.
35. Kahn, "They Don't Appreciate the Real Blues in France," 9.
36. Kahn, "They Don't Appreciate the Real Blues in France."
37. Schwartz, "Preaching the Gospel of the Blues," 148.
38. Schwartz, "Preaching the Gospel of the Blues," 146.
39. Schwartz, "Preaching the Gospel of the Blues."
40. Schwartz, "Preaching the Gospel of the Blues," 147.
41. Schwartz, "Preaching the Gospel of the Blues."
42. Wynn, "Why I Sing the Blues," 14-15.
43. Stewart-Baxter, "Preachin' the Blues" (1953), 4.
44. Gold, "Big Bill Broonzy," 15.

45. Gold, "Big Bill Broonzy," 5.
46. Stewart-Baxter, "Preachin' the Blues" (1951), 13.
47. Stewart-Baxter, "Date with the Blues," 5-6.
48. Stewart-Baxter, "Date with the Blues," 5-6.
49. Borneman, "One Night Stand: Big Bill Talkin," *Melody Maker*, September 29, 1951, 11.
50. Stewart-Baxter, "Preachin' the Blues" (1951), 13.
51. Gregory, "Lomax in London," 162.
52. Borneman, "Big Bill Talkin'."
53. Borneman, "Big Bill Talkin'."
54. Quote taken from Borneman, "Big Bill Talkin"; Stewart-Baxter, "Preachin' the Blues" (1951).
55. Stewart-Baxter, "Preachin' the Blues" (1951), 13.
56. Panassié, "Big Bill Doesn't Sell His Music," 9.
57. Borneman, "Big Bill Talkin'."
58. Sweetman, "Big Bill Broonzy in France and England."
59. Wald, *Josh White*, 221.

Chapter Seven

1. Michael van Isveldt, interview with the author, June 10, 2016, Amsterdam, the Netherlands.
2. Henry Sonnenschein, Superior Court of Cook County, Decree for Divorce, No. S1S6478, Chicago, IL, June 18, 1951, in box 1, van Isveldt Collection.
3. Letter from Big Bill Broonzy to Alan Lomax, April 11, 1953, folder 09.04.10, Lomax Collection.
4. Broonzy's marriage certificate to Rose Lawson is dated July 11, 1956. See File 2405936, Historical Cook County, Illinois Office of Cook County Clerk.
5. Pim van Isveldt, interview by Louis van Gasteren, August 1, 2004, in van Gasteren, "How Did I Come to Make These Recordings?," 38.
6. Korner, "Big Bill Broonzy," 1.
7. Van Gasteren, "How Did I Come to Make These Recordings?," 30-31.
8. Van Rijn, "Lowland Blues," 223-27.
9. Van Rijn, "Lowland Blues," 228.
10. Van Isveldt, interview by van Gasteren, 39.
11. Big Bill Broonzy to Win Stracke, January, 24 1953, MSM-15,096, Old Town School of Folk Music Items and Sound Recordings.
12. Big Bill Broonzy to Win Stracke, January, 24 1953, MSM-15,096, Old Town School of Folk Music Items and Sound Recordings.
13. Letter from Big Bill Broonzy to Pim van Isveldt, March 2, 1956, and April 28, 1956, box 1, van Isveldt Collection.
14. Broonzy discussed these logistical problems in multiple letters contained within the van Isveldt Collection.
15. Letter from Big Bill Broonzy to Pim van Isveldt, September 26, 1956, box 1, van Isveldt Collection.

16. Wald, *Josh White*, 221.
17. Wald, *Josh White*, 226, 243-44.
18. Wald, *Josh White*, 243-44.
19. Wald, *Josh White*, 247.
20. Trixie Stevens to Pim van Isveldt, 1957, box 1, van Isveldt Collection.
21. Letter from Big Bill Broonzy to Trixie and David Stevens, 1956, box 1, van Isveldt Collection. See also Wald, *Josh White*, 220-21. In the winter of 1957-58, White found a month-long residency (presumably with help from Broonzy) at the Gate of Horn in Chicago, where he took the time to visit and lend money to his very ill friend; see Wald, *Josh White*, 250-51.
22. Winant, *World Is a Ghetto*, 272-73.
23. Poiger, *Jazz, Rock, and Rebels*, 7.
24. Schroer, *Recasting Race after World War II*, 6.
25. Big Bill Broonzy to Pim van Isveldt, November 5, 1956, box 1, van Isveldt Collection.
26. "Paris: Big Bill Broonzy Interview," May 13, 1952, Lomax Audio Archive.
27. Big Bill Broonzy, *Black, Brown, and White*, Vg134, LP30037, February, 1951.
28. Broonzy, *Big Bill Broonzy Interviewed by Studs Terkel*.
29. Gold, "Big Bill Broonzy," *Down Beat*, February 6, 1958, 38.
30. Gold, "Big Bill Broonzy," *Down Beat*, February 6, 1958, 38.
31. Van Rijn, "Lowland Blues," 224.
32. Van Gasteren, "How Did I Come to Make These Recordings?," 30-31.
33. Letter from Big Bill Broonzy to Pim van Isveldt, November 1955, box 1, van Isveldt Collection.
34. Letter from Big Bill Broonzy to Pim van Isveldt, February 26, 1956, box 1, van Isveldt Collection.
35. Letter from Big Bill Broonzy to Pim van Isveldt, June 21, 1953, box 1, van Isveldt Collection.
36. Nederlands Jazz Archeif, "Work of Michiel de Ruyter: Big Bill Broonzy."
37. Nederlands Jazz Archeif, "Work of Michiel de Ruyter: Big Bill Broonzy."
38. Letter from Big Bill Broonzy to Pim van Isveldt, February 23, 1956, March 2, 1956, and April 28, 1956, box 1, van Isveldt Collection.
39. Letter from George Adins to Pim van Isveldt, May 6, 1957, box 1, van Isveldt Collection.
40. Letter from Big Bill Broonzy to Pim van Isveldt, May 2, 1957, box 1, van Isveldt Collection.
41. R. Cohen, *Rainbow Quest*, 8-19.
42. "Broonzy's Blues Excite British," *Baltimore Afro-American*, November 26, 1955.
43. Elizabeth Rannels, "Have You Heard," *Chicago Daily Tribune*, October 21, 1951; "Have You Heard," *Chicago Daily Tribune*, December 13, 1953; William Leonard, "Tower Ticker," *Chicago Daily Tribune*, November 28, 1951; "Tower Ticker," *Chicago Daily Tribune*, July 2, 1952; "Russell Nype Sings Well in Marine Room," *Chicago Daily Tribune*, November 9, 1952; "Moulin Rouge Features Show with Big Cast," *Chicago Daily Tribune*, December 6, 1953; "Blue Angels Show Lively and Colorful," *Chicago Daily Tribune*, December 20, 1953; "On the Town," *Chicago Daily Tribune*, February 27,

1955; "Folk Song Program Hits Roosevelt U. on Dec. 13," *Chicago Defender*, December 11, 1956.

44. Izzy Rowe's Notebook, "The Postman Rings Twice," *Pittsburgh Courier*, May 2, 1953. A Big Bill Broonzy performance is advertised in "Jazz History, Concert Set in Park Forest," *Chicago Daily Tribune*, April 28, 1955; Charles Edward Smith, "Blow Hot, Blow Sweet," *New York Times*, November 4, 1956; John S. Wilson, "Country 'Blues': Bill Broonzy's Singing Is Living History," *New York Times*, September 15, 1957; "Unbound Jazz: Invention of LP Gave Jam Sessions Space," *New York Times*, March 16, 1958.

45. Broonzy sent van Isveldt a business card in 1957 displaying the name and address of the tavern; box 1, van Isveldt Collection. Initially, the origin of this ephemera was unclear, but it became apparent once corroborated with his obituary from the *Chicago Tribune*; see *Chicago Daily Tribune*, August 16, 1958, 12.

46. Old Town School of Folk Music, "Biography of a Hunch."

47. The history of Circle Pines Center is discussed on its website: http://www.circlepinescenter.org/history.php.

48. Schultz, "Send Your Kids to Summer Camp at Circle Pines"; Harold Henderson, "Camp Co-Op," *Chicago Reader*, July 27, 1989.

49. Vera King, quoted in Henderson, "Camp Co-Op."

50. Perchard, "Tradition, Modernity, and the Supernatural Swing," 25-45.

51. Cressant, "'Big Bill' Broonzy," 17.

52. Letters from Big Bill Broonzy to Pim van Isveldt, January 17, March 2, April 4, June 1, September 7, September 26, November 5, December 11, 1956; March 29, September 18, December 18, 1957; January 1, March 3, 1958, box 1, van Isveldt Collection.

53. Letter from Big Bill Broonzy to Pim van Isveldt, June 1, 1956, box 1, van Isveldt Collection.

54. Letter from Big Bill Broonzy to Pim van Isveldt, June 1, 1956, box 1, van Isveldt Collection.

55. House, "Keys to the Highway," 214.

56. The front page of the *Chicago Daily Tribune* explained the unprecedented rainfall that wrecked the city that weekend. Since Friday, July 12, nearly six inches of rain had flooded Chicago's streets, basements, and storefronts, with numerous lightning strikes reported across the city—fitting, perhaps, for the last recording session for such a legendary musician. See "Heavy Rains Swamp City! 48 Hurt as Theater Tent Falls; Flood Basements; Traffic Disrupted; Many Trees Down; River up 6 Feet; Water Emptied into Lake," *Chicago Daily Tribune*, July 14, 1957, 1.

57. Bill Randle, liner notes to *The Bill Broonzy Story*.

58. Bill Randle, liner notes to *The Bill Broonzy Story*.

59. Asbell, "Whisper of Big Bill Broonzy," 13.

60. Letter from Big Bill Broonzy to Pim van Isveldt, January 18, 1958, box 1, van Isveldt Collection.

61. Steiner, "Beyond the Impression," 7.

62. "Maybe I'll Sing Again Says Big Bill," 1.

63. "Maybe I'll Sing Again Says Big Bill," 1; "Stars All Set to Help Big Bill," 20.

64. Gold, "Big Bill Broonzy Benefit Concert," 37–38.

65. The British musician Lonnie Donegan had helped introduce skiffle—a hybrid form of jazz, blues, and folk originating in the early twentieth-century United States—to British audiences. He was a huge admirer of Broonzy's and helped organize the second of the two British concerts. See "Maybe I'll Sing Again Says Big Bill," 1.

66. Asbell, "Whisper of Big Bill Broonzy," 13.

67. Letter from Big Bill Broonzy to Pim van Isveldt, March 18, 1958, box 1, van Isveldt Collection.

68. Big Bill Broonzy to David and Trixie Stevens, July 1958, quoted in "£500 'Blues' for Broonzy," 1.

69. "Bill Broonzy, Famed Blues Singer, Dies," *Chicago Daily Tribune*, August 16, 1958, 12.

70. "£500 'Blues' for Broonzy," 1.

71. "Bill Broonzy, Famed Blues Singer, Dies," 12; "Big Bill Broonzy Sang, Wrote Blues," *New York Times*, August 16, 1958, 17; "Radio Show Plans Tribute to Bill Broonzy," *Chicago Defender*, August 18, 1958, A2; "Wake Services Tonight for Big Bill Broonzy," *Chicago Defender*, August 19, 1958, A6; "Big Bill Broonzy Succumbs: 'Even the Elements Know a Great Big Man Is Gone,'" *Norfolk Journal and Guide*, August 23, 1958, C1; "Big Bill Broonzy, Famed Blues Singer, Dies at 65," *Baltimore Afro-American*, August 30, 1958, 7; "Final Note for Blues Singer Bill Broonzy," *Pittsburgh Courier*, August 30, 1958; "£500 'Blues' for Broonzy," 1; Littleton, "There's No Argument," 11; "Tangents: Big Bill Broonzy," 42; Letter from David and Trixie Stevens to Pim van Isveldt, September 3, 1958, box 1, van Isveldt Collection; Letter from Yannick Bruynoghe to Pim van Isveldt, October 19, 1958, box 1, van Isveldt Collection.

72. "Tangents: Big Bill Broonzy," 42.

Chapter Eight

1. Clapton, *Clapton*, 30; Werner, "Eric Clapton," 28.

2. Clapton, *Clapton*, 34.

3. On "public memory," see note 32 to the introduction.

4. See H. Howard Taubman, "Negro Music Given at Carnegie Hall," *New York Times*, December 24, 1938; "Spiritual Swing at Carnegie Hall," *Baltimore Afro-American*, December 2, 1939; "From Spirituals to Swing to Be Heard," *Chicago Defender*, December 9, 1939; Gama Gilbert, "TAC Jazz Session at Carnegie Hall," *New York Times*, December 25, 1939; Billy Rowe, "Broadway in Glowing Tribute to Negro Music," *Pittsburgh Courier*, January 6, 1940; Broonzy, "Baby I Done Got Wise," 9; Isleton, "Big Bill Broonzy," 7.

5. Lomax, *Land Where the Blues Began*, 459–79; Lomax and Fleming, interview by Julian Marshall.

6. Lomax, *Land Where the Blues Began*, 459.

7. Lomax, *Land Where the Blues Began*, 473.

8. Lomax, *Land Where the Blues Began*, 460.

9. An embellished and highly romanticized original transcription of the interview was published in 1948, and each man's identity was masked by a pseudonym. See Lomax, "I Got the Blues."

10. Lomax, "I Got the Blues," 38.

11. Lomax, "I Got the Blues," 52.

12. Filene, *Romancing the Folk*, 59-62.

13. Lomax, *Land Where the Blues Began*, 426.

14. Lomax, *Land Where the Blues Began*, 446.

15. Lomax, *Land Where the Blues Began*, 448.

16. Lomax, *Land Where the Blues Began*, 456.

17. Lomax, *Land Where the Blues Began*, 439.

18. Broonzy, "Baby I Done Got Wise," 10.

19. Broonzy's autobiography is filled with remembrances of his life in the South and the ways in which those experiences formed a bridge into his then-current embodiment of the blues as folk. In addition, the reader is introduced to Broonzy's music, the motivations behind his compositions, and the historical moment from which they arose. Bruynoghe and Broonzy, wherever possible, attempted to link the majority of these back to Broonzy's life on the plantation, carefully selecting anecdotes from Broonzy's past in an attempt to prove his legitimacy as one of the last great country blues singers. Even though by 1955 he had lived in Chicago far longer than he had in the Deep South, as much as one-half to two-thirds of the book discusses plantation life, manual labor, Jim Crowism, and southern romanticism, while deeper investigations into his life as a black pop star are limited to a chapter.

20. Charles Edward Smith, "Blow Hot, Blow Sweet," *New York Times*, November 4, 1956.

21. Broonzy, *Big Bill Blues*, 29.

22. Interview transcript, folder 09.04.10, Lomax Collection.

23. John Hammond introduced Alan Lomax to Robert Johnson's "unpublished masters" in the late 1930s, when he discovered the recordings working for CBS Records. In 1939, Lomax found them again and began tracing Johnson's roots back to the Mississippi Delta. See Lomax, *Land Where the Blues Began*, 13.

24. Towering black intellectuals including W. E. B. Du Bois, Carter G. Woodson, E. Franklin Frazier, and Booker T. Washington began writing about the importance of black culture beginning in the first three decades of the twentieth century. White intellectual circles, however, did not quite engage these elements until the 1940s, with the appearance Melville J. Herskovits's highly controversial *The Myth of the Negro Past* in 1941. By the 1960s, American historians began rewriting the history of the black experience.

25. Schwartz, *How Britain Got the Blues*, 40.

26. See Big Bill Broonzy, *Horny Frog*, American Recording Company Records, 7-05-57, 1937; and *Flat Foot Susie With Her Flat Yes Yes*, Columbia Records 30135, 1938.

27. Bruynoghe, "Chicago," 67.

28. Broonzy, *Big Bill Blues*, 116-18, 122-23.

29. Broonzy, *Big Bill Blues*, 151-52.

30. Broonzy, *Big Bill Blues*, 151.

31. Ford, *Blues Bibliography*, 179.

32. Bruynoghe, "Chicago," 69.

33. Bruynoghe, "Chicago," 67-76.

34. Bruynoghe, "Chicago."

35. A revised American edition first emerged in 1964 with a new foreword by the producer Charles Edward Smith, an expanded introduction by Bruynoghe, and an up-to-date discography of Broonzy's recorded works. See Broonzy, *Big Bill Blues*, rev. ed.

36. Bruynoghe, "Introduction to the American Edition," ibid., 9.

37. Charles Edward Smith was an esteemed early jazz critic and record producer with strong ties to Moses Asch and Folkways Records. See Smith and Ramsey, *Jazzmen*; Olmstead, *Folkways Records*; Raeburn, *New Orleans Style and the Writing of Jazz History*.

38. Outside of the advertisements marketing blues records in black newspapers, Broonzy's name does not appear as part of a featured story until 1938 and 1939, when he appeared at Carnegie Hall. See H. Howard Taubman, "Negro Music Given at Carnegie Hall," *New York Times*, December 24, 1938; "Spiritual Swing at Carnegie Hall," *Baltimore Afro-American*, December 2, 1939; "From Spirituals to Swing to be Heard," *Chicago Defender*, December 9, 1939; Gama Gilbert, "TAC Jazz Session at Carnegie Hall," *New York Times*, December 25, 1939; Billy Rowe, "Broadway in Glowing Tribute to Negro Music," *Pittsburgh Courier*, January 6, 1940.

39. Smith, foreword to Broonzy, *Big Bill Blues*, rev. ed., 13.

40. Smith, foreword to Broonzy, *Big Bill Blues*, rev. ed., 14.

41. Filene, *Romancing the Folk*, 49.

42. Smith, foreword to Broonzy, *Big Bill Blues*, rev. ed., 11-12.

43. Robert Ford's *A Blues Bibliography* contains approximately 160 entries on Big Bill Broonzy alone. Dozens of the entries are from European jazz publications. See Ford, *Blues Bibliography*, 178-82.

44. Charters was initially a jazz enthusiast and historian who in his early twenties in the 1950s moved to New Orleans to conduct field research for a book on jazz. See Charters, *Jazz in New Orleans*. Like his European counterparts, however, Charters quickly discovered that the blues was a parallel genre to jazz and was still popular in the black South. He abandoned jazz altogether after his first book to concentrate on the blues, and his fieldwork and analysis of recordings were compiled in the classic *The Country Blues*, 179.

45. Charters, *Country Blues*, 179.

46. Charters, *Country Blues*, 19.

47. Charters, *Country Blues*, 166-81. In 1931, Broonzy recorded his very first solo tracks, "Station Blues" and "How You Want It Done," for Paramount Records (13084), and the company mistakenly listed the performer as "Big Bill Broomsley."

48. Charters, *Country Blues*, 169.

49. Charters, *Country Blues*, 172-75.

50. Charters, *Country Blues*, 176.

51. Rowe, *Chicago Blues*, 15.

52. Rowe, *Chicago Blues*, 40-78.

53. Rowe, *Chicago Blues*, 59.

54. Alan Lomax, for example, had broadcast *Blues in the Mississippi Night* in February 1951 on a program titled *Adventures in Folk Song* for the BBC. The following year,

the jazz aficionado Max Jones featured Broonzy on a jazz program for the BBC called *Jazz Club*. See Schwartz, *How Britain Got the Blues*, 45-46.

55. Gordon, *Can't Be Satisfied*, 158.

56. Chess Records became eager to tap into the wave of posthumous fanfare erupting after Broonzy's death, hiring Muddy Waters to record covers of Broonzy's popular folk-blues songs. Both Benjamin Filene and Robert Gordon have aptly discussed the irony in Waters's regressive transformation from the king of Chicago electric blues to Muddy Waters the folk singer. See Filene, *Romancing the Folk*, 119-20; and Gordon, *Can't Be Satisfied*, 164. To push their analysis further, Waters and Broonzy had been close friends for over fifteen years and had established a mentor-mentee relationship, and this relationship was as strong personally as it was professionally.

57. Waters, *Muddy Waters Sings Big Bill Broonzy*.

58. Quoted in Gordon, *Can't Be Satisfied*, 73.

59. The *Living Blues* founder and editor Jim O'Neal captured this very famous photograph in the mid-1940s. See Gordon, *Can't Be Satisfied*, 204.

60. Schwartz, *How Britain Got the Blues*, 56.

61. Schwartz, *How Britain Got the Blues*, 56; Gordon, *Can't Be Satisfied*, 157-59.

62. Carson, *Jeff Beck*, 19.

63. House, *Blue Smoke*, 143. House also analyzes images from a 1956 Belgian film (*Low Lights, Blues Smoke*) featuring Broonzy in a dimly lit cellar club in Brussels. See House, *Blue Smoke*, xiv.

Epilogue

1. *The Man Who Brought the Blues to Britain*, television documentary, BBC Four, May 2013.

2. Michael van Isveldt, interview by the author, Amsterdam, the Netherlands, June 17, 2016.

3. Michael van Isveldt, interview by the author, Amsterdam, the Netherlands, June 17, 2016; see also van Isveldt Collection.

4. At fourteen, Michael confided to one of his teachers that he was indeed the son of Big Bill Broonzy, only to have the teacher reject the claim in disbelief. Michael was devastated because he had never shared that secret beyond his close family and friends.

5. Van Isveldt interview.

6. Peter van Brummelen, "Big Bill Broonzy's enige nazaat werkt bij Cosmic in Amsterdam," *Het Parool* (Amsterdam, NL), February 17, 2006.

7. Michael van Isveldt, interview by the author, Amsterdam, the Netherlands, June 17, 2016.

8. Michael van Isveldt, interview by the author, Amsterdam, the Netherlands, June 17, 2016.

9. Van Brummelen, "Big Bill Broonzy's enige nazaat werkt bij Cosmic in Amsterdam." Around this time, the biographer Bob Riesman began contacting Michael about his own work on Broonzy; Riesman, *I Feel So Good*.

10. Michael van Isveldt, interview by the author, Amsterdam, the Netherlands, June 17, 2016.
11. Michael van Isveldt, interview by the author, Amsterdam, the Netherlands, June 17, 2016.
12. Michael van Isveldt, interview by the author, Amsterdam, the Netherlands, June 17, 2016.
13. Bettina Weller, interview by the author, Amsterdam, Netherlands, June 17, 2016.
14. Van Isveldt interview.
15. Hesse, *My Belief*, 167.
16. Ward, *Just My Soul Responding*, 3.
17. Kelley, "But a Local Phase of a World Problem," 1047.
18. Five years after Broonzy's death, the pioneering black studies scholar Amiri Baraka offered one of the first attempts at examining African American jazz and blues through an African American studies approach, employing Broonzy's music to make several arguments. See L. Jones (Baraka), *Blues People*.

Bibliography

Archival Collections

American Federation of Musicians, Chicago Chapter Files, The Blues Archive, Chicago Public Library, Chicago, IL
Gunter Boas Collection, Lippmann+Rau Musikarchiv, Eisenach, Germany
Chicago History Museum, Chicago, IL
Illinois Office of Cook County Clerk
Alan Lomax Audio Archive, Association for Cultural Equity, New York, NY
Alan Lomax Collection, American Folklife Center, Library of Congress, Washington, DC
Old Town School of Folk Music Items and Sound Recordings, Chicago History Museum, Chicago, IL
Pullman Company Archives, Newberry Library, Chicago, IL
John Steiner Papers, Special Collections Research Center, University of Chicago Library, Chicago, IL
United States Census, 1900, 1910, 1920, 1930, 1940
Michael van Isveldt Private Collection, Amsterdam, the Netherlands
Vice President for Student Affairs, Department of Residence, Personnel Files, Record Series 7/4/2, Special Collections, Parks Library, Iowa State University, Ames, IA

Newspapers

Baltimore Afro-American, 1939–58
Chicago Daily Tribune, 1947–58
Chicago Defender, 1915–58
Chicago Tribune, 2007
Cleveland Gazette, 1919
Het Parool, 2006
Iowa State Daily, 1951–64
Kansas City Advocate, 1919
Kansas City Plaindealer, 1943
New York Amsterdam News, 1938–58
New York Times, 1938–2008
Norfolk Journal and Guide, 1958–61
Pine Bluff Commercial, 1919
Pine Bluff Daily Graphic, 1919
Pittsburgh Courier, 1940–58
Savannah Tribune, 1919
Topeka Plain Dealer, 1919
Washington Bee, 1919

Books, Articles, and Other Sources

Abbott, Lynn, and Doug Seroff. "'They Cert'ly Sound Good to Me': Sheet Music, Southern Vaudeville, and the Commercial Ascendency of the Blues." *American Music* 14, no. 4 (1996): 402–54.

Absher, Amy. *The Black Musician in the White City: Race and Music in Chicago, 1900-1967*. Ann Arbor: University of Michigan Press, 2014.
Albertson, Chris. *Bessie*. New Haven, CT: Yale University Press, 2003.
"All Recording Stops Today." *DownBeat*, August 1, 1942.
American Business Consultants. *Red Channels: The Report of Communist Influence in Radio and Television*. New York: Counterattack, 1950.
Asbell, Bernie. "The Whisper of Big Bill Broonzy." *Melody Maker*, February 8, 1958.
Ayers, Edward. *The Promise of the New South: Life after Reconstruction*. New York: Oxford University Press, 1992.
Baker, Houston. *Modernism and the Harlem Renaissance*. Chicago: University of Chicago Press, 1987.
Baldwin, Davarian L. "Chicago's New Negroes: Consumer Culture and Intellectual Life Reconsidered." *American Studies* 44, nos. 1-2 (2003): 121-55.
———. *Chicago's New Negroes: Modernity, the Great Migration and Black Urban Life*. Chapel Hill: University of North Carolina Press, 2007.
———. "Introduction: New Negroes Forging a New World." In *Escape from New York: The New Negro Renaissance beyond Harlem*, edited by Davarian L. Baldwin and Minkah Makalani, 1-27. Minneapolis: University of Minnesota Press, 2013.
Baldwin, Davarian L., and Minkah Makalani, eds. *Escape from New York: The New Negro Renaissance beyond Harlem*. Minneapolis: University of Minnesota Press, 2013.
Barlow, William. *Looking Up at Down: The Emergence of Blues Culture*. Philadelphia: Temple University Press, 1989.
Bastin, Bruce. *Crying for the Carolines*. London: Studio Vista, 1971.
———. Red River Blues: *The Blues Tradition in the Southeast*. Urbana: University of Illinois Press, 1986.
Bean, Annemarie, James V. Hatch, and Brooks Macnamara, eds. *Inside the Minstrel Mask: Readings in Nineteenth Century Blackface Minstrelsy*. Hanover, NH: Wesleyan University Press, 1996.
Beauchamp, Lincoln T., ed. *BluesSpeak: The Best of the Original Chicago Blues Annual*. Urbana: University of Illinois Press, 2010.
Bechet, Sidney. *Treat It Gently: An Autobiography*. 2nd ed. New York: De Capo, 2002.
Blackmon, Douglas A. *Slavery by Another Name: The Re-enslavement of Black Americans from the Civil War to World War II*. New York: Doubleday Books, 2008.
Bluestone, Daniel. "Chicago's Mecca Flat Blues." *Journal of the Society of Architectural Historians* 57, no. 4 (1998): 382-403.
Bogdanov, Vladimir, Chris Woodstra, and Stephen Thomas Erlewine, eds. *All Music Guide to the Blues: The Definitive Guide to the Blues*. San Francisco: Backbeat Books, 2003.
Bohländer, Carlo. "The Evolution of Jazz Culture in Frankfurt: A Memoir." In *Jazz and the Germans: Essays on the Influence of "Hot" American Idioms on 20th Century German Music*, edited by Michael J. Budds, 167-78. Hillsdale, NY: Pendragon, 2002.
Bontemps, Arna, and Langston Hughes, eds. *The Book of Negro Folklore*. New York: Dodd, Mead, 1958.

Borneman, Ernest. "One Night Stand: Big Bill Talkin." *Melody Maker*, September 29, 1951.

Bradford, Perry. *Born with the Blues: The True Story of the Pioneering Blues Singers and Musicians in the Early Days of Jazz*. New York: Oak, 1965.

Broonzy, Big Bill. *Amsterdam Live Concerts 1953: Unissued Live Concerts Recorded by Louis Van Gasteren*. CD 275. Munich Records, 2006.

———. "Baby I Done Got Wise." *Jazz Record*, March 1946.

———. *Black, Brown, and White*. Vg134. LP30037. February, 1951.

———. *Big Bill Blues: William Broonzy's Story as Told to Yannick Bruynoghe*. 1964. Reprint, New York: Da Capo, 1992.

———. *Big Bill Blues: William Broonzy's Story as Told to Yannick Bruynoghe*. Rev. ed. New York: Oak, 1964.

———. *Big Bill Broonzy: Complete Recorded Works, Vol. 12 (1945-1947)*. Document Records BDCD-6047, 1995.

———. *Big Bill Broonzy in Concert with Graeme Bell & His Australian Jazz Band, Germany, September 1951*. Jasmine Records CD JASMCD 3007, 2002.

———. *Big Bill Broonzy Interviewed by Studs Terkel*. Chicago, November 14, 1956. Folkways LP FG 3586, 1957. Transcribed in *Jazz Journal* 11, no. 5 (1958): 36.

———. *The Bill Broonzy Story*. Recorded July 12-13, 1957. MGV Records LP MGV 3000-5, 1960.

———. *The Complete Vogue Recordings*. Vogue Europe CD B0002VYE3G, 2005.

———. "Excerpts from Big Bill's Letters to Yannick Bruynoghe." *Living Blues* 55 (1982-83): 22-23.

———. *Flat Foot Susie With Her Flat Yes Yes*. Columbia Records 30135, 78 rpm. Originally released in September 1938.

———. *Horny Frog*. American Recording Company Records 7-05-57, 78 rpm. Originally released in January 1937.

———. "The Truth about the Blues" (1952). *Living Blues* 55 (Winter 1982): 17-20.

Broonzy, Big Bill, Memphis Slim, and Sonny Boy Williamson. *Blues in the Mississippi Night*. Recorded and edited by Alan Lomax. Rounder Select CD 82161-1860-2, 2003, audio CD. Originally released in 1947.

Brundage, W. Fitzhugh, ed. *Beyond Blackface: African Americans and the Creation of American Popular Culture, 1890-1930*. Chapel Hill: University of North Carolina Press, 2011.

———. "Working in the 'Kingdom of Culture.'" In *Beyond Blackface: African Americans and the Creation of American Popular Culture, 1890-1930*, edited by W. Fitzhugh Brundage, 1-42. Chapel Hill: University of North Carolina Press, 2011.

Bruynoghe, Yannick. "Chicago: Home of the Blues," in *Just Jazz 2*, edited by Sinclair Traill and Gerald Lascelles, 67-76. London: Peter Davis, 1958.

Burnim, Mellonee V. "Spiritual." In *African American Music: An Introduction*, 2nd ed., edited by Mellonee V. Burnim and Portia K. Maultsby, 50-72. New York: Routledge, 2015.

Burnim, Mellonee V., and Portia K. Maultsby, eds. *African American Music: An Introduction*. 2nd ed. New York: Routledge, 2015.

Byrd, Frank. "Harlem Rent Parties." WPA Federal Writers Project Collection. Manuscript Division, Library of Congress, Washington, DC, 1938.

Calt, Stephen. "The Anatomy of a 'Race' Label—Part 2." *78 Quarterly* 1, no. 4 (1989): 9-30.

Carson, Annette. *Jeff Beck: Crazy Fingers*. San Francisco: Backbeat Books, 2001.

Cashmore, Ellis. *Beyond Black: Celebrity and Race in Obama's America*. London: Bloomsbury Academic, 2012.

Charters, Samuel B. *The Country Blues*. 1959. Reprint, New York: Da Capo, 1975.

———. *Jazz in New Orleans: An Index to the Negro Musicians of New Orleans*. Belleville, NJ: Walter C. Allen, 1958.

Chicago Blues Museum. *The Soul of Bronzeville: The Regal, Club De Lisa and the Blues*. Temporary exhibit at the Du Sable Museum of African American History, Chicago, June-December 2009.

Chicago Commission on Race Relations. *The Negro in Chicago: A Study of Race Relations and a Race Riot*. Chicago: University of Chicago Press, 1922.

City of Chicago. *City Planning in Race Relations: Proceedings of the Mayor's Conference on Race Relations, February, 1944*. Chicago: Mayor's Committee on Race Relations, 1944.

Clapton, Eric. *Clapton: The Autobiography*. New York: Broadway Books, 2007.

Cobb, James. *The Most Southern Place on Earth: The Mississippi Delta and the Roots of Regional Identity*. New York: Oxford University Press, 1992.

Cockrell, Dale. *Demons of Disorder: Early Blackface Minstrelsy and Their World*. New York: Cambridge University Press, 1997.

Cohen, Lizabeth. *Making a New Deal: Industrial Workers in Chicago, 1919-1939*. New York: Cambridge University Press, 1990.

Cohen, Ronald D. *Rainbow Quest: The Folk Music Revival and American Society, 1940-1970*. Amherst: University of Massachusetts Press, 2002.

Cohen, Ronald D., and Rachel Clare Donaldson. *Roots of the Revival: American and British Folk Music in the 1950s*. Urbana: University of Illinois Press, 2014.

Cook, James W. "Finding Otria: On the Geopolitics of Black Celebrity." *Raritan* 34, no. 2 (2014): 84-111.

Cressant, Pierre. "'Big Bill' Broonzy." *Jazz Hot* 59 (1951): 17.

Cullen, Jim. "Fool's Paradise: Frank Sinatra and the American Dream." In *Popular Culture in American History*, edited by Jim Cullen, 203-28. Oxford, UK: Blackwell, 2001.

———, ed. *Popular Culture in American History*. Oxford, UK: Blackwell, 2001.

Cunningham, Jimmy, Jr. "J. Mayo 'Ink' Williams." In *The Encyclopedia of Arkansas History and Culture*, September 23, 2013. http://www.encyclopediaofarkansas.net/encyclopedia/entry-detail.aspx?entryID=5411.

Dance, Stanley. "The Perennial Blues." *Saturday Review*, May 11, 1957.

Daniels, Douglas H. "The Significance of Blues for American History." *Journal of Negro History* 70 (1985): 14-23.

Davis, Angela. *Blues Legacies and Black Feminism: Gertrude "Ma" Rainey, Bessie Smith and Billie Holiday*. New York: Vintage Books, 1999.

Demlinger, Sandor, and John Steiner. *Destination Chicago Jazz*. Chicago: Arcadia, 2003.

DeVeaux, Scott. "Bebop and the Recording Industry: The 1942 AFM Recording Ban Reconsidered." *Journal of the American Musicological Society* 41, no. 1 (1988): 126-65.

Dixon, Robert W., John Godrich, and Howard W. Rye. *Blues and Gospel Records: 1890-1943*. New York: Oxford University Press, 1997.

Donaldson, Rachel C. *"I Hear America Singing": Folk Music and National Identity*. Philadelphia: Temple University Press, 2014.

———. "Music for the People: The Folk Music Revival and American Identity." PhD diss., Vanderbilt University, 2011.

Downey, Clifford J. *Images of Rail: Chicago and the Illinois Central Railroad*. Chicago: Arcadia, 2007.

Drake, St. Clair, and Horace R. Cayton. *Black Metropolis: A Study of Negro Life in a Northern City*. New York: Harcourt, Brace, 1945.

Du Bois, W. E. B. "An Essay toward a History of Black Men in the Great War." *Crisis* 18 (1919): 72.

———. *The Souls of Black Folk*. Chicago: A. C. McClurg, 1903.

Dugan, James, and John Hammond. "An Early Black-Music Concert from Spirituals to Swing." *Black Perspective in Music* 2, no. 2 (1974): 191-207.

Dunaway, David King. *How Can I Keep from Singing? The Ballad of Pete Seeger*. New York: Villard Books, 2008.

Evans, David. *Big Road Blues: Tradition and Creativity in the Folk Blues*. Berkeley: University of California Press, 1982.

———, ed. *Ramblin' on My Mind: New Perspectives on the Blues*. Urbana: University of Illinois Press, 2008.

Filene, Benjamin. *Romancing the Folk: Public Memory and American Roots Music*. Chapel Hill: University of North Carolina Press, 2000.

First, Sara Babcox. "The Mechanics of Renown; or, The Rise of Celebrity Culture in Early America." PhD diss., Michigan University, 2009.

Ford, Robert. *A Blues Bibliography*. New York: Routledge, 2007.

Fry, Robert Webb, II. "We Are the Blues: Individual and Communal Performances of the King Biscuit Tradition." PhD diss., Florida State University, 2010.

Gaines, Kevin. *Uplifting the Race: Black Leadership, Politics, and Culture in the Twentieth Century*. Chapel Hill: University of North Carolina Press, 1996.

Gamson, Joshua. *Claims to Fame: Celebrity in Contemporary America*. Berkeley: University of California Press, 1994.

Gioia, Ted. *The History of Jazz*. 2nd ed. New York: Oxford University Press, 2011.

Gold, Don. "Big Bill Broonzy." *DownBeat*, February 6, 1958.

———. "Big Bill Broonzy Benefit Concert." *DownBeat*, January 9, 1958.

Gordon, Robert. *Can't Be Satisfied: The Life and Times of Muddy Waters*. Boston: Little, Brown, 2002.

Gordon, Robert, and Bruce Neverov, eds. *Lost Delta Found: Rediscovering the Fisk University-Library of Congress Coahoma County Study, 1941-1942*. Nashville: Vanderbilt University Press, 2005.

Grayson, Lisa. *Biography of a Hunch: The History of Chicago's Legendary Old Town School of Folk Music*. Chicago: Old Town School of Folk Music, 1992.

Green, Adam. *Selling the Race: Culture, Community, and Black Chicago, 1940-1955*. Chicago: University of Chicago Press, 2007.

Gregory, E. David. "Lomax in London: Alan Lomax, the BBC and the Folk-Song Revival in England, 1950-1958." *Folk Music Journal* 8, no. 2 (2002): 136-69.

Gregory, James N. *The Southern Diaspora: How the Great Migrations of Black and White Southerners Transformed America*. Chapel Hill: The University of North Carolina Press, 2005.

Gronow, Pekka. "The Record Industry: The Growth of a Mass Medium." *Popular Music* 3 (1983): 53-75.

Grossman, Richard R. *Land of Hope: Chicago, Black Southerners, and the Great Migration*. Chicago: University of Chicago Press, 1989.

Guralnick, Peter. *Searching for Robert Johnson: The Life and Legend of the "King of the Delta Blues Singers."* New York: Penguin Books, 1989.

———. *Sweet Soul Music: Rhythm and Blues and the Southern Dream of Freedom*. New York: HarperCollins, 1986.

Gussow, Adam. "Racial Violence, 'Primitive Music,' and the Blues Entrepreneur: W. C. Handy's Mississippi Problem." *Southern Cultures* 8 (2002): 56-77.

———. *Seems like Murder Here: Southern Violence and the Blues Tradition*. Chicago: University of Chicago Press, 2002.

Hale, Grace Elizabeth. "Hear Me Talking to You: The Blues and the Romance of Rebellion." In *Beyond Blackface: African Americans and the Creation of American Popular Culture, 1890-1930*, edited by W. Fitzhugh Brundage, 239-58. Chapel Hill: University of North Carolina Press, 2011.

———. Panel comments on "New Perspectives on Race and Music in the American South" at the Southern Historical Association's annual meeting, November 5, 2010.

Halker, Clark. "A History of the Local 208 and the Struggle for Racial Equality in the American Federation of Musicians." *Black Music Research Journal* 8, no. 2 (1988): 207-22.

Hamilton, Marybeth. "The Blues, the Folk, and African American History." *Transactions of the Royal Historical Society* 11 (2001): 17-35.

———. "Sexuality, Authenticity, and the Making of the Blues" *Past and Present* 169, no. 1 (2002): 132-60.

Hammond, John. *From Spirituals to Swing: Box Set*. Vanguard CD B00000JT6C, 1999.

———. *On Record*. New York: Summit Books, 1977.

Handy, W. C. *Father of the Blues: An Autobiography*. New York: Da Capo, 1941.

Harold, Ellen, and Peter Stone. "Big Bill Broonzy." Association for Cultural Equity. Accessed April 20, 2016, http://www.culturalequity.org/alanlomax/ce_alanlomax_profile_broonzy.php.

Heap, Chad. *Slumming: Sexual and Racial Encounters in American Nightlife, 1885-1940*. Chicago: University of Chicago Press, 2009.

Herskovits, Melville J. *The Myth of the Negro Past*. New York: Harper and Brothers, 1941.

Hesse, Hermann. *My Belief: Essays on Life and Art*. Edited by Theodore Ziolkowski. Translated by Denver Lindley, with two essays translated by Ralph Manheim. London: Triad Paladin Grafton Books, 1989.

Hill, Mark E. "Color Differences in the Socioeconomic Status of African American Men." *Social Forces* 78, no. 4 (2000): 1437-60.

Hine, Darlene Clark, and John McCluskey Jr., eds., *The Black Chicago Renaissance*. Urbana: University of Illinois Press, 2012.

House, Rodger Randolph. *Blue Smoke: The Recorded Journey of Big Bill Broonzy*. Baton Rogue: Louisiana State University Press, 2010.

———. "Keys to the Highway: William 'Big Bill' Broonzy and the Chicago Blues in the Era of the Great Migrations." PhD diss., Boston University, 1999.

Huggins, Nathan Irving. *Harlem Renaissance*. New York: Oxford University Press, 1971.

Hunter, Tera. *To 'Joy My Freedom: Southern Black Women's Lives and Labors after the Civil War*. Cambridge, MA: Harvard University Press, 1997.

Hutchinson, George. *Harlem in Black and White*. Cambridge, MA: Harvard University Press, 1996.

Isleton, Bill. "Big Bill Broonzy: Selected Discography." *Jazzology* 2 (January 1947): 7.

Johnson, Guy B. "Double Meaning in the Popular Negro Blues." *Journal for Abnormal and Social Psychology* 22 (April-June 1927): 534-37.

Johnson, Robert. *The Complete Recordings*. Columbia CD C2K 64916, 1990.

Jones, LeRoi (Amiri Baraka). *Blues People: Negro Music in White America*. New York: William Morrow, 1963.

Jones, Peter. "Horst Lipmann: Offering Musicians a Chance to Be Heard." *Billboard* 92, no. 52 (1980): 6-14.

Josephson, Barney, and Terry Trilling-Josephson. *Café Society: The Wrong Place for the Right People*. Urbana: University of Illinois Press, 2009.

Kahn, Henry. "They Don't Appreciate the Real Blues in France." *Melody Maker*, February 2, 1952.

Kaye, Andrew M. *The Pussycat of Prizefighting: Tiger Flowers and the Politics of Black Celebrity*. Athens: University of Georgia Press, 2004.

Keil, Charles. *Urban Blues*. Chicago: University of Chicago Press, 1966.

Kelley, Robin D. G. *Africa Speaks: America Answers: Modern Jazz in Revolutionary Times*. Cambridge, MA: Harvard University Press, 2012.

———. "'But a Local Phase of a World Problem': Black History's Global Vision, 1883-1950." *Journal of American History* 86, no. 3 (1999): 1045-77.

———. "Notes on Deconstructing the Folk." *American Historical Review* 97, no. 5 (1992): 1400-1408.

———. *Race Rebels: Culture, Politics, and the Black Working Class*. New York: Free Press, 1994.

———. *Thelonious Monk: The Life and Times of an American Original*. New York: Free Press, 2009.

Kenney, William Howland. *Chicago Jazz*. New York: Oxford University Press, 1993.

———. *Recorded Music in American Life: The Phonograph and Popular Memory*. New York: Oxford University Press, 1999.

King, B. B. *Blues All around Me: The Autobiography of B. B. King*. New York: Avon Books, 1996.

Knight, Althea. "He Paved the Way for T.O.B.A.," *Black Perspective in Music* 15, no. 2 (1987): 153-81.

Korner, Alexis. "Big Bill Broonzy: Some Personal Memories." *Jazz Journal* 11, no. 3 (1958): 1.

Kyriakoudes, Louis M. *The Social Origins of the Urban South: Race, Gender, and Migration in Nashville and Middle Tennessee, 1890-1930*. Chapel Hill: University of North Carolina Press, 2003.

Lahmon, W. T., Jr. *Raising Cain: Blackface Performance from Jim Crow to Hip-Hop*. Cambridge, MA: Harvard University Press, 1998.

Laing, Dave. "MacColl and the English Folk Revival." In *Legacies of Ewan MacColl: The Last Interview*, edited by Allan F. Moore and Giovanni Vacca, 153-70. Farnham, UK: Ashgate, 2014.

Leadbitter, Mike, and Neil Slaven. *Blues Records, January 1943 to December 1966*. London: Hanover Books, 1968.

Levine, Lawrence. *Black Culture, Black Consciousness: Afro-American Folk Thought from Slavery to Freedom*. 1977. 30th anniversary ed. New York: Oxford University Press, 2007.

———. "The Musical Odyssey of an American Historian." In *Music and History: Bridging the Disciplines*, edited by Jeffrey H. Jackson and Stanley C. Pelkey, 3-20. Jackson: University of Mississippi Press, 2005.

Lewis, David Levering. *W. E. B. Du Bois: Biography of a Race, 1868-1919*. New York: Owl Books, 1993.

———. *W. E. B. Du Bois: The Fight for Equality in the American Century, 1919-1963*. New York: Holt, 2000.

———. *When Harlem Was in Vogue*. New York: Knopf, 1981.

"L500 'Blues' for Broonzy: Problem for the Jazz Federation." *Melody Maker*, August 23, 1958.

Lipsitz, George. *Time Passages: Collective Memory and American Popular Culture*. Minneapolis: University of Minnesota Press, 1990.

Littleton, Humphrey. "There's No Argument—The Money Is Big Bill's." *Melody Maker*, September 9, 1958.

Litwack, Leon. *Trouble in Mind: Black Southerners in the Age of Jim Crow*. New York: Vintage Books, 1999.

Locke, Alain. "The New Negro." In *The New Negro: Voices of the Harlem Renaissance*, edited by Alain Locke, 3-16. New York: Albert and Charles Boni, 1925.

———, ed. *The New Negro: Voices of the Harlem Renaissance*. New York: Albert and Charles Boni, 1925.

Lomax, Alan. "I Got the Blues." *Common Ground* 8, no. 4 (1948): 38-52.

———. *The Land Where the Blues Began*. New York: Doubleday Books, 1993.

Lomax, Anna, and Don Fleming. Interview by Julian Marshall. *On Point*, NPR, August 8, 2003. http://www.onpointradio.org/2003/08/capturing-the-blues.

Lomax, John A. *Negro Folk Songs as Sung by Leadbelly: "King of the Twelve-String Guitar Players of the World."* New York: Macmillan, 1936.

MacColl, Ewan. *Journeyman: An Autobiography*. Manchester: Manchester University Press, 2009.

Maddox, Colby, and Bob Reisman. *Win Stracke: Chicago's Troubadour*. Chicago: Old Town School of Folk Music, 2000.

Malone, Bill C. "Writing the History of Southern Music: A Review Essay." *Mississippi Quarterly* 45 (1992): 385-404.
Malone, Bill C., and David Stricklin. *Southern Music / American Music*. Rev. ed. Lexington: University of Kentucky Press, 2003.
Marshall, P. David. *Celebrity and Power: Fame in Contemporary Culture*. Minneapolis: University of Minnesota Press, 1997.
"Maybe I'll Sing Again Says Big Bill." *Melody Maker*, March 15, 1958, 1.
Melrose, Lester. "My Life in Recording." *American Folk Music Occasional* no. 2 (1970): 59-61.
Miller, Karl Hagstrom. *Segregating Sound: Inventing Folk and Pop Music in the Age of Jim Crow*. Durham, NC: Duke University Press, 2010.
Minton, John. *78 Blues: Folksongs and Phonographs in the American South*. Jackson: University Press of Mississippi, 2008.
Mississippi Blues Trail. "Tommy Johnson." Accessed February 27, 2017, http://www.msbluestrail.org/blues-trail-markers/tommy-johnson.
Morris, Ronald L. *Wait until Dark: Jazz and the Underworld, 1880-1940*. Bowling Green, OH: Bowling Green University Press, 1980.
Muir, Peter C. *Long Lost Blues: Popular Blues in America, 1850-1920*. Urbana: University of Illinois Press, 2010.
Mullen, Patrick B. *The Man Who Adores the Negro: Race and American Folklore*. Urbana: University of Illinois Press, 2008.
"Music: Spirituals to Swing." *Time*, January 2, 1939.
"Musician's Plight." *Time*, May 7, 1956.
Nederlands Jazz Archeif. "The Work of Michiel de Ruyter: Big Bill Broonzy." Accessed May 12, 2014, http://mdr.jazzarchief.nl/producent/broonzy/.
Odum, Howard W. "Folk-Song and Folk-Poetry as Found in the Secular Songs of Southern Negroes." *Journal of American Folklore* 24 (July-September 1911): 255-94.
Odum, Howard W., and Guy B. Johnson. *The Negro and His Songs*. Chapel Hill: University of North Carolina Press, 1925.
———. *Negro Workaday Songs*. Chapel Hill: University of North Carolina Press, 1927.
Old Town School of Folk Music. "Biography of a Hunch: Opening Night." Accessed December 13, 2015, http://www.oldtownschool.org/history/night.html.
Oliver, Paul. "Big Bill Broonzy on 'Vogue.'" *Music Mirror* 3 (1956): 4-6.
———. "Blue-Eyed Blues: The Impact of the Blues on European Culture." In *Approaches to Popular Culture*, edited by C. W. E. Bigsby, 227-40. Bowling Green, OH: Bowling Green University Press, 1978.
———. *Blues Fell This Morning: Meaning in the Blues*. London: Cassell, 1960.
———. *Savannah Syncopators: African Retentions in the Blues*. New York: Stein and Day, 1970.
———. *Songsters and Saints: Vocal Traditions on Race Records*. New York: Cambridge University Press, 1984.
———. *The Story of the Blues*. 2nd ed. Boston: Northeastern University Press, 1997.
———. "Taking the Measure of the Blues." In *Cross the Water Blues: African American Music in Europe*, edited by Neil A. Wynn, 23-38. Jackson: University Press of Mississippi, 2007.

Olmstead, Tony. *Folkways Records: Moses Asch and His Encyclopedia of Sound*. New York: Routledge, 2003.

O'Neal, Jim, and Amy van Singel. *The Voice of the Blues: Classic Interviews from "Living Blues" Magazine*. New York: Routledge, 2002.

Palmer, Robert. *Deep Blues*. New York: Viking, 1981.

Panassié, Hugues. "Big Bill Broonzy: Und Grand Chanteur de Blues." *La Revue du Jazz* 7 (1949): 218-19.

———. "Big Bill Doesn't Sell His Music—He Gives It Away." *Melody Maker*, September 15, 1951.

Perchard, Tom. "Tradition, Modernity, and the Supernatural Swing: Re-reading 'Primitivism' in Hugues Panassié's Writing on Jazz." *Popular Music* 30, no. 1 (2011): 25-45.

Poiger, Uta G. *Jazz, Rock, and Rebels: Cold War Politics and American Culture in a Divided Germany*. Berkley: University of California Press, 2000.

Portelli, Alessandro. *The Death of Luigi Trastulli and Other Stories: Form and Meaning in Oral History*. Albany: State University of New York Press, 1990.

Prial, Dunstan. *The Producer: John Hammond and the Soul of American Music*. New York: Picador, 2007.

Radano, Ronald. "On Ownership and Value." *Black Music Research Journal* 30, no. 2 (2010): 363-70.

Raeburn, Bruce Boyd. *New Orleans Style and the Writing of Jazz History*. Ann Arbor: University of Michigan Press, 2009.

Ransby, Barbara. *Eslanda: The Large and Unconventional of Life Mrs. Paul Robeson*. New Haven, CT: Yale University Press, 2013.

Reid, Ira D. "Mrs. Bailey Pays the Rent." In *Ebony and Topaz: A Collectanea*, edited by Charles S. Johnson, 144-48. New York: National Urban League, 1927.

Riesman, Bob. *I Feel So Good: The Life and Times of Big Bill Broonzy*. Chicago: University of Chicago Press, 2011.

Rowe, Mike. *Chicago Blues: The Music and the City*. New York: Drake, 1973.

———. *Chicago Breakdown*. New York: Drake, 1975.

Roy, William G. *Reds, Whites, and Blues: Social Movements, Folk Music, and Race*. Princeton, NJ: Princeton University Press, 2010.

Runstedtler, Theresa. *Jack Johnson, Rebel Sojourner: Boxing the in the Shadow of the Color Line*. Berkley: University of California Press, 2012.

Russell, Tony. "Clarksdale Piccolo Blues." *Jazz and Blues*, November 1971.

Sacre, Robert. "Yannick Bruynoghe." *Living Blues* 60-61 (Summer-Fall 1984): 71-72.

Schroeder, Patricia. *Robert Johnson, Mythmaking, and Contemporary Culture*. Urbana: University of Illinois Press, 2004.

Schroer, Timothy L. *Recasting Race after World War II: Germans and African Americans in American-Occupied Germany*. Boulder: University Press of Colorado, 2007.

Schultz, Stan. "Send Your Kids to Summer Camp at Circle Pines: A Unique Co-Op Camp That Teaches Great Values." *Lifestyle: Associated Content*, 2007.

Schwartz, Roberta Freund. *How Britain Got the Blues: The Transmission of American Blues Style in the United Kingdom*. Burlington, VT: Ashgate, 2007.

———. "Preaching the Gospel of the Blues: Blues Evangelists in Britain." In *Cross the Water Blues: African American Music in Europe*, edited by Neil A. Wynn, 145-66. Jackson: University Press of Mississippi, 2007.

Smith, Charles Edward. "Big Bill and the Country Blues." In *Big Bill Blues: William Broonzy's Story as Told to Yannick Bruynoghe*, by Big Bill Broonzy, 11-25. 1964. Reprint, New York: Da Capo, 1992.

Smith, Charles Edward, and Frederic Ramsey Jr. *Jazzmen*. New York: Harcourt Brace Jovanovich, 1939.

Spear, Allan H. *Black Chicago: The Making of a Negro Ghetto, 1890-1920*. Chicago: University of Chicago Press, 1969.

Springer, Robert. "The Blues in France." In *Cross the Water Blues: African American Music in Europe*, edited by Neil A. Wynn, 235-49. Jackson: University Press of Mississippi, 2007.

"Stars All Set to Help Big Bill." *Melody Maker*, March 8, 1958, 20.

Steiner, John. "Beyond the Impression." *Record Research* 17 (March-April 1958): 7.

Sternheimer, Karen. *Celebrity Culture and the American Dream: Stardom and Social Mobility*. New York: Routledge, 2011.

Stewart-Baxter, Derrick. "A Date with the Blues." *Melody Maker*, September 15, 1951.

———. "Preachin' the Blues." *Jazz Journal* 4, no. 11 (1951): 13-14.

———. "Preachin' the Blues: Big Bill Broonzy." *Jazz Journal* 6, no. 2 (1953): 4.

Sugrue, Thomas. *Origins of the Urban Crisis: Race and Inequality in Postwar Detroit*. Princeton, NJ: Princeton University Press, 1997.

Sweetman, Ron. "Big Bill Broonzy in France and England." Jazz Journalist Association Library, 2003. http://www.jazzhouse.org/library/?read=sweetman2.

Szwed, John. *Alan Lomax: The Man Who Recorded the World*. New York: Viking, 2010.

"Tangents: Big Bill Broonzy." *DownBeat*, October 8, 1958, 42.

Terkel, Louis "Studs." Liner notes to *Muddy Waters Sings Big Bill Broonzy / Folk Singer*. BGO BGO 397, 1998, compact disc.

Terkel, Louis "Studs," John de Graaf, and Alan Harris Stein. "The Guerilla Journalist as Oral Historian: An Interview with Louis 'Studs' Terkel." *Oral History Review* 29, no. 1 (2002): 87-107.

Titon, Jeff Todd. *Early Downhome Blues: A Musical and Cultural Analysis*. Urbana: University of Illinois Press, 1977.

Toll, Robert C. *Blacking Up: The Minstrel Show in Nineteenth Century America*. New York: Oxford University Press, 1974.

Tuttle, William M., Jr. *Race Riot: Chicago in the Red Summer of 1919*. New York: Atheneum, 1975.

U.S. Congress, Committee on the Judiciary. *Designating the Year Beginning February 1, 2003, as the "Year of the Blues."* 107th Cong., 2nd sess., 2003, 107.

Uzzel, Robert L. *Blind Lemon Jefferson: His Life, His Death, and His Legacy*. Fort Worth, TX: Eakin Books, 2002.

van der Tuuk, Alex. *The Rise and Fall of Paramount Records: A History of the Wisconsin Chair Co. and Its Recording Activities*. Denver: Mainspring, 2003.

van Gasteren, Louis. "How Did I Come to Make These Recordings?" Essay in liner notes to Big Bill Broonzy, *Amsterdam Live Concerts 1953: Unissued Live Concerts Recorded by Louis Van Gasteren*. Munich Records CD 275, 2006.

Van Rijn, Guido. "Lowland Blues: The Reception of African American Blues and Gospel Music in the Netherlands." In *Cross the Water Blues: African American Music in Europe*, edited by Neil A. Wynn, 218-34. Jackson: University Press of Mississippi, 2007.

Wald, Elijah. *Escaping the Delta: Robert Johnson and the Invention of the Blues*. New York: HarperCollins, 2004.

———. *Josh White: Society Blues*. Amherst: University of Massachusetts Press, 2000.

Ward, Brian. *Just My Soul Responding: Rhythm and Blues, Black Consciousness, and Race Relations*. Berkeley: University of California Press, 1998.

Waters, Muddy. *Muddy Waters: The Complete Plantation Recordings: The Historic 1941-42 Library of Congress Field Recordings*. MCA/Chess Records, 1993.

———. *Muddy Waters Sings Big Bill Broonzy*. Chess Records LP 1444, 1960.

Werner, Jann. "Eric Clapton." In *The Rolling Stones Interviews: Talking with the Legends of Rock and Roll, 1967-1980*, edited by in Pete Herbs, 24-31. New York: HarperCollins, 1981.

Whiteis, David. "The Blues Reality of Maxwell Street." In *BluesSpeak: The Best of the "Original Chicago Blues Annual,"* edited by Lincoln T. Beauchamp, 22-25. Urbana: University of Illinois Press, 2010.

Williams, Chad L. *Torchbearers of Democracy: African American Soldiers in the World War I Era*. Chapel Hill: University of North Carolina Press, 2010.

Winant, Howard. *The World Is a Ghetto: Race and Democracy since World War II*. New York: Basic Books, 2001.

Wintz, Cary D. *Black Culture and the Harlem Renaissance*. Houston: Rice University Press, 1988.

Wolcott, Victoria. *Remaking Respectability: African American Women in Interwar Detroit*. Chapel Hill: University of North Carolina Press, 2001.

Wolfe, Charles, and Kip Lornell. *The Life and Legend of Leadbelly*. New York: Da Capo, 1999.

Wynn, Neil A., ed. *Cross the Water Blues: African American Music in Europe*. Jackson: University Press of Mississippi, 2007.

———. "'Why I Sing the Blues': African Culture in the Transatlantic World." In *Cross the Water Blues: African American Music in Europe*, edited by Neil A. Wynn, 3-22. Jackson: University Press of Mississippi, 2007.

Index

Abott, Robert, 40
Algemene Vereniging Radio Omroep (AVRO), 133
Altheimer, Josh, 82
American Federation of Musicians (AFM): Chicago Local 208 chapter, 80; and 1942 recording strike, 88–89; as a segregated union, 66
American Society of Composers, Authors, and Publishers (ASCAP): role in 1942 recording strike, 88; as a segregated organization in early music recording, 65–66
Ames (Iowa), 96, 110–14
Anderson, Mozelle, 69, 72
Apollo Theater, 46, 82, 86, 103
Armed Forces Radio Service, 117
Armstrong, Louis, 53, 85, 103, 113
Asch, Moses (Mo), 98, 106, 117, 203n37
Authenticity: and Alan Lomax, 100–101, 154; in *Big Bill Blues*, 157–65; defined, 194n8; as part of celebrity, 6; in recording marketing strategies, 6; in studies of the blues, 11, 158, 165

"Baby I Done Got Wise," 87, 156–57
Baker, Josephine, 9
Barber, Chris, 145
Barnes, George, 81
"Barrel House Rag," 73
Basie, William J. (Count Basie), 2–3, 86–87, 156
Bechet, Sidney, 106, 119, 124–25; on spirituals, 23
Beck, Jeff, 149, 168; and Broonzy's public memory, 170–71
Belcher, Jerry, 18
Bell, Graeme, 124

Berliner, Emile, 51
Bernay, Eric, 3
"Big Bill Blues," 56, 63, 64, 69, 159
Big Bill Blues: Broonzy and Yannick Bruynoghe as authors, 157, 183n16; as part of Broonzy's public memory, 158–64
"Big Bill's Boogie," 85
"Black Brown and White," 12, 108, 127, 138–39, 160, 199n27
Black consciousness: and black agency, 2, 6, 13; and Broonzy, 20, 27–28, 29, 41–42, 45; and celebrity culture, 13; defined, 181n13; in New Negro Renaissance, 10, 30, 34
Black identity: and the Black Metropolis, 43; and Broonzy, 4, 58, 77, 98; and celebrity culture, 10, 172; and community formation, 10–11; and the folk music revival, 98
Black Metropolis (Bronzeville), 4, 10, 37; blues music in, 49, 52, 58, 76, 97; as center for black music, 52–53, 71–72, 74, 153; as a center for race, class, and gender development, 40, 43, 45; and commercialized leisure, 54, 57, 65, 83; as a community study, 37, 187n36, 187n49; defined, 3, 35–36; and Great Depression, 70; Old vs. New Settler ideology in, 40, 188n50; as part of New Negro Renaissance, 10, 34, 43, 50, 68; and "Spend Your Money Where You Can Work" campaign, 71
Black Patti Records, 71
Black Swan Records, 60
Blake, William (Blind Blake), 45, 49, 55–57, 64–66, 93, 169, 190n56; impact on Broonzy, 60–63

Bluebird Records, 42–43, 78, 84
Blues, 15; and authenticity, 11, 23, 61, 100–101, 154–58, 165; Chicago (urban) blues, 2–4, 11–12, 43, 51–53, 68, 69–81, 84, 90, 111; classic blues, 4, 7, 24–25, 31, 47, 61, 117, 141; and community, 3, 10, 13, 22, 50–51, 53, 92–95, 145, 190n56; and the consumer marketplace, 43, 50, 61, 76; country blues, 2, 5, 11, 49, 54, 61–62, 64–66, 82, 102–3, 138; defined, 6–8, 11, 15, 23–24, 50, 178–79; Delta blues, 3, 11, 84, 86, 91, 93–94, 190n50, 193n69; and the folk music revival, 8, 12, 23, 97–114, 134–41, 151–55, 196n58, 202n19, 204n56; and "From Spirituals to Swing," 1, 82–83; Hokum, 46; and identity, 184n25; and Jim Crow racism, 21, 23, 107–10, 138–40; jump blues, 85; and literary analysis, 13, 182n35; and the New Negro, 7, 10–11, 48, 50, 58, 182n29; as part of southern music, 17–18, 19, 24, 184n28, 190n57; popularity of, 24–25; and public memory, 12, 14, 148–72; and recording industry, 24, 49, 58–59, 78–80, 85–90; relationship to jazz, 8, 12, 52–53, 78–80, 85, 87–88, 115–30, 133–47, 156–57, 192–93n52, 203n44; at rent parties, 42, 56–58; rhythm and blues, 85; and Robert Johnson, 6–7; on sheet music, 24; studies of, 151–68, 205n18; as transnational music, 5, 12, 115–30, 131–47, 174, 201n65

Blues Fell This Morning, 163

Blues in the Mississippi Night, 106, 108–9, 128, 151–52

Boas, Gunter, 125, 197n34
Borneman, Ernest, 121, 126, 128–29
Boyd, Eddie, 92
Bradley, Andrew J., 35
Bradley, Frank, 18
Bradley, James, 30
Bradley, Lee Conley. *See* Broonzy, Big Bill

Bradswell, Frank, 69
Broadcast Music Incorporated (BMI), 88
Broonzy, Annie (second wife), 47
Broonzy, Big Bill: addresses in Chicago, 31; and Alan Lomax (*see* Lomax, Alan); and American Federation of Musicians, 80, 88, 192n34; in Ames, 96, 112–14, 121, 194n5; in Arkansas, 3, 10, 17–19, 30; arrival in Chicago, 31–33; and Arthur Blake (Blind Blake), 62–63; and authenticity, 101, 105, 154–55, 157–58, 165; background, 18, 183n7, 184n28, 196n54, 196n55, 196n58; and benefit concerts, 145–46; and *Big Bill Blues* (see *Big Bill Blues*); and black consciousness, 6, 15, 106–10, 178–79, 185n61, 205n18; and Blind Lemon Jefferson, 49, 55–56, 62; and *Blues in the Mississippi Night* (see *Blues in the Mississippi Night*); and cancer, 143–46; and celebrity, 4–6, 9–10, 12, 15, 19, 22, 33, 59, 86–87, 96, 114, 116, 121, 123–24, 132, 141–43, 147, 154, 158, 170–72, 178, 190n57; Charlie Jackson (Papa Charlie), 49, 60–61; and Chicago blues, 4, 53, 68, 69, 73–74, 76, 82, 96, 123; and *Chicago Defender*, 37, 64; and Circle Pines Center, 142–43; and commercialized leisure, 8, 43, 50; and community, 11, 68; and consumer marketplace, 11, 68; and country blues, 5, 12, 67, 82, 84, 101, 103, 105, 123; death, 146–47, 186n80; and death of brother, James, 30; as didact, 8, 12, 115–16, 121, 128, 142; in Europe, 114, 116–30, 133–47; and the folk music revival, 4–5, 7–8, 96–114, 118–19, 126, 128, 141; in "From Spirituals to Swing," 1–3, 6, 8, 82, 101–3, 122; on gender and sexuality, 45–48; and Georgia Tom Dorsey, 72–73; and Great Migrations, 4, 32; as a guitarist, 2, 49, 54, 57, 62, 64, 76, 91, 123, 145; and hokum, 73; and Hugues Panassie (*see* Panassie,

220 Index

Hugues); and "I Come for to Sing," 96, 112, 121, 141; and identity, 4–5, 10, 12–13, 44, 49–50, 55–59, 67, 69, 76–78, 80–81, 83–84, 99, 114–16, 123–25, 130, 147, 172, 192–93n52; introduction to music, 17–19, 23; and jazz, 8, 78, 85–87, 115–30; and Jim Crow racism, 4, 10, 19–21, 30, 36, 38, 41–42, 45, 84, 137–40, 183n16; and J. Mayo Williams, 60, 63, 66; and John Hammond (see Hammond, John); and Josh White (see White, Josh); jump blues, 85; as a laborer, 35, 38, 68, 74, 96; as leader in Chicago blues community, 42, 91–95, 96; and Lester Melrose (see Melrose, Lester); and Louis Armstrong, 113; marriages, 21, 47, 131–32, 197n23; and Maxwell Street, 54; and Mettie Belcher (Bradley; mother), 46; and Michael De Ruyter (see de Ruyter, Michiel); and Michael van Isveldt, 84, 131, 173–79, 204n4; and Muddy Waters (see Morganfield, McKinley); and music industry, 1, 5, 10, 12, 20–22, 42–43, 49, 51, 60, 63–64, 67, 72, 75–76, 80–82, 85–90, 96, 123, 134–36; on music royalties, 65–67; as New Negro, 7, 10–11, 33–34, 37, 43–44, 48, 50; and Old Town School of Folk Music (see Old Town School of Folk Music (Chicago)); and People's Songs, Inc., 103–4, 106, 110–11; and Pim van Isveldt, 132–34, 139, 141, 143–44, 174; and public memory, 101, 148–72, 203n35, 203n38, 204n56; and religion, 20–21; at rent parties, 43, 55–58; and respectability, 12, 38–40, 42–44, 47–48; respect for Minnie Douglas (Memphis Minnie), 47; and Robert Johnson, 2, 6–7; service in the Army, 25–29; and Tampa Red, 3, 70, 72; as transnational musician, 9, 12; as vocalist, 2, 57, 64, 76–77, 85, 145; and World War I, 25–26, 29, 183n7; 184n47; and Yannick Bruynoghe (see Bruynoghe, Yannick)

Broonzy, Rose (née Allen, third wife), 47, 131, 188n72, 197n23

Broonzy, Rose (née Lawson, fourth wife), 47, 132, 174, 188n70, 197n23, 198n4

Brown, Robert C. (Washboard Sam), 43, 75, 78, 90, 92

Brunswick Records, 74, 90

Bruynoghe, Yannick: background, 120; as Belgian jazz writer, 119; and *Big Bill Blues*, 157–65, 183n16, 202n19, 203n35; and Broonzy, 120, 135, 140; and Broonzy's European tours, 121–22, 135. *See also* Public memory

Burnett, Chester (Howlin' Wolf), 91, 141, 158, 163

Byas, Don, 85

Café Society, 3, 46, 82, 98, 103

Cahill, Marie, 24

Carr, Leroy, 45, 75, 166

Carter, Louis, 19, 20

Celebrity culture: and black identity, 5–6, 9, 13, 15, 59, 147, 171–72, 178; in blues culture, 68–69, 84, 86, 110; Broonzy as part of in Europe, 132–36, 139, 141–43, 170; Broonzy as part of in U.S., 4–5, 8–13, 57, 69, 74, 84, 86, 97, 102, 104–5, 108, 114, 116, 121, 127, 154; Broonzy learning about, 17–19, 22, 57, 74; and consumer marketplace, 11, 13; defined, 5–6; historiography of, 182n23; son Michael as steward of, 173, 177

Charters, Samuel Barclay, 166–67

Chatman, Peter (Memphis Slim), 43, 76, 90–92, 106, 146, 151, 161–63

Chess, Leonard, 95

Chess, Philip, 95

Chess Records, 95, 142, 143, 169, 204n56

Chicago. *See* Black Metropolis (Bronzeville)

Index 221

Chicago Blues, 167
Chicago Music Publishing Company, 60, 65–66, 72
Chicago Whip, 59
Circle Pines Center, 142–44, 200n47
Clapton, Eric, 131; Broonzy's public memory, 148–50, 168; influenced by Broonzy, 148
Columbia Phonograph Company, 51, 52
Columbia Records, 2, 69, 85, 89, 103, 119
Commercialized leisure: and black identity, 50, 172; and the Black Metropolis, 10, 36, 39, 55; and Broonzy, 42, 49, 57, 68, 92; and community respectability, 40, 43; defined, 8, 187n49; and the Great Migrations, 54; and Paramount Records, 65–66
Congress of Industrial Organizations Political Actions Committee (CIO-PAC), 110
Consumer Marketplace: and blues music, 11, 90; and Broonzy, 11, 50, 105, 187; and commercialized leisure, 50; and community formation, 40, 45; and the New Negro Renaissance, 10–11, 13, 105; and southern music, 50
Cox, Ida, 25, 47, 55, 64, 65
Coyler, Ken, 146

Davis, John ("Blind"), 81, 133, 134
Davis, Walter, 76, 77
Decca Records, 43, 71, 106
de Ruyter, Michiel, 133, 140
Dickerson, Althea, 49
Dixon, Willie, 141
Donegan, Lonnie, 145, 201n65
Dorsey, Thomas A. (Georgia Tom), 69, 72; background of, 72; with Broonzy, 73–74; with Ma Rainey and Tampa Red, 72–73
Douglas, Minnie (Memphis Minnie), 90, 93, 161; Broonzy's respect for, 47
"Down in the Basement Blues," 65

Du Bois, W.E.B.: on double consciousness, 28, 181n13; on returning black veterans of World War I, 27; on spirituals, 22

Easton, A. Amos (Bumble Bee Slim), 76
Edison, Harry (Sweets), 3
Edison, Thomas, 51
Embrey, Gertrude (first wife), 21, 29, 47
Eric Clapton Unplugged, 149
Estes, John ("Sleepy"), 76, 119, 126, 161
Europe, James Reese, 9, 119

Feinberg, Leonard, 112–13
Fisk Jubilee Singers, 9
Folk music revival, 15; and *Blues in the Mississippi Night*, 109; Broonzy as participant in, 4, 14, 99, 110; and Broonzy's public memory, 165; defined, 97–98; in England, 117, 119; John and Alan Lomax's influence on, 99–104; Robert Johnson's importance to, 7; as a social movement, 97, 194n6, 194n8
Folkways Records, 142, 164, 166, 203n37
"From Spirituals to Swing" (1938), 1–8, 82, 98, 101–2, 104, 122, 149, 156, 164, 169–70
"From Spirituals to Swing" (1939), 82, 98, 103, 149, 151, 156, 164, 170

Gertrude, Rainey (Ma Rainey), 24, 25, 47, 55, 57, 61, 64, 65, 72, 126
Gillum, William McKinley (Jazz Gillum), 76
Glasser, Joe, 122
"Gonna Tear it on Down," 56, 63
Goodman, Benny, 85–86
Gordon, Robert Winslow, 98, 100
Great Depression: and blues in Europe, 9; and Broonzy, 72, 78, 81; and Great Migrations, 76; and impact on recording industry, 69, 71–72, 75, 78, 80, 84, 166, 189n39; and labor, 98; and New Negro Renaissance, 34

222   Index

Great Migrations: Broonzy as participant, 4, 11, 90, 157–58; and Chicago, 91, 152; defined, 31, 35, 78; and music business, 59
Green, Lilian (Lil), 11, 43, 46, 120
Guthrie, Woody, 98, 104, 110, 111, 118

Hall, Vera, 119
Hamilton, Frank, 142
Hammond, John: and Broonzy, 104, 110, 170; and folk music revival, 101–2, 110; and "From Spirituals to Swing," 2–3, 82, 98; and Robert Johnson, 7, 118, 202n23
Handy, W.C., 23, 24
Hays, Lee, 110, 111
"Hey, Hey," 148, 149, 169
Hines, Earl, 53
"Hit The Right Lick," 76
"Horny Frog," 46, 76, 160
Hot Club de France, 119, 120, 122, 124
Hot Club of Frankfurt, 124, 125
House, Eddie (Son House), 21, 23, 66, 93, 102, 106, 158, 190n57
"House Rent Stomp," 56, 63, 64, 69, 127
House Un-American Activities Committee (HUAC), 111, 118
Hudtwalcker, Olaf, 124, 125
Hughes, Langston, 36, 55

"I Can't Be Satisfied," 56
"I Come for to Sing," 14, 96, 111, 121, 141. *See also* Roble, Chet; Stracke, Win; Terkel, Louis (Studs)
"I Feel So Good," 125
"I Love My Whiskey," 85
Iowa State College (University), 96–97, 112–13, 122
"It Hurts Me too," 144
"It's a Lowdown Dirty Shame," 81

Jackson, Mahalia, 135, 146, 147; as pioneer of gospel music, 73
Jacobs, Walter (Little Walter), 90, 92, 96, 141, 147, 163, 168

Jacqueline (girlfriend), 147
Jazz, 74, 103, 171; bebop, 87, 120, 126; big band, 85–86, 156; and Broonzy, 5, 80, 86–87, 89, 102, 112, 115–30, 116, 142; Chicago, 53, 82, 90–91, 94, 102, 156; and Chicago blues, 12, 52, 78, 125, 127; and consumer marketplace, 58; in Europe, 4, 8, 12, 101, 115–30, 136, 139–40, 203–4n54; and the New Negro, 7, 61; New Orleans (traditional), 1, 23, 53, 120, 124, 127, 143, 156; New York, 71, 74, 82; and Papa Charlie Jackson, 60; and public memory, 155–67; and recording industry, 52, 88–89; and relationship to blues, 85, 115–30; studies of, 47, 87–88, 91, 119–22, 127, 143–47, 155–67, 203n37, 203n44, 205n18
Jazz Journal, 127
Jazz Record, 87, 156
Jefferson, Lemon Henry (Blind Lemon), 5, 23, 49, 55–57, 60, 61–63, 64, 65, 66, 68, 80, 93, 101, 102, 103, 166, 169
Jim Crow racism, 2, 3, 11, 20, 84, 87; and *Big Bill Blues*, 158–60, 202n19; and blues, 21, 23, 50, 105; and *Blues in the Mississippi Night*, 106–10, 152; and Broonzy, 10, 20–21, 30, 33, 41–42, 67, 104, 112, 114, 128, 153–54; and celebrity, 5, 17, 20, 22, 181n19; and Lomax, Alan, 150, 153–54; and migration, 35, 38; and music, 4, 14, 21–22, 100; and World War I, 26–28
"Joe Turner Blues," 144
Johnson, Big Bill. *See* Broonzy, Big Bill
Johnson, Eldridge, 51
Johnson, Jack, 9
Johnson, James P., 2
Johnson, Lonnie, 23, 75, 93, 96, 117, 161, 166
Johnson, Pete, 2, 87, 106
Johnson, Robert, 2, 5, 6, 7, 23, 93, 102, 103, 119, 158, 162, 166, 190n57, 193n69, 202n23
Johnson, Tommy, 60, 190n50

Jones, Floyd, 92, 168
Jones, Max, 121, 126, 127, 204nn3-4
Joplin, Scott, 23

"Keep Your Hands Off Her," 76, 125
"Key to the Highway," 31, 76
KFFA (Helena, Arkansas), 91, 93
King, Riley (B.B.), 30, 91
Kraber, Tony, 98

LaMothe, Ferdinand Joseph (Jelly Roll Morton), 53, 74, 119, 126
Lane, Larry, 96, 141
Ledbetter, Huddie (Lead Belly), 98, 104, 117, 120, 122; compared to Broonzy, 110-11; as example of authenticity, 100-102
Lenoir, J.B., 92, 96, 146-47
Library of Congress, 21, 60, 91, 93; Archive of American Folksong, 98, 117, 183n7, 193n69
Lippmann, Horst, 124
Locke, Alain, 34
Lomax, Alan: and authenticity, 100, 154, 194; and *Blues in the Mississippi Night*, 106-10, 151, 203-4n54; and Broonzy's public memory, 149, 151-55, 157-58, 165, 196n2; in Europe, 115, 128-29, 131, 145-46; and folk music revival, 98, 103, 106, 117, 194n8; and *The Land Where the Blues Began*, 7, 154, 160, 192n38; and Lead Belly, 99-101; and Library of Congress Archive of American Folk Song, 21, 117; and music, 87; and politics, 104; and racism, 99; recording of Muddy Waters, 91, 93, 193n69; relationship with Broonzy, 27, 33, 47, 81, 101, 103-04, 110, 115, 122, 135, 183n7, 183n16, 186n80, 192n38, 192-93n52; on Robert Johnson, 7, 103, 202n23
Lomax, John: as folk music pioneer, 98-99, 194n8; and Lead Belly, 99-101; and Library of Congress Archive of American Folk Song, 99

London Jazz Club, 127, 134
"Long Tall Mama," 76
Luandrew, Albert (Sunnyland Slim), 90
Lunsford, Bascom Lamar, 98, 194n8

MacColl, Ewan, 118-19, 196n9
Maxwell Street Market, 10, 44, 53-54, 168
McGhee, Walter Brown (Brownie), 106, 118
McRae, Teddy, 86
Melody Maker, 123, 125, 127, 129, 145, 146
Melrose, Lester, 68, 89, 95, 104, 110; background, 69, 74-75; and Chicago's music community, 69, 74, 99; in the Jim Crow South, 84; and relationship with Broonzy, 69, 75-80, 84-85, 91-92, 94, 99, 122; and reorganization of music industry, 90
Mercury Records, 85, 95
Miller, Rice (Sonny Boy Williamson II), 91, 141
Morganfield, McKinley (Muddy Waters), 92, 96, 119, 131, 147, 163; background, 93; and Broonzy's public memory, 149, 158, 168-70, 171, 204n56; friendship with Broonzy, 93-94

National Broadcasting Company, 51
new generation of Chicago blues, 90-91, 95, 141, 193n75
New Masses, 82
New Negro: and blues, 8, 182n29; Broonzy as, 7, 10-11, 30-31, 48, 58, 178; and celebrity culture, 5; in Chicago, 10-11, 14, 32-33, 44, 105; and the consumer marketplace, 11, 50; defined, 10, 34, 186n5; and leisure, 10-11, 50; as a movement, 7-8, 10, 13, 33-34, 68; Williams, J. Mayo as, 59, 190n42; and World War I, 29
The New Negro, (Locke), 34
New York Amsterdam News, 85, 87

224 Index

Odum, Howard, 99
Okeh Records, 52, 72
Old Town School of Folk Music (Chicago), 142, 173
Oliver, Joe (King), 53, 74
Oliver, Paul, 121, 126, 163

Panassie, Hugues, 119; descriptions of Broonzy's artistry, 143; as early jazz writer/critic, 119–20; as organizer and promoter for Broonzy's in Europe, 120, 122–23
Paramount Records, 43, 52, 56, 59–66, 69, 71, 72, 74, 82, 190n41, 190n50, 193n69
Patterson, Ottilie, 146
Patton, Charley, 66, 93, 158, 190n50
People's Songs, Inc., 103, 104, 106, 110–11
Pettis, Arthur, 69
Public memory: and *Big Bill Blues*, 157–65; and the blues, 11–12; and Broonzy, 14, 99, 149, 156, 162, 166–68, 170–72; defined, 182n32; and Lomax, Alan, 151–56; and Waters, Muddy, 169–70
Pullman Company, 35, 38, 46

Race records, 52, 58–59; defined, 25
Ragtime, 20, 23, 51, 53, 60, 62, 64, 73
Randle, Bill, 144, 184n28
RCA Victor, 69, 78, 80, 82, 89, 90
Red Channels, 118
Rent parties: and black identity, 49, 58; and Broonzy, 4, 43–44, 55–57, 58, 63, 64; defined, 55–57; as part of commercialized leisure in black Chicago, 43, 53, 55, 72; and public memory, 161, 168
Respectability: and behavior, 44, 48; and Broonzy, 38, 47–48, 56; and Old Settler vs. New Settler class formation, 39–43; and racial uplift ideology, 38
Rhythm & Blues (R&B), 123, 148, 164

Richards, Keith, 149
Rider, See-see, 17–18, 62, 110, 190n57
Robeson, Paul, 9, 118, 179
Roble, Chet, 141, 147
Rodgers, Jimmie, 23
Rogers, Jimmy, 23, 90, 92, 168
Rooduijn, Hans, 139
Rowe, Mike, 149; and Broonzy's public memory, 167–68
Rushing, Jimmy, 2

Sampson, Sammy. *See* Broonzy, Big Bill
Sandburg, Carl, 98
"Saturday Night Rub," 57
Seeger, Charles, 96
Seeger, Pete, 96, 98, 110, 111, 118, 142, 144, 146
"See See Rider," 144
Sellers, Brother John, 147
Sharp, Cecil, 98, 99, 118
Shines, Johnny, 90
"Skoodle Do Do," 56, 75
Smith, Bessie, 24, 25, 47, 55, 57, 61, 86, 126
Smith, Mamie, 24, 25, 47
Spirituals, 1, 2, 19, 22, 23, 104, 123, 144
"Starvation Blues," 65
Stevens, David, 136, 146
Stevens, Trixie, 136, 146
Stewart-Baxter, Derrick, 121, 126, 127
Stracke, Win: as Chicago folk music pioneer, 96, 110–12; in "I Come for to Sing," 141; and Old Town School of Folk Music, 142; relationship with Broonzy, 121, 122, 134, 147
Swing Records, 120

"Tadpole Blues," 56, 75
Terkel, Louis (Studs): and Broonzy Benefit Concert, 146; as Chicago folk music pioneer, 96, 110–12; in "I Come for to Sing," 141; relationship with Broonzy, 4, 41, 121, 122, 138, 192–93n52

Index 225

Terrell, Saunders (Sonny Terry), 2, 106, 118
"That Stuff I Got," 73
Theatre Owner's Booking Association (TOBA), 24
The Country Blues, 163, 166, 167, 203n44
"The Duck's Yas Yas Yas," 73
The Hokum Boys, 73
The Land Where the Blues Began, 7, 154, 160
The Stroll: as center for leisure and labor, 54; as center of black music activity, 49, 52–53; as home to J. Mayo "Ink" Williams office, 66; as home to rent parties, 55, 57, 58, 71, 72
Thomas, John, 49, 61–65, 72
"Tight Like That," 73
"Tod Pail Blues," 63
"Trouble in Mind," 125, 144
"Trucking Little Woman," 76
Turner, Joe, 2

van Gool, Wouter, 139
van Isveldt, Michael, xiii; birth, 131–32, 192n45; Broonzy financial support of, 135; as steward of Broonzy's legacy, 134, 173–78, 188n72
van Isveldt, Pim: meeting Broonzy for first time, 132, 174, 176, 177; as mother to Michael, 131, 192n45; relationship with Broonzy, 133–34, 197n23; as steward of Broonzy's legacy, 176, 188n72
Vaudeville, 23–25, 43, 51–53 passim, 57, 60–62 passim, 68, 72, 73, 120; defined, 76, 90
Verve Records, 144–45
Victor Talking Machine Company, 51
Victory Disks (V-Discs), 120

Vocalion Records, 43, 52, 82
Vogue Records, 123

Weller, Bettina, xiii, 176
"What's That I Smell," 73
"When Do I Get to Be Called a Man," 158–59
Whitaker, Hudson (Tampa Red), 3, 43, 70, 75, 90, 93, 96, 161; background, 72; in the Black Metropolis, 72–73; and relationship with Broonzy, 72–74, 146–47, 163
White, Josh, 98, 104, 142; background, 195n48; and Broonzy, 122, 136; in Europe, 117, 118, 120; and folk music revival, 110–11, 199n21
Wilcox, Herbert (Wilcox brothers), 127, 129, 134–36
Williams, J. Mayo (Ink Williams), 49; background, 59–60; and Broonzy, 63, 65, 72, 104, 110, 122; as New Negro, 59, 190n42; and Paramount Records, 60–61; and recording industry, 65–67, 71, 78
Williams, Johnny, 90, 92
Williamson, John Lee (Sonny Boy Williamson I), 94; and *Blues in the Mississippi Night*, 106–8, 151–54; in Chicago's blues community, 76, 90; and relationship with Broonzy, 43–45, 161
Wisconsin Chair Company, 52, 59–60
Work, John W., III, 11, 93, 193n69
World War I, 113–14, 116, 119, 154, 157–58 passim; Broonzy's service, 14, 25–29, 183n7, 184n47
World War II, 9–12 passim, 93, 116, 117–19, 120

www.ingramcontent.com/pod-product-compliance
Lightning Source LLC
Chambersburg PA
CBHW030647230426
43665CB00011B/985